FRANKLIN D. ROOSEVELT AND THE SEARCH FOR SECURITY

FRANKLIN D.

SR *Scholarly Resources Inc.*
Wilmington, Delaware

ROOSEVELT
and the Search for Security

AMERICAN-SOVIET RELATIONS, 1933–1939

By Edward M. Bennett

First published 1985
Second printing 1986
Printed and bound in the United States of America

Scholarly Resources Inc.
104 Greenhill Avenue
Wilmington, Delaware 19805

Bluffton College Library

Library of Congress Cataloging in Publication Data

Bennett, Edward Moore, 1927–
    Franklin D. Roosevelt and the search for security.

    Bibliography: p.
    Includes index.
    1. United States—Foreign relations—Soviet Union.
2. Soviet Union—Foreign relations—United States.
3. United States—Foreign relations—1933–1945.
4. Roosevelt, Franklin D. (Franklin Delano), 1882–1945.
I. Title.
E183.8.S65B46   1985   973.917'092'4   85-10850
ISBN 0-8420-2246-5
ISBN 0-8420-2247-3 (pbk.)

Contents

Preface

AMERICAN-SOVIET RELATIONS in the 1930s did not meet the minimum requirements of the times, but the problem was not uniquely Russia's. In the face of Adolf Hitler's challenge to the Versailles order, after 1933 the United States failed to sustain adequate and reassuring relations with any of the major powers. Indeed, for many world leaders the foreign policies of Franklin D. Roosevelt were incomprehensible, producing reactions of dismay, frustration, and often anger. In refusing to condone any changes in the international peace structure emanating from force, Roosevelt could not come to terms with an aggressive Germany, Italy, or Japan, nor could he offer the commitments elsewhere required to discourage aggression or make the United States a trustworthy ally.

Although he understood the dangers confronting international society, neither Roosevelt's isolationism nor his internationalism encouraged him to assume the responsibilities that came with great power, especially with America's major role in creating the peace structure then under assault. Unable to formulate a direct response to the threats of aggression, he moved between broad appeals to the status quo and specific, limited maneuvers that were usually lacking in substance. One such maneuver was his recognition of Russia in November 1933. For Roosevelt recognition alone would give the aggressors pause by bringing Russia again into the mainstream of world politics and enabling that country, along with others, to create a balance of power capable of preserving the peace.

Maxim Litvinov, Russia's foreign minister and leading proponent of collective security, expected no less of recognition, declaring before a New York audience in late 1933: "Who can doubt but that the united voices of the two giants will compel themselves to be taken into consideration, and that their joint efforts will weight the scales to the benefit of peace." As early as 1934 Litvinov saw that the countries which favored the status quo could prevent war only by standing together. Convinced that direct diplomacy with Berlin and Tokyo would achieve nothing, he advanced a collective security plan consisting of periodic conferences of the major countries opposed to aggression to perfect joint economic and other policies designed to warn the aggressors. Litvinov advised Ambassador William C. Bullitt that war in Europe was inevitable unless the United States accepted Russia's peace plan or a similar one. In Washington, Bullitt likewise reminded the American people that the next war would not be localized, that the United States and Russia would be in it together. Except for an alliance with France, Russia's search for collective security had achieved nothing. With no country interested in any realistic program to stop aggression, the USSR, Litvinov concluded, would rely on its own armed forces. Ultimately, that nation would seek its security in a pact with Germany.

Litvinov's appeal for collective security was as direct a challenge to the Roosevelt administration as was Hitler's burgeoning assault on the Versailles structure. This volume delineates in detail America's failure to respond, focusing both on Roosevelt's idiosyncrasies, his occasional attempts at personal diplomacy, and the public and bureaucratic pressures that rendered any effective agreement with the Kremlin impossible. Ostensibly, Russia's refusal to pay its debts to the United States alone stood in the way of any closer understanding. Actually the failure of American-Soviet relations in the 1930s had more pervading causes. Those relations demonstrated above all the inability of the United States to deal realistically with a country that pursues policies or harbors ideologies at odds with those of the United States. Secretary of State Cordell Hull exemplified the problem as he attempted repeatedly to prevent the president from dealing with the Russians. The State Department was totally opposed to any collaboration with the USSR; most of its members saw nothing to be gained in any agreement with the Soviets. Among many informed Americans the distrust of Russia was profound.

Such impediments, added to the highly declaratory nature of American reaction to events abroad, left Roosevelt little room for policy creation. Both Bullitt and his successor, Joseph Davies, reminded Roosevelt from Moscow that Russia was a key element in the European peace structure; their admonitions had no effect on national policy. By 1937 American-Soviet relations comprised largely commentary on one another's public statements. That year at the State Department East European Affairs was absorbed into European Affairs; even the files were dispersed or destroyed. Thereafter the Russians received less and less assurance from Roosevelt, but even that little they accepted with both hands. They listened carefully to the public declarations of Roosevelt and Hull for some clue that the United States intended to take a stand against Germany and Japan. If Hull's preachments promised nothing, the Russians hailed them simply because they placed the United States morally against aggression. Similarly, Roosevelt's naval-building program offered some reassurance, although it was tied to no specific foreign commitments. Nothing, however, could bridge the policy gap, one reinforced finally by the Nazi-Soviet Pact. The Soviet-American separation, an unintended triumph for Hitler, was profound as Europe went to war in September 1939.

Norman A. Graebner
Charlottesville, Virginia
May 1985

Acknowledgments

THERE IS A certain necessary sameness in acknowledgments for assistance rendered in producing a book because we all find that mentors, relatives, friends, students, colleagues, and professional archivists provide invaluable advice, information, and motivation for historical studies. In an earlier work, I noted the role my wife Margery played as research assistant, editor, and critic, based on her own experience as a teacher and historian. Once again she has served in all these capacities, with great patience and tender loving care.

My doctoral students at Washington State University helped me form more distinct views of the twenties, thirties, and forties through their research papers, seminar discussions, and dissertations, all of which were of exceptional quality. Thus to Gary M. Ross, Willard Barnes, Harry R. Heubel, Roger Bjerk, Michael Blayney, Marlin Freiderich, Denise O'Neal Conover, Peter Buckingham, Robert Swartout, John Engram, Vanida Tuttle, Dwight Tuttle, and Michael Polley I owe a debt as equally concerned colleagues. A special note goes to Douglas Burleigh, who decided to terminate his graduate career to teach high school after having written a perceptive master's thesis on William C. Bullitt, and to my M.A. candidates Merle Shulte Kunz, Tom Noer, George Knudsen, Harvey Young, and Peter Chapin, each of whom provided some perspective through their seminar papers or theses.

The staff at Hyde Park; the Department of State section at the National Archives and Federal Records Center at Suitland, Maryland; and the Library of Congress were so helpful that they deserve special mention, along with the Houghton Library staff at Harvard College Library for allowing me access to the papers of Joseph C. Grew. Numerous individuals at the University of Illinois, Texas A&M, and Washington State University libraries worked to make the research task simpler by acquiring materials. I am also indebted to the Houghton Library for their permission to cite the Grew papers and to three people with whom I discussed Franklin Delano Roosevelt and his foreign policy perspective: Eleanor Roosevelt, Madame Frances Perkins, and Herbert Feis. I talked with Mrs. Roosevelt at Hyde Park in the summer of 1959 and again when she came to give a public address at the University of Illinois. Madame Perkins was kind enough, during a visiting lectureship at Illinois, to let me join her for dinner, at which time she answered questions quite candidly about FDR and others whom she knew at the cabinet and ambassadorial levels. At the National Archives in the spring of 1958, Herbert Feis joined other researchers for open discussions of New Deal diplomacy.

My final indebtedness is a particularly special one. I dedicate this volume to my friend, mentor, and colleague Norman A. Graebner, who directed the initial efforts of a neophyte historian in learning his craft and whose help and friendship have been unstinting.

Introduction

FRANKLIN DELANO ROOSEVELT has been called elusive, enigmatic, secretive, boyish in his enthusiasm, peevish, a realist, an idealist, and a pragmatist. All of these characteristics were displayed in his Russian policy, plus one more—curiosity. He wondered what sort of man was Joseph Stalin, were the Soviet leaders bold experimenters, what were the people like in that vast country, and the largest question of all: Could Russia be used as an instrument of peace in a troubled world plagued by new ideologies far more threatening, in Roosevelt's view, than the Soviet experiment?

Nazism and Japanese militarism were more dangerous because they were being put forward by those nations whose governments were bent on spreading their doctrines by force, whereas by 1932 the Soviet Union had focused its attention on propaganda and attempts to foster native Communist movements. Roosevelt expressed a Holmesian confidence in the ability of Americans to resist ideologies alien to their culture and experiences. He did not believe that they could be taken in by persuasion and was far more worried about the prospect of another world war that would disrupt economic recovery, spread obnoxious doctrines by conquest, and destroy democracy in the process.

How clearly did Roosevelt perceive these threats and alternatives when he began his presidency? Through an examination of his Russian policy, it is possible to illustrate that his future vision was better than most American political leaders of his time. He entered office on the heels of Japan's Manchurian adventure and sufficiently after Adolf Hitler's entrance to control in Germany to perceive that the dangers emanating from those two areas were serious. Immediately, as President-elect, Roosevelt sent William C. Bullitt to Europe to examine ways to stop Japanese expansion, through economic pressure, and to see how

Russia might be used to block Japan or possibly frighten its leadership into easing off on plans to conquer China. As soon as he was sworn in, Roosevelt moved to discover ways he could fit the Russians into his broader foreign policy goals. By the time Maxim Litvinov arrived in Washington to discuss recognition, Germany had become a second focal point of FDR's recognition objectives.

Roosevelt desired to make the Russians tie into his overall thrust for peace and security. Although he did not develop specific policies to implement his objectives, which were interwoven into a host of foreign and domestic policy perceptions, the fundamental aim of his foreign policy was to preserve the peace and, failing this, to ensure national security. From the beginning he groped to work American-Soviet relations into this larger framework.

One source of difficulty in developing a more effective foreign policy by the Roosevelt administration was the president's philosophy of politics. He was a political pragmatist inclined to visions of how things should be, although he was unwilling to specify long-term plans on how to reach his ultimate goal. For example, having determined that preservation of the peace was his objective, Roosevelt opened every door that might lead to a course that would ensure this as long as he was positive that there were no hidden dangers. If there were the possibility of overwhelming opposition to any plan to guarantee the peace, or if it involved commitments that would create contests he was unlikely to win with the congressional isolationists, he did not even reach for the handle of that particular door. This meant that often in his approaches to create a secure peace he was restricted either to rhetorical responses to the foreseen threats or to very cautious agreements to "consult" with others interested in his objectives, announcing clearly that consultation did not necessarily mean action.

Roosevelt believed that, if the aggressor nations were convinced he knew what they were all about and if he warned them often enough that they could not succeed with their plans for conquest, eventually they might back off, especially if their economic well-being could be threatened. If the president could get across to Germany and Japan that, under certain circumstances, the United States would be forced to fight and if he could keep them off balance in their estimates of exactly at what point the Americans would intervene actively, then war might be averted, and the dissentient powers might seek accommodation with their opponents. Where Russia fit into Roosevelt's peace plans became apparent almost as soon as he met with former Secretary of State Henry L. Stimson after Herbert Hoover's defeat. The president hoped to use the Russians as an instant bloc to Japan's aggression and to work cooperatively with them to discourage Hitler.

In keeping with his pragmatism, Roosevelt did not have a predetermined opinion of the Soviets' social and political systems, and he found their experiment "interesting." How he intended to deal with the Russian question was revealed only piecemeal and was subject to change. He had a "hopscotch" mind; he would often set forth a position that he was prepared to abandon or modify at the slightest appearance of opposition or change if another course suddenly appealed to him. These were the marks of a political pragmatist and were traits that made him an effective leader in domestic situations but often confused his subordinates assigned the task of implementing American foreign policy. Even more frustrating were the shifts of position he ordered when he was moved by whimsy or intuition. The deficiencies of a pragmatic approach were described by Herbert Feis, formerly a State Department economic adviser, when one of my colleagues asked him if he could explain "the well-springs of American policy, the long-range plan, concerning the Spanish Civil War." Feis responded that it was the same as general U.S. foreign policy. "There was none. It was day to day, crisis to crisis diplomacy."[1] And so it was with FDR's Russian policy.

Crisis-to-crisis diplomacy was symptomatic of American foreign policy in the 1930s. The fault was not Roosevelt's alone; the perspective not only dripped down from the top, it also perked up from the bottom. A latter-day Foreign Service officer, assessing the position of his colleagues during this decade, observed that "diplomats tended to drift with occurrences abroad, treating them as isolated squalls that would eventually blow over without affecting conditions on remote American shores. Furthermore, they supported Washington's traditional practice of noninvolvement in European politics."[2] Unable to comprehend the totalitarian trends and dislocations, they tended, in Charles E. Bohlen's words, to adhere to the maxim "Don't get involved," which began in the 1920s and became in the 1930s a stratified role for them as "clerks on the end of a wire."[3] Secretary of State Cordell Hull added to the process of noninvolvement. The Foreign Service officers' purpose, "as defined by . . . Cordell Hull, was to provide accurate and impartial information, protect the lives and property of Americans in foreign countries, and carry out the department's instructions."[4] On one occasion an ambassador wrote directly to Hull for information as to what

---

[1]Interview with Herbert Feis, spring 1958, National Archives, Washington, DC.

[2]Hugh DeSantis, *The Diplomacy of Silence: The American Foreign Service, the Soviet Union, and the Cold War, 1933–1947* (Chicago: University of Chicago Press, 1980), p. 56. This is an indispensable analysis of the influences that shaped the Foreign Service officers' cultural background and their role in approaching the USSR.

[3]Ibid., pp. 21–22.

[4]Ibid., p. 22.

was America's foreign policy, and the secretary responded that he should read his and the president's speeches, for it was all outlined in those public statements. Roosevelt gave the same advice, at one point suggesting to Hull that he circularize the ambassadors to that effect.

In the 1930s and 1940s, Hull contributed greatly to the confusion surrounding American policy. Quite often U.S. presidents have selected their secretaries of state for their weaknesses rather than their strengths, and one suspects that Roosevelt had something like this in mind when he settled on Hull to head the Department of State. He symbolized the rewards available to southern Democrats who were loyal to the party; brought the prestige of his reputation as a gentle man with vague ideas of international cooperation to the cabinet; and had the advantage, from the president's viewpoint, of not having been associated with any particular experience in the field of foreign policy, with the exception of reciprocal trade agreements. After Hull settled into the office, he generally urged excessive caution and opposed doing anything that would rock the boat. He constantly tightened the reins on the president's proposed commitments to support consultative pacts in the disarmament talks at Geneva and warned FDR not to get ahead of public opinion, which often meant not leading when leadership was mandatory.

In America's dealings with the Russians, the Hull-Roosevelt relationship was critical. Hull never trusted the Soviets and acted as a brake on an outgoing policy toward them; sometimes he was willing to work with them but only if they played the game by his rules, which seldom happened. The secretary of state's legalistic-moralistic approach to foreign policy was so much a part of his makeup that even Roosevelt, who had inclinations in that direction himself, grew weary of it.

Among the president's foibles that bothered Hull were his tendency to select people outside the Department of State to perform special missions for him, his inclination to play events for dramatic effect, and his secretiveness about the results of his investigations. Hull did not particularly like, for political or personal reasons, some of the appointments that Roosevelt made to the Department of State. He especially resented the privilege accorded to Bullitt, and later to Joseph E. Davies and others, to correspond directly with the president on matters relating to foreign policy.

Roosevelt's initial approach to resuming relations with the Soviet Union provided an excellent illustration of how he antagonized his secretary of state. First, he forced Hull to accept Bullitt as special assistant secretary of state. Then the president initiated his contacts with the Russians through Bullitt and Farm Credit Administration Director Henry Morgenthau, Jr., without keeping Hull fully informed. Although Roosevelt followed the formalities of communication with the Department of State, he kept the Russian negotiations under his control from the outset and took them over personally shortly after Litvinov arrived in Washington. He made a grandstand play by inviting the Soviet representative to the White House before the State Department could pin the commissar down on some of the issues to be decided, especially the question of debts owed by Russia to either the U.S. government or American citizens. Thus, in the very first contact with the Russians, FDR established a pattern for the conduct of American-Soviet relations which kept his State Department partially in the dark on what he was doing and why.

In part, Roosevelt's seemingly capricious approach stemmed from his style in implementing foreign policy. Although he sometimes enjoyed keeping friends and enemies alike guessing as to the course he would pursue, there were other occasions when he simply did not know what he wanted to do to gain his general objective of preserving the peace. In some measure this related to his pragmatism; he was reluctant to try fathoming a foreign policy plan that depended on precisely defined goals and alternative courses of action. Again his approach was pragmatic. In response to a letter from an admirer, who asked the president to give some permanency to American foreign policy and a long-range plan that the public could use as a guide, Roosevelt replied: "Frankly, I do not know how to effect a permanency in American foreign policy."[5] He also said he did not know that he would do so even if he knew how because he had learned from Woodrow Wilson that the public could not be attuned to the highest note in the scale without becoming discomforted. According to James MacGregor Burns, part of Roosevelt's problem in developing his foreign policy was that "on crucial operating questions . . . and above all the commitments to be undertaken by the United States, he was uncertain."[6]

The irony of the American-Soviet relationship of the 1930s was that Roosevelt knew precisely what he wanted from the Russians; they were to play a role in blocking the aggressive designs of the Axis powers. However, despite constant probing and prodding, he could not find a way to collaborate with them except on Soviet terms, which he did not feel free to accept. In the inverse, Soviet leaders desired the same objectives and experienced similar frustration. The incredible thing was that neither set of leaders gave up trying until the attempt to promote collective security gave way to Axis ambitions and war on September 1, 1939.

---

[5]Letter of January 30, 1934, PPF 359, Foreign Affairs Folder, Franklin D. Roosevelt Papers, Franklin D. Roosevelt Library, Hyde Park, New York.

[6]James MacGregor Burns, *Roosevelt: The Lion and the Fox* (New York: Harcourt, 1956), p. 352.

Abbreviations

DSF   Department of State Files
FO   Foreign Office (London)
FRUS *Foreign Relations of the United States*
OF   Official File
PPF   President's Personal File
PSF   President's Secretary's File

I

Resuming Relations with the Russians: Nothing To Fear but Fear Itself

"HE COULD NOT UNDERSTAND what all the fuss was about. Franklin had absolute confidence in the good sense of the American people to judge for themselves, and to judge accurately."[1] This was Eleanor Roosevelt's recollection of her husband's response to the opponents of Russian recognition. This was no doubt true, but he also was just about sure that the "fuss" was coming from discredited elements in the society and was positive that he had nearly unchallengeable support where it counted before he announced his decision to resume relations with the Russians, a term he preferred to recognition. Franklin D. Roosevelt had no intention of moving beyond what the public would accept in his operation of external affairs, particularly during the period when the domestic crisis was so acute. Roosevelt was the ultimate political animal; he attacked his opponents when he was reasonably certain of success and remained passive or retreated when he or his advisers believed that the timing was wrong for boldness. In his search for a Russian policy, he was well aware of what the fuss was about, and he set out to neutralize the fussers.

Roosevelt knew that dealing with external affairs required attention to domestic opposition. The foundation of his foreign policy program was cemented in his perception of the leadership role that the president must play. He summed it up succinctly in a note to Ray Stannard Baker:

---

[1]Interview with Eleanor Roosevelt, summer 1959, Hyde Park, New York. Mrs. Roosevelt also said that her husband considered reversing the nonrecognition policy from the outset because he thought it ridiculous, not in keeping with American traditions, and possibly useful in blocking aggression and aiding recovery.

Theodore Roosevelt lacked Woodrow Wilson's appeal to the fundamental and failed to stir, as Wilson did, the truly profound moral and social convictions. Wilson, on the other hand, failed where Theodore Roosevelt succeeded in stirring people to enthusiasm over specific individual events, even though these specific events may have been superficial in comparison with the fundamentals.[2]

This observation was important because it stated a perspective to which Roosevelt adhered throughout his term in office. He tried to be a moralist and a realist at the same time but not always with the best results.

Roosevelt believed almost instinctively that, if he could marshal the forces of international opinion as Woodrow Wilson had tried to do and failed, then the world crisis could be overcome by using Theodore Roosevelt's technique of stirring enthusiasm over individual specific events. First, however, the president had to make sure that the event was significant enough to draw attention, that the opposition to his intended action was not so formidable as to make him lose the battle, and that the end was worth the struggle. Only inside this framework is it possible to understand Roosevelt's focus on the recognition question for a year before he moved on it, as well as his hot and cold attitude toward the Soviet Union throughout the 1930s.

When Roosevelt entered the White House, guaranteeing peace and security became the first concern of his foreign policy. He suggested supporting a plan, one that various newspapers called bold. It aimed at strengthening security throughout the world by removing the weapons of offense, which thereby would strengthen the weapons of defense, a process, said the president, "by which you give security to every nation, including the small nations."[3] Once other countries realized that this was foolproof protection against aggressors and the easiest possible way to save money while maintaining adequate defense, Roosevelt was confident it would be simple to gain international agreement. Several of the president's advisers and well-wishers wrote to congratulate him on his splendid move toward peace, but none of them challenged his proposal at its most obvious weak point: What was to be done if some nations preferred aggression to guaranteed security? During his presidency, this policy was one of many logical schemes Roosevelt would provide to defend the world from itself by asking the

---

[2]Quoted in Arthur M. Schlesinger, Jr., *The Age of Roosevelt*, vol. 1, *The Crisis of the Old Order, 1919–1933* (Boston: Houghton Mifflin, 1957), p. 482.

[3]Press Conferences of Franklin D. Roosevelt, 1, No. 19, May 10, 1933, p. 234, Franklin D. Roosevelt Library, Hyde Park, New York.

powers to bury self-interest in pursuit of the common good. However, not one of these was really destined to work.

Appealing to American concern for the underdog was not just a political ploy on the president's part; he really believed such considerations were legitimate objectives of U.S. foreign policy. This was partly due to his own education and development and partly to the simple fact that he was an American, more sophisticated in his view of the external world than most but with normal perceptions of the U.S. role in defending the weak. This did not mean that Roosevelt thought that the United States should rush into war; rather, he shared the concern of his fellow citizens for expressing interest and using American influence on behalf of those with whom he sympathized. In this, he was the national spokesman of liberal opinion and conscience instead of a statesman judging his nation's vital interests. It was a part he fitted comfortably and enjoyed. Eleanor Roosevelt said of her husband that he genuinely cared for people who he believed needed defending against those who wielded the preeminence of power and who did not take into consideration the needs of the little guy. This attitude extended to small countries trying to protect their interests against the great powers.[4] Roosevelt's penchant for New Dealism in foreign policy was corroborated by Frances Perkins.[5]

Searching for the best route to obtain his objectives, Roosevelt experimented. Often, however, he vacillated and found opposition sometimes where it did not exist or could be turned aside by more forthright leadership. Certainly one reason for the president's caution resulted from his fear of the congressional response to a forward foreign policy. He especially wished to avoid a conflict with those whose seats on Capitol Hill were in the Senate. These legislators acted as both reflectors and formulators of public opinion and generally considered themselves to be oracles of the people. At best they considered the president to be primus inter pares with them in his role as a foreign policymaker and less than equal as a molder of public opinion.

In his relationship with the isolationist senators, President Roosevelt's position was delicate. For the most part the leading progressive isolationists, including Senators William E. Borah, George W. Norris, and Hiram W. Johnson, were among his warmest supporters on many of his pet domestic programs. To alienate them would hurt his legislative agenda without aiding materially in breaking down the isolationist barrier. At the same time, some of the nation's leading intellectuals lent support to the isolationist cause as they kept up a barrage of advice

---

[4]Interview with Eleanor Roosevelt.
[5]Interview with Frances Perkins, spring 1958, University of Illinois, Urbana, Illinois.

to the president and Congress. A typical communication from Yale Professor Edwin M. Borchard underscored the problem:

> I firmly believe that the United States will be unable to accomplish anything useful by another intervention in Europe. . . . It is not the mission of the United States . . . to produce European peace by war on behalf of one group, even if that mission could be accomplished. If Europe cannot keep the peace alone, let them take the consequences. Let us not be dragged down with them.[6]

Republican spokesmen championed the tradition of insularity for a decade; Roosevelt, once elected, challenged them. Raymond Leslie Buell thought the president's Wilson Foundation address of December 1933 somewhat oversimplified when FDR foretold the need of the 90 percent of the people in the world who supported peace to work on the 10 percent who did not, but this nonetheless indicated that he would not follow the dangerous pattern of isolation, which he had extolled prior to his election.[7] Although the words seemed promising for those who hoped for international cooperation, Buell warned: "The task still remains, . . . of converting the President's words into deeds."[8] When he might do this remained, until near the end of his second administration, the prime question concerning his foreign policy.

Roosevelt confronted a self-evident problem. Solving the domestic crisis would do little good if the rest of the world disintegrated; the United States was not immune to the effects of a general global disorder. But how could he treat the broader disorders without first healing the internal wounds? Did he have enough energy and power to tackle both ills? Should he be candid or should he approach the world crisis as he did the internal one by first calming the public's fears and then isolating the crises for separate treatment? The president chose not to alarm the public. In his fireside chats and public statements, he presented an optimism on the success potential of the London Economic Conference, the Geneva Disarmament Conference, and general developments abroad, which he did not always believe. This was due to his desire to give the American people a more positive image of external events, at least in part because they had enough to worry about in the depths of their domestic problems without being depressed over a world headed for economic disaster and possibly war.

---

[6]Borchard to Senator Key Pittman, May 22, 1933, Committee Papers, U.S. Senate Committee on Foreign Relations, SEN 734-10 (112B), National Archives, Washington, DC.

[7]Raymond Leslie Buell, "An Epoch Making Address," *Foreign Policy Bulletin* 13 (January 5, 1934): 1–2.

[8]Ibid., p. 2.

In his private correspondence and conversations, the president was more realistic. He wrote to friends and diplomats, expressing his desire for international conditions to improve but stating his fear that his hopes might be ill founded unless somebody altered the slide toward war. Early in his first administration he illustrated this concern when he wrote to William E. Dodd, ambassador to Germany:

> Walter Lippmann was here last week and made the interesting suggestion that about 8 per cent of the population of the entire world, i.e., Germany and Japan, is able, because of imperialistic attitude, to prevent peaceful guarantees and armament reductions on the part of the other 92 per cent of the world. . . . I feel that the situation is even more serious than the papers have discovered it to be.
>
> I sometimes feel that the world problems are getting worse instead of better.[9]

John Cudahy, U.S. ambassador to Poland, sent Roosevelt a bright prediction in December 1933, suggesting that the situation in Germany would prove to be only a manifestation of the peculiar need of the Germans who loved display and pageantry. The president, however, proved less sanguine than his correspondent:

> I do hope you are right in what you say of preparations in Germany. The chief problem is, of course, whether the marching of the general spirit of things is heading consciously or sub-consciously toward an idea of extension of boundaries. I am, of course, hopeful that some form of Arms Control Commission can be agreed upon, but the news in regard to this and other arms matters is not at this moment particularly encouraging.[10]

Cudahy thought that the Germans liked to wear uniforms and march to the strains of martial music in order to let off steam. FDR was concerned that too often when Germans put on uniforms and began marching they marched across someone's border.

Where could the president move in a foreign policy initiative that would affect the immediate Japanese threat and the growing German one? Roosevelt's answer was recognition of Russia. The resumption of a friendly relationship would bring this large and potentially powerful nation, with its vast human and natural resources, into the balance in preserving the peace. The Soviet Union already was threatened by

---

[9]FDR to Dodd, October 28, 1933, PPF 1043, William E. Dodd Folder.
[10]FDR to Cudahy, January 8, 1934, PPF 1193, John Cudahy Folder.

Japan's machinations, and the Russians had to be concerned over a rearmed and belligerent Germany on their western borders. If the Soviets could be assured that the United States was not an enemy, perhaps they could be persuaded to cooperate in pressuring the real enemies of the peace. Roosevelt may have considered the importance of resuming relations with Russia when he was a candidate for the presidency, but he did not begin an active investigation of the prospects until he was president-elect. After he took the oath of office he confronted the question, asking "Can I do it; and, if so, how?"

II

As early as May 1932 recognition became a subject of consideration by members of the Roosevelt team. Adolf A. Berle participated with several others who drew up a memorandum for FDR, outlining the critical issues he would have to act on if he won the election. Under the heading of foreign problems, they considered Russian recognition in a purely economic sense. In this section they advised Roosevelt that the USSR provided the largest actual market available at the moment. While shortages in the wheat crop and needs for practically everything that the United States manufactured were apparent, legal restrictions caused by nonrecognition posed a significant barrier to the resumption of trade relations. Because Russia lacked credit or surplus items for export, it could not pay for American products without some credit arrangements. Italy and Germany shared a large portion of the Soviet market because they provided extensive credits. Berle recorded that such giant corporations as General Electric, Standard Oil of New Jersey, and International Harvester were prepared "to encourage negotiations looking toward the recognition of Russia, the settlement of the Russian-American claims, and the resumption of commercial relations with Russia."[11]

Berle discounted propaganda as any longer providing a reason to abjure relations with the Soviet Union because encouragement of a world revolution had taken second place to Russian preoccupation over the success of the Five-Year Plan. He argued that there were trade opportunities with the Soviets that only recognition could guarantee and urged that recognition should be studied and "in any such study, purely doctrinaire ideas, as, that communism automatically outlaws a nation, should be discarded."[12] Others who participated in either drawing up the memorandum or discussing it with Roosevelt were Raymond

---

[11]Beatrice Bishop Berle and Travis Beal Jacobs, eds., *Navigating the Rapids, 1918–1971: From the Papers of Adolph A. Berle* (New York: Harcourt, 1973), p. 49.
[12]Ibid.

Moley, James R. Angell, Rexford G. Tugwell, and Samuel I. Rosenman. Berle noted that the ideas set forth in the memorandum were generally adopted.[13] The prospect of recognizing Russia was therefore an item of consideration with no apparent dissent by the Brain Trust in late May 1932, and it had all been brought out in discussions with the president.

Roosevelt permitted the news of his reopening of the Russian question to be released to the *New York Times* in December 1932. During the next year he evaluated the reactions and allowed members of his administration to speak on the side favoring recognition, as Moley did.[14] Some observers who viewed events in Washington assumed that President Roosevelt had taken a courageous stand in the face of powerful opposition, but this assumption had little foundation in fact. One regular attendant at the White House press conferences believed that steps were not taken to recognize Russia before November 1933 because of the administration's preoccupation with internal problems.[15] While this may be a reason for the delay, it was not the predominant one; FDR's desire for information and preparation was at least equally important.

As always, Roosevelt conducted his careful study through diverse sources. Secretary of State Cordell Hull requested Professor Jerome Davis, a theologian at Yale University and longtime advocate of recognition, to prepare a memorandum for the president on the subject.[16] Professor Davis advised that too much should not be made of the advantage of collaborating with Russia in the Far Eastern situation, although recognition could not help but be a warning to Japan. In favor of resuming relations, he used most of the standard arguments such as common sense, traditional U.S. policy, and fifteen years of de facto control by the Soviet government. He suggested that immediate recognition provided an opportunity to win the Soviets' goodwill, which he judged a distinctly important psychological advantage, and opposition would die out when confronted by an accomplished fact. Davis informed the president that business solidly supported the move:

> Already for the first time in its history the American-Russian Chamber of Commerce, composed of 150 of our leading business concerns, have voted unanimously for recognition. Letters from

---

[13]Ibid.

[14]"Should the United States Government Recognize Soviet Russia?" *Congressional Digest* 12 (October 1933): 240.

[15]Ernest K. Lindley, *The Roosevelt Revolution* (New York: Viking, 1933), p. 225.

[16]Thomas R. Maddux, *Years of Estrangement: American Relations with the Soviet Union, 1933–1941* (Tallahassee: University Press of Florida, 1980), p. 5. Davis sympathized with the Soviet experiment, worked avidly for recognition, and lobbied to become the first U.S. ambassador to the USSR.

some 150 other large business concerns to me brought only four
responses that were definitely opposed to recognition.[17]

His assertion of the support rendered from business concerns was a
particularly accurate index of the position of a number of large man-
ufacturing companies that hoped to gain something from furnishing
the equipment Russia needed for its industrial and agricultural development programs.[18]

In July 1933 Undersecretary of State William Phillips prepared
a memorandum for the president, in which he outlined "the problems
pertaining to Russian-American relations which, in the interest of
friendly relations between the United States and Russia, should be
settled prior to the recognition of the Soviet government."[19] Phillips
emphasized the items that Robert F. Kelley of the State Department
stressed so strenuously in his own evaluations recommending against
recognition.[20] The problems Phillips called to the president's attention
concerned world revolutionary activity, repudiated debts, and confiscated property, "difficulties arising out of the profound differences
between the economic and social structure of the two countries, especially the state monopoly of foreign trade, and the treatment by the
Soviets of foreign nationals subject to their laws and practices."[21] The
undersecretary urged the president not to grant recognition until these
issues had been settled:

> The experience of countries which have extended recognition to
> the Soviet government has shown pretty conclusively . . . that as

---

[17]Davis memorandum, OF 220-A, Russia Miscellaneous, Box 4, 1933, Franklin D.
Roosevelt Papers. There are many letters in this file, offering assistance and advice on
recognition from people who had been in the Soviet Union, most of whom favored
recognition.

[18]See especially Peter Filene, *Americans and the Soviet Experiment, 1917–1933* (Cambridge, MA: Harvard University Press, 1967); and Joan Hoff-Wilson, *Ideology and Economics: U.S. Relations with the Soviet Union, 1918–1933* (Columbia: University of Missouri
Press, 1974). Hoff-Wilson denied the influence of business on recognition which was
accurate but missed the importance of business support in making the move palatable
to important elements in America. President Roosevelt cared less for the results in trade
than for the business support, although he hoped for some economic benefit from it.

[19]Phillips to FDR, July 27, 1933, PSF, Box 15, Franklin D. Roosevelt Papers.

[20]John Richman, in *The United States and the Soviet Union: The Decision to Recognize*
(Raleigh, NC: Camberleigh Hall, 1980), pp. 35–41ff., pointed out the antagonism of the
Russian Section, Kelley in particular, toward recognition, which placed too much emphasis on the anticommunism that underlay the opposition and not enough on the natural
suspicion of a group of men who had seen the USSR in action and were totally convinced
that not much good would come of recognition if it were anticipated or advertised as
capable of producing desirable results resting on friendship, enhanced trade, or promoting
security interests.

[21]Phillips to FDR, July 27, 1933, PSF, Box 15.

long as these obstacles remain, official relations, established as a result of recognition, tend to become, in view of the extraordinary nature of these obstacles, the source of friction and ill will rather than the mainspring of cooperation and good will. . . . Until a substantial basis of mutual understanding and common principles and purposes has been established, official intercourse, with its increased contacts, is bound to lead to friction and rancor.[22]

The most cautious newspaper evaluation that the president received regarding opinion on his recognition policy came from the Department of State where enthusiasm for restoration of relations was, to say the least, not great. In mid-October Undersecretary Phillips forwarded to Roosevelt a confidential memorandum prepared by the Division of Current Information. Phillips cautioned the president not to take the evaluation as definitive because it covered only the previous thirty days, and during that time, out of 300 newspapers examined, there was little editorial comment on recognition: "However, as far as it goes, the memorandum seems to indicate that the New England and North Atlantic States do not appear to be enthusiastically in favor of recognition; that the majority of the Southern and Mid-western States are in favor of recognition and that the Pacific Coast States are somewhat indifferent."[23]

Roosevelt's approach to Russian recognition fitted the pattern of his conduct of diplomacy throughout his tenure in the White House. He used the Department of State for data and the more formal preparations for his diplomacy but relied on other information and initiated probes and proposals on the subject anywhere he found a likely source of intelligence. For example, within three weeks of his inauguration, he enlisted the White House press corps in his investigation of the Soviet Union. The president dined with some newsmen on the evening of March 19, 1933 and proposed to Fred Storm, dean of the White House press corps, and some of the others that they should check their sources for him on any matters relating to Russia. Roosevelt achieved two goals by this effort: the press was informally apprised of the seriousness of his intent on the Russian question, and he made them feel that they were on the inside concerning a delicate diplomatic maneuver. Storm replied by letter the next day, promising to send the president a report, scheduled to arrive from Eugene Lyons, as soon as he received it.[24]

---

[22]Ibid.

[23]Ibid., October 19, 1933, OF 220, Russia.

[24]Stephen T. Early to Marguerite (Missy) LeHand (Roosevelt's secretary), March 20, 1933, Record Group 59, DSF 861.00/1152.

Eleanor Roosevelt affirmed that she helped in her husband's investigation through contacts with friends who knew something of the Russian situation. On one particular occasion she arranged for Esther Lape of the American Foundation to secure an appointment with the president,[25] probably at Mrs. Lape's request. The latter wrote to the president on July 21, 1933, stating that she did not know how much detail Mrs. Roosevelt had passed on to him concerning the appointment; therefore, she enlightened him on several points she thought would be of interest. In addition to members of her committee, the group she wished to meet with the president included representatives of the American-Soviet Chamber of Commerce and "certain businessmen of the country eminently qualified to speak, not only by reason of their business weight and direct experience but also by reason of their personal calibre." She assured Roosevelt that she and her group could provide him with important practical information on the USSR which would be of value in his study of the recognition question. The president bluntly informed Mrs. Lape that she alone would be welcome to visit him but not the rest of her entourage, for their visit "would be taken as an out and out announcement of recognition." He was careful in the early stage of his investigation to keep it low-keyed and not to permit any organization to make him appear inclined toward its position.[26]

Eleanor Roosevelt recalled a conversation with her husband in which he mentioned both his curiosity about Russia and Joseph Stalin and his belief that recognition would serve several purposes. She said that the president thought nonrecognition was an irrational and hysterical response, generated in part by the "Red Scare." Mrs. Roosevelt believed that he moved carefully, as he usually did, seeking all sorts of opinions so that he could assess the public's mood on the question, and that he planned to go ahead with the matter unless there was some overwhelming block that he could not foresee.[27]

President Roosevelt used selectively gratuitous sources of information that came to his attention. Appeals from supporters were numerous and included longtime advocates of recognition such as Hugh L. Cooper, Alexander Gumberg, and Raymond Robins. In particular, Gumberg continued a campaign that he had launched in the 1920s and used every contact he had to keep the Russian question alive during the period when Roosevelt was considering it. Because Gumberg's Republican connections were with the wing of the party willing

---

[25]Interview with Eleanor Roosevelt.
[26]Esther Lape to FDR, July 21, 1933, and response of July 28, 1933, OF 220-A.
[27]Interview with Eleanor Roosevelt.

to support FDR's programs, he was able to use them to get prerecognition people in to see the president. In this way Philip La Follette secured an interview with FDR for Robins after Robins returned from a trip to the USSR.[28]

Religious opinion also concerned Roosevelt, and he carefully assessed its impact on recognition. He knew that some Protestant and Catholic groups opposed recognition, while the Jewish community remained more neutral.[29] The Central Conference of American Rabbis, however, petitioned the president on behalf of recognition.[30] The Department of State sent Roosevelt a memorandum dealing with the religious question, thus prompting him to call for Bullitt. In order to avoid the charge that the United States was dealing with an avowed enemy of God, the department suggested that certain promises concerning freedom of religion should be extracted from the Russians before negotiations began.[31]

Eleanor Roosevelt said that her husband certainly must have considered the political implications of the religious question as he examined the prospects for recognition, and one should remember FDR's own deep religious feelings which, while not usually directed at the organized church, were nonetheless strong.[32] Henry Morgenthau, Jr., remarked on the president's concern and that expressed by members of his administration; Roosevelt was not going to proceed toward recognition unless he was sure that religious opinion would not be significantly alienated by his action.[33] In this context, the president engaged in one of the most bizarre behind-the-scenes negotiations of his political career and as a result secured the confidence he needed to deal with the issue. He informed religious leaders that he would emphasize religious freedom for Americans and would work to free religious prisoners in Russia. In view of these commitments, an outspoken critic of recognition, Father Edmund A. Walsh of Georgetown University, agreed to support the move to recognize the Soviet Union. His cooperation emerged as one of the president's major coups in preparing the public

---

[28]James K. Libbey, *Alexander Gumberg and Soviet-American Relations, 1917–1933* (Lexington: University Press of Kentucky, 1977), p. 119.

[29]Filene, *Americans and the Soviet Experiment*, p. 88. Filene maintained that throughout the 1920s the Jewish community in the United States had mixed feelings about the USSR because of religious suppression in Russia counterbalanced by Soviet efforts to reverse the anti-Semitism previously prevalent in Russia.

[30]Ibid., p. 263.

[31]Memorandum, October 16, 1933, OF 799, William C. Bullitt Folder.

[32]Interview with Eleanor Roosevelt.

[33]Morgenthau Diaries, Farm Credit Diary, April 1933, p. 17, Henry Morgenthau, Jr., Papers, Franklin D. Roosevelt Library, Hyde Park, New York.

for recognition and in ensuring minimal opposition from some of the important pressure groups.[34]

As the president examined the ramifications of the recognition question, he tried to disarm opponents, discover the degree of opposition, feel out the Russians, and assess the advantages, both for internal political bonus points and for his foreign policy objectives. Not until these issues had been evaluated did Franklin Roosevelt contact Soviet President Mikhail Kalinin, suggesting that it was time to discuss differences of opinion.

III

Several of the individuals involved in the Department of State's preparation of the documents and memoranda on American-Soviet relations have blamed Roosevelt for not following their advice in the recognition negotiations and thereby laying the groundwork for subsequent difficulties. These critics were at least partly at fault, for they provided considerable opposition to recognition and were excessively cautious concerning any approach to the Russians. When it became obvious that the president was determined to proceed with the resumption of relations, they still dragged their feet, and Roosevelt knew it, which merely reinforced his image of the State Department and his stereotype of many of its professionals as striped-pants cookie pushers, dilettantes, closet Republicans, faint hearts, and mossbacks. This image was corroborated and encouraged by several close associates of the president. Felix Frankfurter, who was particularly suspicious, wrote to FDR, suggesting that the professionals in the Department of State were not the types to carry out his policies.[35]

One who came in for special criticism was Robert Kelley, Head of the Division of Eastern European Affairs, who also directed a small group known as the Russian Section, which kept track of events in the Soviet Union, both in the United States and through the American legation in Riga, Latvia, which was known during the nonrecognition era as the "window on Russia." Kelley, among others in the department, was disturbed by the prospect of resuming relations with Russia because of the Soviets' revolutionary objectives. There are two schools of thought on Kelley's opposition. One view emphasizes his innate conservatism and credits him with handling the recognition question from a determined antagonism, which ensured that nothing would come

---

[34]Edward M. Bennett, *Recognition of Russia: An American Foreign Policy Dilemma* (Waltham, MA: Blaisdell, 1970), pp. 94–97.

[35]Richman, *United States and the Soviet Union*, p. 68.

of the resumption of relations.[36] Herbert Feis, on the other hand, has contended that, despite Kelley's opposition, he accepted the president's decision and provided research that would assure the careful drafting of a final agreement.[37] Kelley and several others within the State Department were alarmed and uneasy that the president, in his haste to conclude recognition, would overcommit the United States or fail to reach a settlement on debts or other issues under negotiation.

Anti-Soviet bias within the Department of State rested on foundations that went beyond simple innate conservatism. Jefferson Caffrey and Sumner Welles believed that the Russians were attempting to become involved in the Western Hemisphere, especially Cuba, and recognition would help them. The Soviet bogeyman was very real to Caffrey and Welles, and they did not want to open the closet door to him.[38]

A leading actor in Roosevelt's Russian policy was William C. Bullitt, somewhat of a mystery man who reemerged dramatically in

---

[36]The supporters of this view adopt the essentials of the argument presented by Daniel Yergin in his study *Shattered Peace: The Origins of the Cold War and the National Security State* (Boston: Houghton Mifflin, 1977). Yergin contended that after 1945 the Riga axiom dominated America's Russian policy and that it rested on the premise that Soviet behavior was grounded on its Marxist ideology and sought world conquest, a position that gained credence because George Kennan and others who were part of Kelley's Russian Section disliked and distrusted the Russians from the outset. The most specific focus on Kelley as the evil genius who trained this group appears in Richman, *United States and the Soviet Union*, p. 89. The author argued that Kelley, by his bureaucratic genius, ensured a continuing anti-Soviet bias, and that "the world we live in today is to a large extent shaped by this [bureaucratic] talent he had. Bullitt was his greatest creation." Richman wrote that Bullitt entered the State Department with strong and sentimental ties to Russia, and, when he left the Soviet Union three years later, his views were indistinguishable from Kelley's. According to Louis Wehle, Bullitt's conversion was much earlier, before he even had met Kelley, and that Bullitt's disenchantment had been expressed to Wehle during the summer of 1932. Louis B. Wehle, *The Hidden Threads of History: Wilson Through Roosevelt* (New York: Macmillan, 1953), p. 713. There is a large body of literature that attacks the Foreign Service officers for their conservatism and hauteur and often ignores the defensive nature of their cliquishness. They were experts in a field that was little understood by most Americans, they adhered to an international protocol that their countrymen found pretentious, and they were isolated in foreign environments that often made them appear to be misfits in the nation they served. They learned lessons in the adoption of protective coloring, which enabled them to hide their divarication from fellow Americans, often meaning that they would not recommend policy if it meant going against the political trend of the time at home. Given these realities, Foreign Service officers seldom openly opposed those policies put forth to them with which they disagreed. Thus researchers tend to blame them for their anti-Soviet position without seeing them in the larger context of the problems they dealt with in establishing an identity for their expertise.

[37]Herbert Feis, *Characters in Crisis* (Boston: Little, Brown, 1966), p. 308.

[38]Richman supported the innate conservatism notion. in Richman, *United States and the Soviet Union*, pp. 53–64; Maddux found the concern about communism present but visualized it as merely one factor in a general suspicion that related to others, in Maddux, *Years of Estrangement*, pp. 17–25; and Hugh DeSantis found the opposition based in part on inertia, timidity, and ethnocentrism, in DeSantis, *Diplomacy of Silence*, pp. 21–33.

the president's life after a brief acquaintance during the Wilson admin-istration. Frances Perkins, who knew FDR very well and Bullitt slightly, judged that they probably enjoyed the aspect of intrigue because a boyish secretiveness appeared inherently in both men. Madame Perkins professed to have had only an observer's knowledge of Bullitt but characterized him as exuberant, brilliant, and erratic in his judg-ments.[39] His mercurial enthusiasm, once devoted to the high principles and flowing idealistic rhetoric of Wilson, was easily kindled by FDR's political magnetism and liberal perspective. Wilson had bitterly dis-appointed Bullitt with his surrender of principle at Paris, but Bullitt's hopes were restored as he visualized Roosevelt picking up Wilson's tattered mantle and wearing it with more authority and constancy.

Bullitt went to Europe to assess the current developments, at first on his own, then with FDR's approval, and finally at the president's urging. During the trip after Roosevelt became president-elect, Bullitt attempted to ensure Japan's isolation and the defeat of its expansionist objectives by securing assurances from Great Britain and France that they would not make loans to Japan and by examining the prospects for resuming relations with Russia.[40] Roosevelt and Bullitt believed that, if Japan's source of loans could be shut off, the Japanese economy could not sustain operations in China. They also knew that Japan was aware of former Secretary of State Henry L. Stimson's assertion before he left office that there could be only one reason for the United States to recognize the Soviet regime and that was to cooperate with the Russians in stopping Japan's incursions in the Far East.

An interesting and disparate group participated in planning for the resumption of relations with Russia. Several of them, including Secretary Hull, Assistant Secretary of State R. Walton Moore, and Kelley, were skeptical of the results recognition might produce. Under-secretary of State Phillips, although not optimistic, was more willing to view recognition with an open mind. All of the State Department memoranda, including Bullitt's, urged caution and suggested concern lest the eagerness to raise trade quotas and arrange commercial agree-ments might rush negotiations to a conclusion without adequate con-sideration of other problems which plagued the nations already in diplomatic communication with the Soviets.[41] An outsider, from the department's point of view, Morgenthau also played a leading role in

---

[39]Interview with Perkins. Bullitt proved his self-esteem and impetuous nature when, as a minor member of the Paris Peace Commission, he called a press conference to announce his resignation and told reporters he would go lie on the Riviera and watch the world go to hell.

[40]Bullitt to Missy LeHand, January 24, 1933, PPF 1124, Bullitt Folder.

[41]Feis, *Characters in Crisis*, pp. 308ff.

the recognition drama. Becoming involved because of his position as a confidant of the president and as director of the Farm Credit Administration, his inclusion related to the economic aspects of recognition, illustrating the hope that, in addition to manufactured products, farm surpluses might be sold to the Russians.

Morgenthau exemplified Roosevelt's habit of bouncing ideas off friends and advisers who were not always aware of what they were being asked, but in April 1933 the president surprised Morgenthau with his consideration to send someone to Moscow as trade commissioner to "break the ice" between the United States and the Soviet Union.[42] Then in July the president, in another discussion, proposed that the Russian question should be brought into "the front parlor." He told Morgenthau that he had a plan but refused to elaborate and suggested that Morgenthau "send for Skvirsky[43] and tell him that we have the whole Russian question under consideration and that the delay in no way is prejudicial."[44]

Until Morgenthau lunched with Bullitt on September 7, he did not realize what the president had in mind. Before this he thought Roosevelt wanted a trade agreement or something of that sort. Bullitt assumed that Morgenthau knew more of the president's plans, but when Morgenthau did not seem to understand what Bullitt was talking about, the special assistant to the secretary explained that the negotiations with Russia involved far more than just lending money to buy goods. He further told Morgenthau that any dealings with the Russians at this point bore a direct relationship to U.S. relations with Japan.[45]

After ensuring against European financing of Japan's war machine, Bullitt and Roosevelt were ready to carry out the next phase of their plan to frustrate Japanese expansionism. As Bullitt outlined the scenario, Japan would interpret the loan to Russia as a forerunner of U.S. intentions to provide the USSR with the wherewithall to purchase airplanes and war materiel. He told Morgenthau of Japanese plans to attack Russia, which made the matter of mutual interest because the Japanese were a serious menace to the United States and would have

---

[42]Farm Credit Diary, April 1933, p. 17.

[43]Boris Skvirskii was associated with Amtorg, an acronym for the American Trade Organization, as Soviet trade representative but actually was in charge of unofficial Soviet diplomatic dealings in the United States. Skvirskii's name was transmitted to Roosevelt by Bullitt in a letter from London, although Bullitt mistakenly referred to him as Svirsky. Bullitt to FDR, July 8, 1933, PSF, London Economic Conference Folder. Russian spellings, unless they are commonly used names in the literature of American-Soviet relations, will follow the 1950s transliteration system of the Library of Congress, which I believe is still the best rendition of Russian to English; thus, Skvirskii instead of Skvirsky.

[44]Farm Credit Diary, July 1933, p. 61.

[45]Ibid., September 27, 1933, pp. 63–64.

to be watched closely. As Morgenthau sorted out the various bits of information provided to him by Bullitt and related it to what the president had told him earlier, he finally understood that Bullitt was discussing the Russian question in terms of recognition.[46]

President Roosevelt then made a dramatic approach. On October 19, 1933 he had Morgenthau and Bullitt confront Boris Skvirskii with an invitation to ask his government, through his "most secure code," that, if the Russians agreed with the idea of discussing the resumption of relations, to send a high-ranking official. Bullitt made Skvirskii promise absolute secrecy if for any reason either side decided not to pursue the matter. Skvirskii asked: "Does this mean recognition?" Bullitt parried with another question: "What more can you expect than to have your representative sit down with the President of the United States?"[47]

IV

Russian leaders were determined to use recognition as a deterrent to aggressive designs on their territory by the Japanese. The Soviets also believed that resumption of relations between their country and the United States might give Adolf Hitler cause to wonder how far the collaboration might go in trying to curb his ambitions for expansion in Europe. Roosevelt and Soviet President Kalinin focused their attention on the issue of preserving the peace as an overriding concern for their willingness to resume relations. Roosevelt referred to the force of 285 million Americans and Russians aligned on the side of peace, and Kalinin agreed, as he noted, that their separation had helped encourage forces wishing to disturb the peace.[48]

Bullitt had asked for a high Soviet official to direct the discussions, and the Russians, in their desire to impress the world with the importance of recognition, could not afford to send anyone of lesser stature than the commissar of Foreign Affairs, Maxim Litvinov, who departed from Europe on November 1, 1933 in a confident mood. Earlier he had predicted to reporters in Berlin on October 28 that an agreement could be reached in one-half hour. In the same interview the Russian assured reporters that friendly relations between his country and America could

---

[46]Ibid. See also Bennett, *Recognition*, p. 162, for information on Japanese plans to attack Russia.

[47]Farm Credit Diary, October 19, 1933, p. 72.

[48]*FRUS: Diplomatic Papers: The Soviet Union, 1933–1939* (Washington, DC: Government Printing Office, 1952), p. 17.

not help but influence Russo-Japanese relations.[49] In Litvinov, Roosevelt and Department of State personnel had a worthy adversary. No one who knew him in the slightest should have underestimated Litvinov. He was to some degree petty and did not like intellects who were capable of competing with him; it was one reason why he did not have a good personal relationship with Giorgii Chicherin when the latter was commissar of Foreign Affairs. Louis Fischer recalled of Litvinov that he was "full-blooded, virile, and tempestuous," as well as a cold-blooded realist.[50] It was said that he could go in the water and come out dry.[51] The contest of will and skill pitted this survivor of revolutionary politics against the squire of Hyde Park and might be referred to as the tale of two foxes. Roosevelt attempted to disarm the suspicious Russian with charm and guile and was partially successful.

Negotiations on recognition bogged down at the State Department. On November 8, after a morning of stalemate, Hull took Litvinov to the White House where FDR changed the climate of the negotiations and in essence shifted their location too. He exuded the Roosevelt charm and less belligerently reviewed the issues that the United States considered essential to restoring relations. The religious agreement, the president said, was necessary to placate Catholics as well as his critics in Congress. He explained to Litvinov the need to ensure domestic support rather than to focus on the State Department's insistence that the concession would be necessary for normal relations. This moved Litvinov to report to Moscow that Roosevelt was truly frightened by the opponents of recognition.[52] The president also attempted to impress Litvinov with his fairness by acknowledging the weakness of the moral position concerning Tzarist debts and by agreeing that, while it was not possible to insist on demanding the removal of the Comintern from Russia, it would be best to move it to Geneva, the seat of the League of Nations.[53]

Although State Department personnel continued to play a part in the negotiations, beginning on November 10 they met in the White

---

[49]*New York Times*, October 29, 1933. Robert Paul Browder suggested that Litvinov's comment on settling matters in Washington in half an hour may have been intended to convey the impression that prolonged discussions implied concessions on his part, thereby making recognition more acceptable to American public opinion. See Robert Paul Browder, *The Origins of Soviet-American Diplomacy* (Princeton: Princeton University Press, 1953), p. 127. It is also possible that Litvinov wanted the world to know that the negotiations were serious and to speculate on what was being discussed, which in fact is what happened.

[50]Louis Fischer, *Men and Politics* (New York: Duell, Sloan & Pierce, 1941), pp. 128–29.

[51]Robert Dallek, *Franklin D. Roosevelt and American Foreign Policy, 1932–1945* (New York: Oxford University Press, 1979), p. 80.

[52]Maddux, *Years of Estrangement*, p. 21.

[53]Ibid.

House. By the end of the first session, according to Phillips, the president had Litvinov in a more pliable mood than he had shown at the department. Roosevelt suggested a meeting alone with Litvinov that same evening so they could, "if need be, insult each other with impunity."[54] During this session they reached agreement on the question of religious freedom and propaganda, which Litvinov had refused to settle at the State Department. FDR took the department memoranda on freedom of religion for American nationals in Russia, the rights of Americans visiting or living in Russia, and the statements on propaganda and hammered out specific agreements on each one with relative ease, which speaks to the legwork done at the Department of State.[55] Certainly FDR skillfully orchestrated the process, but in part the success may be accredited to the skill of his opponent. Litvinov's obduracy was reserved for the department partly because he wanted the world to know that the Russians had worked out their arrangements in Washington directly with President Roosevelt. Phillips and Hull suggested that this was because Litvinov was on an ego trip.

By and large FDR followed the Department of State's format in the recognition discussions until he took up the debt question, at which point his departure from recommended procedure was complete and disastrous. The president indicated before the discussions began that more than any other phase he cared less for the financial portion of the negotiations, as talks on the debt were protracted and trying to his patience.[56]

When the Tzarist regime was overthrown in 1917, the new Soviet government was in no position to assume the obligations of its predecessor without inviting economic collapse, and for this and other reasons announced its intent not to honor the financial liabilities undertaken by that government. The new leadership contended that monies from these loans had been used to oppress the Russian people. Neither American citizens nor the U.S. government were among the heaviest investors in the Tzarist enterprises, but substantial sums were loaned to Russia in order to prosecute World War I. Some Americans, for the same purpose, had participated in Tzarist bond issues and those of the succeeding provisional government under Alexander Kerensky. Also, there were certain American businesses with properties in Russia which had been confiscated by the Soviet government. If the debt had to be accepted, the Soviets were determined that it would be arranged in

---

[54]Browder, *Origins*, p. 133.

[55]Orville H. Bullitt, ed., *For the President: Personal and Secret* (Boston: Houghton Mifflin, 1972), pp. 47–48.

[56]Farm Credit Diary, October 23, 1933, p. 76.

such fashion as to ensure that the whole question of debts to the European powers could not be reopened on the basis of the American settlement.

Litvinov agreed to accept the debt in principle, on the understanding that it would be only the amount incurred by the Kerensky government to prosecute the war against Germany, plus a reasonable settlement for legitimate claims by American citizens. He absolutely repudiated the Tzarist debt and that incurred by Kerensky and others to supply the anti-Bolshevik forces after the November revolution. President Roosevelt, proceeding from this basis after much wrangling, informed Litvinov that he believed he could persuade Congress to accept a settlement of $150 million, pared down from the $636,177,226.15 total obligations submitted to FDR by the Treasury Department,[57] but he doubted that it would be satisfied with less. Litvinov, in turn, told the president that he believed that he could convince Moscow to agree to pay $75 million, but it was questionable whether his government would go above that figure. The matter was left open to further discussion, with the signature of both men being affixed to a memorandum acknowledging that a final settlement would be negotiated at a later date and would be limited to a minimum of $75 million and a maximum of $150 million. The method of payment and the specific provisions concerning interest payments were also left to subsequent adjudication.[58]

Why FDR decided to be less than exact on the debt question is a subject of considerable conjecture and may never be known for sure.[59] The simplest explanation of the president's action stems from his confidence, after the other issues were settled, that this last and possibly least important concern should not delay an agreement that lay within his grasp. There is also the possibility that because of Roosevelt's busy schedule he could not afford to spend much time on the matter, and for purposes of prestige he could not turn it back to the Department of State for protracted discussions. In any case, by this time he was suspicious of the department's commitment to resume relations.

Certain questions arise in any attempt to assess the outcome of the debt negotiations. Would an airtight agreement on debts have made any difference? Would the Soviets have paid if they were bound by a firmer and clearer commitment? The answer is probably not. But the

[57]*FRUS: Diplomatic Papers*, vol. 2, *General, British Commonwealth, Europe, Near East, Africa, 1933* (Washington, DC: Government Printing Office, 1949), pp. 787–88.

[58]*FRUS: Soviet Union*, pp. 25–26.

[59]Speculations on the subject may be found in Donald G. Bishop, *The Roosevelt-Litvinov Agreements: The American View* (Syracuse: Syracuse University Press, 1965), chaps. 5, 9; and Richman, *United States and the Soviet Union*, provides various citations in which the central thesis is that the debt question was consciously manipulated by Kelley to ensure that no close relationship would ensue after recognition.

unfortunate way in which the subject was handled at the conference table gave them an excuse for not paying and left Roosevelt exposed to the subsequent criticism of his opponents for this glaring failure in an otherwise apparently successful effort. Thereafter, Litvinov steadfastly refused to consider payment unless it came in the form of a loan or unrestricted credits, which amounted to the same thing. The president, for a combination of political and legal reasons, could not agree to this. It seems clear that Litvinov understood that loans were not an acceptable means of repaying the indebtedness. He informed his government on November 15 that he had not agreed to more than $75 million on the Kerensky loan, and that the obligation would be discharged in the form of additional interest on the credit Russia obtained from America.[60] This illustrated that the Russians did not enter into the debt discussion already determined not to pay. Apparently they were willing to settle if the terms were satisfactory.

However, Litvinov did not get all he wanted from recognition, for no clear-cut challenge to the aggressors emerged from the announcements, at least from the U.S. side. Roosevelt was determined to make recognition a block to Japan by freeing the Russians from their concerns over an antagonistic America. He brought up the need for cooperation in this area several times in his discussion with Litvinov on November 17 but did not inform the State Department of this. In addition, Litvinov and FDR reviewed the German threat to the peace and proposed that Moscow and Washington should exchange information about Japan. Litvinov reported optimistically that "America is ready to do everything in order to avert the Japanese danger from us." He admitted that the Americans would not wage war on Russia's behalf, "but the President is ready to give us 100% moral and diplomatic support." FDR went so far beyond what the Department of State recommended that it is small wonder he failed to inform the department of this discussion. Litvinov continued:

> As if reasoning aloud, Roosevelt asked why we did not subscribe to a non-aggression pact to which I gave immediate consent and also approved the idea of a Pacific pact, and Roosevelt on the spot charged Bullitt to busy himself with these questions and to make a report to him. Roosevelt, certainly, understands the unacceptability of even a triangular pact for Japan, but the rejection of Japan unties his hands for the conclusion of a pact with us.[61]

---

[60]Maddux, *Years of Estrangement*, p. 22.
[61]Quoted in ibid., p. 23.

The Soviet commissar tried to persuade Roosevelt to commit himself to an agreement on joint actions should there be a threat to the peace, and he analyzed the American president's response shrewdly and accurately: "Roosevelt, afraid of every doublesided obligation, replied that he prefers to make unilateral statements during the latter situation."[62]

In subsequent negotiations over the next seven years, Litvinov repeatedly returned, in his dealings with Bullitt and his successors, to the substance of this discussion, especially the part referring to a bilateral nonaggression pact. Just as the Americans insisted that Litvinov had committed Russia to a debt settlement in Washington, he reminded a forgetful Bullitt that his president had promised a bilateral agreement intended to give the Japanese cause to worry. During the negotiations in Washington, Litvinov also had the president's expression of concern over German machinations as an indicator that there was a different mood in America from the one that had prevailed since 1919.

V

Recognition was supposed to illustrate, both at home and abroad, FDR's prowess as a political tour de force and to return the United States to the international stage as a leading actor in preserving peace and economic stability. From Roosevelt's perspective he could achieve his ends by political processes that worked for him in domestic affairs. He thought of the Russian diplomats as operating in the same frame of reference as American politicians. Fundamental differences in the philosophical base upon which the communistic and democratic systems rested escaped him and many other administration spokesmen who supported the president's position on recognition.

Roosevelt's own analysis of the foundations of an efficacious foreign policy gives some basis for judging his actions. He expanded the idea of the Good Neighbor to a universal application: American policy was to rest on "fraternal cooperation."[63] He reduced his formula to an analogy of relationships among individuals; "friendship among nations, as among individuals, calls for constructive efforts to muster the forces of humanity in order that an atmosphere of close understanding and cooperation may be cultivated."[64] While some American diplomats operated in the same general mode, this concept of friendship horrified most Russian experts in the Department of State who were fully aware

---

[62]Ibid.
[63]Franklin D. Roosevelt, *On Our Way* (New York: John Day, 1934), p. 110.
[64]Ibid., pp. 110–11.

that Soviet leaders would be genuinely perplexed and suspicious of the American eagle when it tried to nuzzle the Russian bear.

Like President Wilson, FDR tended to oversimplify both problems and solutions in the realm of foreign affairs. In his book *On Our Way*, he recorded the content of the first letters he exchanged with Kalinin and commented: "Thus, through the exchange of these simple letters, after many years the historic friendship between the people of Russia and the people of the United States was restored."[65] It reads like a fairy tale, which it was. Roosevelt compounded the myth when he spoke at the Wilson Day dinner on December 28, 1933, reminding his audience of Wilson's noble dream for world peace. He said that the former president had challenged history, which down to the World War provided a dismal record of wars through the centuries, wars that were made by governments with no voice for the people in the decision making:

> The challenge made the people who create and change governments think. They wondered with Woodrow Wilson whether the people themselves could not someday prevent governments from making war.
>
> It is but an extension of the challenge of Woodrow Wilson for us to propose in this new generation that from now on war by governments shall be changed to peace by peoples.[66]

The thrust of Roosevelt's remarks was intended to alert his fellow citizens and the potential makers of war to a new force. In the modern age, public opinion could be mobilized to cast into Hades any who moved to war against the desires of the people. There were two problems with this reasoning. If the 10 percent of the world he said were bent on war cared little for what the rest of the 90 percent thought, then collective opinion pressure alone would not deter them, and, if he could not secure public support beyond moral condemnation, there was no effective deterrent to those who ignored world public consensus.

Roosevelt's focus on the idea of international friendship as a means of turning aside dissentient powers was nowhere clearer than his public rationalization of resuming relations with Russia. This friendship was clearly supposed to act as a deterrent to aggression by lining up 160 million Russians with 125 million Americans on the side of peace. The president's welcoming speech of January 8, 1934 to Soviet Ambassador Alexander Troianovskii conveyed this idea:

---

[65]Ibid., p. 130.

[66]U.S. Department of State, *Press Releases* (Washington, DC: Government Printing Office, 1933), December 30, 1933.

A deep love of peace is the common heritage of the people of both
our countries, and I fully agree with you that the cooperation of
our great nations will inevitably be of the highest importance in
the preservation of world peace. The successful accomplishment
of this mutual task will be of immediate and lasting benefit not
only to the people of our countries but to all peace-loving peoples
everywhere.[67]

Roosevelt's remarks were thoroughly in keeping with his idea of "peace
by peoples." It was one more step in bringing the 90 percent together
to work on the 10 percent at a time when circumstances dictated the
need to develop a concrete plan to deal with the leadership of the
aggressive nations on the basis of equal military power. This speech
also illustrated the president's hopes to use recognition against Japan,
for he knew that the Russians were emphasizing American-Soviet cooperation against Japanese aggression in their interpretation of the meaning of his demarche. He publicly encouraged this interpretation.[68]

There is overwhelming evidence that recognition came from a
desire to aid in preserving the peace by moving to unite the peace-
loving nations.[69] Supporters of the move saw recognition as aimed
directly against Japan and against Germany by implication. Litvinov
and Bullitt recorded this as the motive expressed to them by Roosevelt.[70]
In the opinion of these leaders, the imperial ambitions of Japan had
to be stopped, but the Roosevelt administration could not decide how
firmly to support threats to Japan through recognition and, as a result,
pushed forward the idea with one hand while pulling it back with the
other. Ultimately, the Japanese considered this vacillation as a sign of
weakness. For this reason the Russians gained more real benefit in the
Far East from the resumption of relations with the United States than
did the Americans.

---

[67]"President Roosevelt's Reply to the Remarks of Alexander Antonovich Troianovskii," ibid., January 13, 1934.

[68]Stanley K. Hornbeck (State Department Asian expert) sent a memorandum to
Cordell Hull, suggesting the technique to be followed by high government officials
concerning U.S. expectations from the recognition discussions. Hornbeck proposed that
no direct mention should be made of events in the Far East because it was known that
the Soviets would attempt to imply that the conversations would have "an important
bearing upon matters of Far Eastern policy" and that on this account Japan was uneasy.
He urged that any impression of cooperation against Japan be avoided. Hornbeck was
unaware of the extent to which FDR was committed to giving precisely that impression.
Hornbeck to Hull, October 28 and 31, 1933, DSF 711.61/333.

[69]That this fitted well into Roosevelt's plans for a "new order" in world politics is
illustrated in Willard Range, *Franklin D. Roosevelt's World Order* (Athens: University of
Georgia Press, 1954). See esp. chapt. 4, "The Rooseveltian Approval to a New Order."

[70]Maddux, *Years of Estrangement*, p. 23; William C. Bullitt, "How We Won the War
and Lost the Peace," *Life* 25 (August 30, 1948): 83–84.

George F. Kennan best expressed Roosevelt's evaluation of the whole recognition process: the president wanted to recognize Russia, he wanted Congress and the public to accept this as a progressive move, and he wished to provide a temporary restraint on Nazi Germany and militarist Japan.[71] Actually FDR hoped that the restraint would be more than temporary, but the important point was that opposing the aggressors was the purpose of the move. Kennan's objection rested on method. He was one of the Russian experts trained by Kelley in the 1920s and was the only one who went to Germany for special training in the language, history, and culture of Russia; most of the others received their special training in France. All of them gained further education through contact with Russian émigrés in Riga, Latvia, the closest thing to old Russia left in the world after the Bolshevik Revolution. Kennan, Loy W. Henderson, and Charles E. Bohlen were the core from the Russian Section who established the first American embassy in Soviet Russia. Kennan touched the keystone deficiency in the making of American foreign policy and certainly the one central to Roosevelt's continuing relationship to Soviet policy. After Kennan's advice was ignored on one of the recognition issues, he learned an important lesson:

> This episode has remained in my mind as the first of many lessons I was destined to receive, in the course of a diplomatic career, on one of the most consistent and incurable traits of American statesmanship—namely, its neurotic self-consciousness and intro-version, the tendency to make statements and take actions with regard not to their effect on the international scene . . . but rather to their effect on those echelons of American opinion, congressional opinion first and foremost, to which the respective statesmen are anxious to appeal.[72]

The only point Kennan overlooked was motive. Roosevelt was not just trying to gain an internal political victory out of recognition. He was actually convinced that he might be able to achieve a master stroke in his drive for peace and security simply by renewing relations with Russia with only the vaguest idea of what should be done to "cooperate" with the Soviet Union in this endeavor.

---

[71]George F. Kennan, *Memoirs: 1925–1950* (Boston: Little, Brown, 1967), p. 57.
[72]Ibid., p. 53.

II

The First Year of American-Soviet Relations: "A Honeymoon Period"

WILLIAM BULLITT became the vehicle (one as it turned out with an erratic steering mechanism) by which President Roosevelt's Russian policy was implemented. As ambassador, Bullitt expressed that mixture of idealism and realism so often found in American diplomatic representatives in the twentieth century. On December 11, 1933, he bounced enthusiastically into Moscow where he remained only ten days before going on to Germany and then to Paris. It was from here that Bullitt sent his first direct report to the president, prefacing his long letter with the remark that he would send an abbreviated version to Secretary Hull but wanted "to set down for your own eye some of the more intimate episodes."[1] The ambassador's account of his first trip makes his later disillusionment more understandable. He was impressed with the little touches in his welcome which indicated special treatment for the Americans. The Soviets had arranged for Bullitt to have the same room he and his mother had occupied in 1914, and he was greeted at the railway station by Litvinov's press secretary Ivan Divilkovskii; Chief of Protocol Dmitri T. Florinskii; Alexander Troianovskii, who was about to become ambassador to the United States; and others.[2] After he presented his credentials to President Mikhail Kalinin, Bullitt gained personal audiences with Stalin, Litvinov, and Molotov. It seemed that all the doors in Russia were open to him, as he was given an unprecedented invitation by Kalinin to visit every part of the country. He thought he had the inside track among all the diplomats in Moscow,

---

[1]Bullitt, *For the President*, p. 61.
[2]Ibid.

which meant that it would be relatively simple to resume the debt negotiations and get on with the business of bluffing Japan and Germany.

The Russian experts within the State Department generally held the same hopes for success that other members of the Roosevelt administration expressed. Those who went to Moscow nurtured "the idea that the Kremlin had trimmed sail on a course of international cooperation."[3] Loy W. Henderson called the first year of American-Soviet relations "a honeymoon period."[4] Dispatches to the Department of State during that time reflected an optimism that belies the charges made later by historians that these people encouraged a consistent and unremitting opposition to the development of any cordial relationship with the Soviet Union.[5] George Kennan, who led the advance party, was the first American to serve in the Soviet Union, and he recalled the prime failing of the U.S. mission after the early days of exhilaration and enthusiasm in Moscow. It is difficult not to see Bullitt and Joseph Davies written between the lines of his complaints which he wrote in 1937:

> I did not despair of the possibility of a limited and unsensational measure of profitable cooperation between the two countries. But I was convinced that even this could be effectively realized only if our part was borne by persons who had the understanding and the qualifications necessary for the task: a gift for self-effacement, a decent educational background, an intellectual humility before the complexities of the Russian world, and, above all, an exceptional capacity for patience. Barring the enlistment of such persons on our part, I could see little future for Russian-American relations other than a long series of misunderstandings, disappointments, and recriminations on both sides.[6]

Kennan did not mean education in its broadest sense; he meant it in Russian language, literature, history, and psychology. This was the kind of training that he, Charles Bohlen, and other Russian experts went through before being posted to the Soviet Union. Ambassadors plucked from the Riviera, the law office, or the business office could never meet Kennan's preparation test for the ambassador's chair in Moscow, and he was absolutely accurate in his assessment. Whatever

---

[3] DeSantis, *Diplomacy of Silence*, p. 27.

[4] Ibid., p. 31.

[5] Richman, *United States and the Soviet Union*, pp. 158–59, 236–37, provides a good example of the suspicion expressed by those who blamed the antis for the failure to develop cooperation with the Russians. William Appleman Williams more accurately placed the blame for the failure on Cordell Hull and William Bullitt. William Appleman Williams, *American-Russian Relations, 1781–1947* (New York: Rinehart, 1952), pp. 241–47.

[6] Kennan, *Memoirs*, p. 74.

the failings of America's professional diplomats, their training was intended to encourage submersion of personal glory to the national interest, while the political appointments sought their positions for a combination of motives which seldom excluded prestige and self-gratification. The Russian experts knew from observation that vanity could not be served in an embassy assignment to Moscow.

Bullitt's staff in the Russian capital launched the resumption of relations with hope for success that marked all of them for future fits of gloom and depression. Most of them did not suffer from the delusion of Roosevelt, Bullitt, and Davies that they were dealing with Russian-speaking Americans, but they did believe that the direction of Soviet policy had perhaps changed and that an acceptable working relationship could be established. As was Bullitt, they were impressed by the unusual cordiality and generosity shown to them by Soviet officials in the early weeks of their mission, and in some measure they failed to understand what was required of them to continue basking in the light of Soviet favor.

Like the fanciful Russian ballets and operas, the American embassy staff was caught up in a world of dreams and then awakened by brutal reality. They plunged into a fever pitch of preparation, including plans for building the embassy compound, arranging offices and living quarters, meeting Russians from the top down, exploring Moscow and the countryside, attending parties, and discussing what they had seen and experienced, all of which was exciting, exhilarating, and unique. Then came the failure of the debt negotiations, Soviet callousness to their comforts, broken stoves unrepaired until spring, telephones that worked sporadically, mysterious calls with only silence on the other end, and purges that swept away the more outgoing and friendly officials of the bureaus with which they dealt. The Americans were suddenly thrust from an apparently warm inner circle to a defensive one surrounded by icy, hostile, ungracious Bolsheviks who would not let callers through the embassy gate. In their memoirs and reminiscences, most who served in Moscow during that first winter never quite admitted the full extent of their shock, but it is implicit. Few openly avowed the responsibility for their situation to the ambassador's overexuberance and frustrated reactions to Litvinov's demands for quid pro quos, but that too emerged between the lines.

Maxim Litvinov told Bullitt in December 1933 that the situation relating to Soviet security was serious and that it concerned Germany as well as Japan. In a strictly confidential message to President Roosevelt on December 24, 1933, Bullitt reported a conversation with Litvinov, during which the Soviet commissar asked if the United States objected to Russia surrendering to French pressure to join the League of Nations. This move would guarantee the security of Soviet western borders when the anticipated attack came from Japan in the east. Bullitt asked Litvinov why the Russians were reversing their stand against joining the league and was told that France desired it so that they could arrange a regional pact that would commit France and Russia to come to one another's aid if attacked by Germany. Litvinov told Bullitt that the USSR had reliable information that Japan would go to war with them in the spring of 1934. Litvinov did not fear an assault by either Germany or Poland unless the war with Japan dragged on for two years, in which case both would join the conflict in concert with the Japanese. Bullitt continued, adding that "he knew preliminary conversations looking forward [to] this eventuality had already taken place between Japan, Germany and Poland. Therefore the Soviet Government although still wishing to keep its hands free and not to join the League of Nations felt it must pay this price if necessary to obtain the agreement from France."[7]

Bullitt went on to ask Litvinov why France was insistent that the USSR join the league as part of the arrangement. Litvinov answered that the French wished to evade the difficulty created by the 1925 Locarno aggrement, which was signed by Germany, Great Britain, France, Belgium, Italy, Czechoslovakia, and Poland and committed these powers to submit disputes to arbitration if normal diplomatic channels failed. Disputes would then be referred to the League of Nations or the Hague Court of International Justice, and the powers would foreswear resolution of problems by force. It was understood that these countries were bound by league provisions to avoid military alliances, except for regional defense arrangements, that would be triggered by an aggression, which the league had not had the opportunity or time to consider. However, the league did not prohibit regional and purely defensive understandings, and therefore the pact could not restrict a Franco-Soviet treaty if it were introduced to the league as a regional understanding. Bullitt told Litvinov that there seemed to be a considerable region between France and the Soviet Union. The commissar replied that the proximity of both to Germany was a sufficient excuse.[8] Thus, alerted to the desperate situation the Russians faced, Bullitt was sure of his ground when he and Secretary of State Cordell Hull agreed that the Russians could be pressured into a debt settlement.

Bullitt reiterated to Roosevelt the Soviets' concern over a possible war, telling the president that nearly all members of the Soviet government and the Communist party, with whom he had talked, stressed

[7]Bullitt to FDR, December 24, 1933, PSF, Box 15.
[8]Ibid.

the impending conflict: "Stalin introduced the chief of staff Egerov to me as 'the man who will lead our army victoriously against the Japanese when they attack us.' "[9] Bullitt said that he repeatedly emphasized, in every discussion of Soviet security problems, that the United States had absolutely no intention of engaging in a war with Japan, and in case of war the American role would be restricted to the use of moral influence: "Nevertheless the Soviet Union is so anxious to have peace that it is obvious that even our moral influence is valued very highly by the Soviet government. It is difficult to exaggerate the cordiality with which I was received by all members of the Government including Kalinin, Molotov, Voroshilov and Stalin."[10]

The wooing of Bullitt was part of the Russian campaign to ensure cooperation. Just as the Americans had carefully sketched biographies of all the Soviets they dealt with in the recognition negotiations, the Russians did their homework on Bullitt. His ego was the target of the first Soviet newspaper article on him when he arrived as ambassador. He was described as a reliable witness and friend whose word on the intentions of the United States could be accepted at face value. *Izvestiia* traced his career and called him a fair observer of Soviet life, an experienced diplomat, not a conservative, and not anti-Soviet.[11] An article of December 14, 1933 proclaimed that the new freindship between the USSR and the United States was a guarantee of peace. Bullitt said that since the Soviet Union and the United States were large and powerful nations who would provoke hostilities in the face of their determined opposition?[12] The Russians concluded that the Americans meant to promote meaningful obstructions to the machinations of the aggressive powers.

Soviet flattery, worried consultations on how the Americans might help to solve Russian security problems, and assurances of the sincerity of Soviet friendship all played a part in the ambassador's optimism concerning a debt settlement. All these factors fed Bullitt's naive assumption that the Russians were so anxious for U.S. moral support that they would do almost anything to please the Americans. He simply did not grasp certain realities of the American-Soviet relationship. The fact that recognition may have assisted in stalling a Japanese attack, while the Japanese war party tested the wind to determine the strength of American-Soviet ties, had nothing to do with reciprocal assistance in any form. The Soviets considered this as the least that they could

[9]Ibid.

[10]Ibid.

[11]"The Career of William Bullitt," *Izvestiia*, December 13, 1933.

[12]"Friendship Between USSR and USA Is a Guarantee of Peace," ibid., December 14, 1933.

expect from recognition, which they assessed as having been unjustly withheld for sixteen years. The subjects of debts and trade were of vital importance to the United States, not the Soviet Union.

Concerning the prospective war with Japan, the higher echelons of the Department of State, including the ambassadors in Moscow, never quite understood the Soviet position. The Russians disliked the prospect of fighting Japan, when they considered that all they had to do was stay out long enough for the imperialist powers to become involved, but they did not fear Japanese power by itself. What frightened the Russians was the possibility of an immediate and prolonged war with Japan for the reasons stated so clearly to Bullitt by Litvinov. The Soviets believed that there were two forces working for them if they could postpone a conflict: first, the aforementioned idea that an imperialist struggle in the Far East was inevitable, thus drawing off Japanese poison in another direction; and, second, that in a very short time they could build a military machine that Japan would be afraid to test in a full-scale war.[13]

Whatever may be said of America's Russian policy in 1934, Roosevelt, Bullitt, and Hull were consistent in their insistence that payment of the Soviet debt was a prerequisite to any further diplomatic cooperation. It is fairly obvious that the Soviet Union, from the outset, had no intentions of paying the debt claims of the United States in total or without some kind of additional concession such as outright loans, extensive credits, or an elimination or substantial reduction of interest payments. The arguments presented in defense of the Soviet position were various and often vague. In essence, the Russians maintained that the debts were not legitimately theirs, having been incurred by previous governments, which they had repudiated and overthrown. To press the issue at a time when every government but Finland was in default on payments to the United States seemed to the Soviets to add luster to their contention that the Americans were not viewing the situation realistically, and that the Soviet position was in line with the rest of the international community.[14]

---

[13]Harold Vanacke detailed several military clashes that took place in 1934 and 1935 as a result of Japanese efforts to test the Soviets' determination to resist. These led to border struggles in 1936 such as the Mongol-Manchurian dispute of February 8–10, 1936; the Japanese counterattack took place from March 25 to 29. According to Vanacke's account, a little indiscretion on the part of either of the commanders would probably have committed the two countries to a war, for which neither side was ready. See Harold M. Vanacke, *A History of the Far East in Modern Times* (New York: F. S. Crofts, 1947), p. 545.

[14]Upon being informed by Bullitt that, as a result of the Johnson Bill, until the Soviets paid their debt the credit markets of the United States would remain closed to them and open to those not in default, Litvinov responded that the USSR would be in good company and could easily make its purchases elsewhere. *FRUS: Soviet Union*, p. 80.

Soviet diplomats made effective use of the argument that, if they paid the United States, they would have to acknowledge the debts to other powers, which they did not believe they could afford to do. They even went so far as to suggest that payment would put them in bad grace with Great Britain and France, whose cooperation they needed in creating a united front against Germany. The inference was that the British and the French did not want the solid front of debt repudiation broken.[15] Litvinov then suggested to Bullitt that, if the United States would grant loans large enough that other countries with claims against the Soviet Union could not match them, a settlement might be reached without danger of the question being opened elsewhere.[16]

Litvinov complained of Bullitt's attempts to blackmail Russia, but this was a two-way street. The commissar told Bullitt that he understood American businessmen well enough to know that eventually the blame for lack of increased trade with the Soviet Union would fall on the Department of State. He was sure that pressure would be brought to bear to overrule the Johnson Bill in the case of the Soviet Union, or to withdraw the resolution of the Export-Import Bank that credits could not be extended to nations in default. Litvinov further explained to Bullitt that he was secure in his belief that the American government would come around to a view that cooperation with the Soviet Union, in the interest of preserving the peace, was more important than debts and would drop the matter, as had been the case with other countries that had debt claims against the USSR.[17]

During the first few months of his assignment in Moscow, Ambassador Bullitt tried various ploys to fulfill what he considered to be his prime task: to clear the deck of the debt in order to establish the friendly relationship that he thought would follow. Herein lay the source of his problem. Bullitt entered his ambassadorial career with such euphoric expectations of the results he could produce in Moscow that it was literally impossible for him not to become disillusioned. There is an ironic, almost fateful, twist in Bullitt's role: in 1919 he went to Russia on a mission that failed, and he blamed Woodrow Wilson; in 1933 he returned with equally high spirits and expectations and failed again, but this time he blamed Litvinov. Perhaps Bullitt's shortcoming was his perception of the historical process. He had been a progressive with all of the expectations usual to progressives, in that history depended on the efforts of the individual and, if the results were unsatisfactory, then someone had to be blamed. Twice disappointed in his Russian

---

[15]Browder, *Origins*, p. 193.
[16]*FRUS: Soviet Union*, pp. 115–16.
[17]Ibid., pp. 111, 80, 109.

adventures he never thought of finding fault with himself. He kept on sticking keys in locks he believed would open doors to friendship with the Soviets, which in turn would affect the whole world. When the door refused to open, he blamed everything except the selector of the keys.

Bullitt sent the State Department an abbreviated report of his long letter to Roosevelt, relaying his impressions of his personal success and that of the United States as he was received in Moscow. On December 12 he lunched en famille with Litvinov, who was delighted by the remarks Bullitt proposed to make on the presentation of his credentials to Kalinin and who said that, as a special politeness, contrary to diplomatic precedent, he would like to give the ambassador an advance copy of the reply that Kalinin would make. After the presentation, Bullitt said he had a lengthy chat with Kalinin and, contrary to rumors that he was a "simple minded old peasant," the Soviet president was delightfully shrewd and followed with great interest President Roosevelt's program in America, which he and everyone in Russia were convinced was genuinely in the interest of workers and farmers. The ambassador also related that "Kalinin was very agreeable to me personally, saying that Lenin had talked to him about me on several occasions, and that he felt as if he were welcoming someone he had known for a long time." A few days later Bullitt met V. M. Molotov and, after a long talk with him, Bullitt decided he had underrated him as he had Kalinin:

> He has a magnificent forehead and the general aspect of a first-rate French scientist, great poise, kindliness and intelligence. He talked freely about the difficulties of the Soviet Union in the Far East, saying that the primary desire of the entire Soviet Government was to avoid war and to obtain time to work out the domestic reconstructing which had scarcely been begun. He said that he feared greatly that Japan would attack this spring; that he considered an eventual attack inevitable and 1935 as the probable limit of peace.[18]

On December 20 the wooing continued as Bullitt dined with a group that included Klementii Voroshilov, Stalin, Molotov, Litvinov, and others whom Stalin assured Bullitt constituted the inside directorate of the Soviet party and government. Bullitt related with relish an exchange of toasts, beginning with Stalin's:

> 'To President Roosevelt, who in spite of the mute growls of the Fishes, dared to recognize the Soviet Union.' His reference to Hamilton Fish created considerable laughter. I then proposed the

---

[18]Ibid., pp. 56–57.

health of President Kalinin and thereupon Molotov raised his glass to me and proposed: 'The health of one who comes to us as a new Ambassador but an old friend.'[19]

Bullitt, well oiled with vodka and compliments, then engaged in a long talk with Stalin, who told him that he needed discarded American steel rails to complete the Trans-Siberian second line to Vladivostok, for which the Russians would pay. The rails were necessary to ensure a more rapid defeat of the Japanese when they attacked. Then, according to Bullitt, Stalin expressed genuine admiration for President Roosevelt, who was universally considered, despite the fact that he led a capitalist country, "one of the most popular men in the Soviet Union." In the context of all this friendship, cooperation, and talk of a victorious war against Japan, the next evening Litvinov brought up the non-aggression pact with Russia, China, and Japan and confided that anything that could be done to make the Japanese believe that the United States was ready to cooperate with Russia, even though there might be no basis for the belief, would be valuable. In this vein, he asked for an American naval squadron, or even a single warship, to visit Vladivostok or Leningrad in the spring. Bullitt said he would take it up with Washington.[20]

II

When Bullitt failed to gain immediate settlement of the debt claims, he returned to this early friendly introduction and sorted out who had been most encouraging. The answer he came up with was everyone. Then why did nothing happen? The person he dealt with in the day-to-day discussions was Litvinov. As everyone else had promised him the moon, surely it must be Litvinov who was not accurately conveying the content of their negotiations. This impression was further cemented when Bullitt returned to Washington in February 1934 and called on Ambassador Troianovskii. Bullitt argued that $150 million must be the minimum settlement paid by Russia because the dollar had been devalued to 60 percent, and that amount represented $90 million at the rate of exchange when the negotiations with Litvinov had taken place in Washington. Bullitt was convinced that Troianovskii accepted his statement as entirely sensible and that for this reason the State Department should not accept one penny less. During the same discussion, Troianovskii showed Bullitt a letter he had received from Baron Shidehara

---

[19]Ibid., p. 59.
[20]Ibid.

Kijūrō which the Russian was convinced had been dictated by Hirota Kōki.[21] The letter said that it would be absolute madness for Japan and the Soviet Union to go to war. Troianovskii told Bullitt he thought that the danger of war in the spring had definitely subsided.[22] Later Bullitt drew two conclusions from this exchange: first, Troianovskii wanted a debt settlement; and, second, the United States, by recognition, had averted a war between Japan and the Soviet Union, for which the Russians owed the Americans something. It meant to Bullitt that cooperation had paid off as he and the president thought it would; they had avoided a Pacific war. Troianovskii's attitude and the success of recognition gave evidence that the Soviet government had in mind paying the debt and that someone was fouling the nest without the knowledge of the men at the top.

In late April, Troianovskii sought an interview with FDR which was attended by Secretary Hull and Assistant Secretary of State R. Walton Moore who was often used by Roosevelt as his go-between with the State Department and by Hull as his contact with the president. The Russian ambassador told the president that Litvinov was prepared to go above the $75 million minimum he had agreed to in Washington. Roosevelt emphasized the devaluation of the currency, which would require an amount closer to the maximum figure of $150 million, and stressed to Troianovskii that any settlement would have to be ratified by the Senate. The Russians had attempted to have the debt discussions transferred to Washington, but the president refused, reminding the ambassador that Bullitt and Litvinov were both familiar with the whole question and should be the ones to settle it. Hull wrote that "there is really nothing concrete to say except that the President leaves the negotiations in your hands without having made any committal or statement conflicting in any way with what you have done or anticipating what you may attempt to do." Hull said that it was all up to Bullitt and suggested, in essence, that if he failed, if Litvinov remained obdurate, Bullitt would no doubt wish the negotiations to be moved to Washington. He reminded Bullitt that he had some aces in the hole as the Swedes had just refused to loan Russia money and relations with Japan were still of concern to the Soviets. Roosevelt added a longhand note to the dispatch, stating that he could not immediately reject Troianovskii, but he had persuaded him that, as all points

---

[21]As Japanese foreign minister and/or premier through most of the 1920s until 1931, Shidehara authored the policy of peaceful penetration of China and was respected in the West for his moderation; therefore, he could be used by Foreign Minister Hirota as an honest broker.

[22]*FRUS: Soviet Union*, p. 65.

of discussion would have to run through Bullitt and Litvinov anyway, it would be less time consuming to have the talks carried on in Moscow.[23]

Bullitt was under pressure to accomplish his task or admit failure and see the negotiations changed to Washington. Secretary Hull let him know that Roosevelt wanted the maximum amount or a figure close to it, that the Senate would scrutinize the fruits of his effort, and that if he did not think he could do the job the State Department was prepared to take over. Thereafter Bullitt was determined either to succeed or find someone to blame for his failure. The ambassador bombarded the department with solutions, complained of Litvinov's intransigence, tried contacting other Soviet officials, and in general played the gadfly. He believed that, if sufficient pressure could be exerted to prove that Litvinov's attitude held back American-Soviet cooperation, the commissar would be forced to change his tack. Bullitt decided that Litvinov was more sure than his comrades that Japan would not attack the Soviet Union and that the United States "no matter how the Soviet Union behaves will attempt to prevent war between the Soviet Union and Japan and will support the Soviet Union in case of war."[24]

The Americans had agreed with the Soviet plan to impress Japan with the visit of a U.S. warship to a Soviet port. Secretary Hull asked Bullitt whether he thought it advisable to refuse the request of the Navy Department to arrange for the USS *Minneapolis* to go to Leningrad as a means of showing the Soviets that the State Department meant business. Bullitt replied that such a visit would be construed as an indication of support for the USSR in its quarrel with Japan and would substantiate Litvinov's contention that aid would be forthcoming without a debt settlement. On these grounds Bullitt opposed the trip, believing that pressure alone would be effective because "I have . . . private information that Stalin and the military authorities feel strongly that cooperation with the United States must be strengthened and not destroyed and I do not consider Litvinov's intransigence irreversible."[25]

At this juncture Bullitt had not given up on persuading Litvinov to accommodate the Americans. In March 1934 he cabled Hull that previous negotiations with the commissar had led him to observe that decisive negations were followed by acquiescence and that he did not

---

[23]Draft of dispatch, Hull to Bullitt, PSF, Russia; altered version sent May 1, 1934, *FRUS: Soviet Union*, p. 87. This was the first attempt by the Russians to establish a practice, which they ultimately achieved, to avoid the embassy in Moscow as middleman and to deal directly with the officials in Washington. This had the advantage for them of creating direct contact with American leaders, which had been denied to U.S. diplomats in Moscow.

[24]*FRUS: Soviet Union*, pp. 115–16.

[25]Ibid., p. 113.

consider the problem insoluble.[26] Bullitt followed the advice President Roosevelt sent him: "I get a lot of chuckles out of the scraps that you and Litvinov have. Keep up the good work."[27] He did.[28] In May he wrote to FDR and again singled out Litvinov as the problem, suggesting that the president might help: "Litvinov was so delighted by your invitation to his son, which I received just before his departure for Geneva, that he talked amicably and seemed ready for concessions; but when I called on Krestinsky to obtain the concessions I was met by a flat refusal even to discuss the matter on the basis of the Department's draft agreement."[29]

Ambassador Bullitt tried to force Litvinov's hand by threatening that, if the Russians failed on the debt payment, there would be no more close cooperation. When the Americans in July refused to sign the bilateral nonaggression pact Litvinov thought he had been promised in Washington and when Litvinov heard of the American intent to block the inclusion of Russia at the forthcoming London Naval Conference, Bullitt pressed his advantage. He tried to keep Litvinov worried about a possible shift in American policy. Telegraphing Hull he recounted a conversation with Litvinov, during which Bullitt intimated that U.S. ties with Japan were getting better and asked if there had been a similar improvement in Soviet-Japanese relations. Litvinov laughed and responded that "the only improvement is that we are not yet at war."[30]

Bullitt claimed his suspicion that Litvinov was not portraying an altogether accurate picture to Stalin and others of their conversations on the debt question was substantiated by one of his conversations with Marshal Voroshilov, then commissar of defense and in command of the Red Army. Voroshilov reportedly told Bullitt that it was his intense desire that relations between the United States and the Soviet Union should not only appear to be friendly and intimate but also should be. As a result, Bullitt was sure Voroshilov would "use his

---

[26]Bullitt to Hull, March 21, 1934, PSF, Box 15.

[27]FDR to Bullitt, May 9, 1934, PSF, Russia, 1933–1936.

[28]There is a large volume of correspondence, of a personal nature, between President Roosevelt and Ambassador Bullitt in PPF 1124, William C. Bullitt, 1933–1944, indicating that in the early 1930s there was a friendly relationship between the two men. The president wrote, telegraphed, or phoned Bullitt frequently when compared to the run-of-the-mill ambassadors, or even others whom the president pushed off on the Department of State. Bullitt was much more intimate in his response to FDR's letters than vice versa and very free with his counsel, which more often than not turned out to be ill advised. He greatly enjoyed this intimacy with the president and, according to Frances Perkins, took advantage of it. Interview with Perkins.

[29]Dispatch, Bullitt to FDR, May 18, 1934, PSF, Box 15.

[30]Bullitt to Hull, July 9, 1934, DSF 711.6112 (AGGRESSOR)/8.

influence with Stalin which is very great to soften Litvinov's obduracy."[31] As he often did, Bullitt relayed his conversation with Voroshilov
directly to Roosevelt, telling the president of his opportunity to conduct
personal talks with Stalin, Voroshilov, and Molotov, and that he hoped
he could brush up on his Russian well enough to accomplish this
without an interpreter, thus enabling him to be far more frank and vice
versa.[32] He also told the president that in the end this would mean "we
shall be able to beat down Litvinov's resistance."[33]

Part of Bullitt's later difficulty with the State Department over
when or whether to moderate the official position on the debt question
rested on his continuing assurances in 1934 that all was not lost. As
late as August he informed Hull that Soviet need and desire for the
friendship of the United States and other Western powers was even
more evident and that ultimately Russia would recognize this and
accede to American demands on the debt. Contrary to Soviet allega-
tions, Bullitt wrote, France and Germany were not vying with one
another for Russian favors by offering substantial credits, there was a
hitch in the sale of the Chinese-Eastern Railway to Japan, and Soviet
foreign affairs were not running smoothly in other areas. These conditions led the ambassador to conclude that "the Soviet desire to come
to an agreement with the United States on the matter of claims and
indebtedness has increased rather than diminished."[34]

On September 9, 1934, Bullitt thought he had found a way to
get by Litvinov. Soviet journalist Karl Radek told the ambassador that
he did not believe that Litvinov was keeping Stalin fully informed on
the proposals from the United States regarding the debt question, and
that this was because Litvinov desired a personal triumph as a bar-
gainer. Radek promised to pursue the matter, and, if Litvinov should
prove to be the problem, he would schedule a meeting between Bullitt
and Stalin. Bullitt was so sure that an arrangement could be made by
this route that he advised postponement of any such drastic action as
dissolving the Export-Import Bank.[35] Hull responded skeptically that
the State Department had no objection to Bullitt meeting with Stalin
but saw little chance for success since Litvinov had won his victory
when he obtained recognition and considered everything else of minor
import.[36]

---

[31]*FRUS: Soviet Union*, p. 124.

[32]Bullitt did not report this plan to Hull, whom he knew to be opposed to "personal"
diplomacy, but he told President Roosevelt, whom he knew to be very much in favor of
such a course.

[33]Dispatch, Bullitt to FDR, August 5, 1934, PSF, Box 15.

[34]*FRUS: Soviet Union*, p. 126.

[35]Ibid., p. 143.

[36]Ibid., p. 146.

Bullitt's hopes that he could settle the matter simply by talking with Stalin were shattered September 15, the same day Hull made his gloomy prediction. Radek notified Bullitt that he had seen Stalin's file of reports, as submitted by Litvinov, and that the foreign commissar had relayed Bullitt's proposals accurately. He further dashed Bullitt's belief in the power of Voroshilov when he related that after Bullitt's tête-à-tête with the marshal he had seen Stalin. While Stalin agreed with Voroshilov "that removal of all obstacles to close cooperation between the United States and the Soviet Union was of prime importance for the maintenance of peace in the Far East," it was even more pressing at that moment to arrange to protect Russia's flank. This could be accomplished by reaching an understanding with the British and French. Thus any arrangement with the United States had to be one that could be offered to the French and English but one that they could not afford to accept. Bullitt concluded: "If we can contrive a formula to meet this particular difficulty I feel that we shall be on our way to a solution although the Soviet Government will doubtless continue to haggle over interest rates."[37] The ambassador, in the meantime, listened to siren songs of better things to come while he told the State Department that the Soviet desire to please the Americans accounted for the postponement of the Seventh Comintern Congress.[38]

III

Peace in Europe and Asia was so obviously in jeopardy that American and Soviet leaders were forced to assess their relationship in terms of what they might do to prevent a rapid move toward war. Roosevelt illustrated his awareness of the external threat as he answered a gloomy report from Ambassador William Dodd in Germany:

> I am glad indeed to have your letter even though your situation cannot exactly be called a rosy one. It confirms my fear that the drift in Germany, and perhaps in other countries in Europe, is definitely downward and that something must break within the next six months or a year. . . . I too am downhearted about Europe but I watch for any ray of hope or opening to give me an opportunity to lend a helping hand. There is nothing in sight at present.[39]

Secretary Hull expressed his concern over Japan's machinations at the preliminary discussions to the London Naval Conference; Japan's

---

[37] Ibid., pp. 147–48.
[38] Telegram, Bullitt to State Department, September 26, 1934, DSF 711.61/504.
[39] FDR to Dodd, August 25, 1934, PPF 1043.

deliberate plan to scrap the 5-5-3 ratio, combined with the fact that "a young, wild, and lawless group of Japanese have seized control and made of their government an international desperado," necessitated that "all questions of policy in the Orient are by Japanese action at London opened up anew and afresh."[40] A logical conclusion from this scenario should have been that American-Soviet relations were thrown into a new perspective because the mutual objective of recognition had not yet been achieved; Japan was still determined to upset the balance of power. The response was to work harder to convince the Soviets that they had to pay their debts before any other significant cooperation could take place.

The reason that Roosevelt and Hull were so adamant in this demand was largely based on internal political motives. Certainly the failure to collect the debt would leave the administration open to charges from those who had opposed recognition that they had analyzed more correctly the results of resuming relations than had the administration. There were also a number of claim holders against the Soviets who would view themselves betrayed. Most important, the administration regarded the debt settlement as a preliminary step to prove the sincerity of the Soviet Union before any further collaboration could be considered. Without such evidence of good faith, the president would lay himself open to attack for not having observed the danger signs when the Russians went back on their word initially on the debt question. Public opinion and political expedience were never out of FDR's mind. Certainly the insistence of Hull and the president that it was imperative that a settlement be reached at the earliest possible date confirms this.[41] As Ambassador Bullitt pointed out to Nikolai Krestinskii and Evgenii Rubinin of the Commissariat of Foreign Affairs, Americans were already suspicious of the sincerity of the Soviet Union, and its intransigence on the debt question only served to heighten that suspicion.[42] Hull made the same point to Troianovskii.[43]

Litvinov was convinced that, if the USSR gave in on American terms and under the kind of pressure Bullitt exerted, it was in for some bad times indeed. The Soviet commissar selected Bullitt as the source of his difficulties with the Americans, probably with more accuracy than Bullitt's selection of him in the inverse. Litvinov wrote to Troianovskii on April 10, 1934: "We must overcome Bullitt's inclination to blackmail, and we can do this only through self-control and composure.

---

[40] Hull to FDR, November 1, 1934, PSF, Departmental Files, Cordell Hull, 1933–1941.

[41]*FRUS: Soviet Union*, pp. 94, 104, 131, 139.

[42]Ibid., pp. 149–51.

[43]Ibid., pp. 130, 134.

We must show that cutting off trade with America does not make the impression on us that Bullitt expected, that it is a blow not against us, but only against those Americans who are interested in trade."[44] According to Litvinov's journal, he considered Bullitt almost from the beginning a bitter enemy and charged that the American ambassador behaved badly during the entire debt negotiations. However, Litvinov also criticized the decision of the Politburo, which he called the Instantsia, to renege on the promise to pay something to the Americans: "Naturally, the Instantsia is not altogether free from blame . . . having made a rash promise we should have kept our word."[45] He thought it ironically amusing that, when the matter was a commercial debt, the members of the Politburo were scrupulous to the point of being silly, but as soon as it was a matter of a state debt they refused to pay despite promises to do so. Litvinov said that he received formal instructions in 1933 from the Politburo on his negotiations with Roosevelt, but, when the Politburo later discovered that they could get away without paying, they could not resist "doing" the Americans. He implied that such maneuvers did not serve well in international relations, but that Stalin and the Caucasian Communists were all traders at heart and loved to bargain.

In the first year of closer contact, future American-Soviet relations swung on the fragile hinge of expectations unfulfilled on both sides. The official Soviet line has emerged variously over the years to a relatively consistent lament: the Americans were not sincere.[46] More precisely, the perception from Moscow also focused on Bullitt as the villain of the insincerity:

> The Americans, for their part, violated the main condition of the gentlemen's agreement, thereby repudiating the Anglo-Saxon tradition, highly revered in Western literature, that a gentleman keeps his word. The Russian Communists proved to be more gentlemanly than the American squires. As if that were not enough, William Bullitt began to blackmail Moscow; according to him, the refusal to make the concessions demanded would worsen the condition of Soviet trade and the position of the USSR in the Far East.[47]

[44]Quoted in Nikolai V. Sivachev and Nikolai N. Yakovlev, *Russia and the United States*, trans. Olga Adler Titelbaum (Chicago: University of Chicago Press, 1979), p. 128.

[45]Maxim Litvinov, *Notes for a Journal* (New York: William Morrow, 1955), pp. 243–44. Despite the cautionary note by E. H. Carr in his introduction, in which he questions the book's authenticity, especially in the later chapters, there is enough similarity of information given to Richard Hottelet and Louis Fischer by Litvinov to make the comments on the debt negotiations and on Bullitt worth repeating.

[46]Sivachev and Yakovlev, *Russia and the United States*, pp. 125–29, 137–43.

[47]Ibid., p. 128.

To a degree the charge was accurate. Bullitt thought he had the Russians in a corner and began to apply the pressure, which he and Hull
both believed would settle the debt question because the Soviets needed
American moral support in their contest with Japan.

It was inside the framework of these political crosscurrents that
the debt negotiations broke down. Bullitt worked through his contacts
close to the president, directly on the president, and on Hull to focus
the necessary blame on Litvinov, while the Soviet commissar played
the middleman on the Russian side. Bullitt's sources of pressure were
considerable. He cultivated Assistant Secretary of State Moore, who
had been a friend of Bullitt's father in their youth, and the Moore-
Bullitt correspondence served Bullitt well, as he found out who was
doing what to whom in the State Department, had a champion close
to Hull, and a voice to the president, with whom Moore met frequently
in the first few years of the Roosevelt administration. Marguerite (Missy)
LeHand was possibly FDR's favorite secretary, and Bullitt wooed her
also. Moore was a romantic old southern gentleman and enjoyed playing Cupid to Bullitt's romancing of Missy. In this fashion, Bullitt made
certain that his anchor within the inner circle was secure and that his
correspondence with Moore could be assured of reaching the president's eyes or ears when the ambassador thought it more politic not
to write directly.[48]

On July 9, 1934, Moore indicated the degree to which Bullitt's
campaign to blame Litvinov for any failure of American-Soviet debt
negotiations was taking effect. Moore wrote Bullitt, accepting Litvinov
as a villain and inserting an unintended barb that must have caused
Bullitt to flinch; he agreed with Bullitt that Troianovskii was to be
trusted. Moore thought the Soviet ambassador was sincere in his belief
that serious debt negotiations might begin in Washington, and the
Russian awaited orders from Litvinov to discuss a settlement. Moore
suggested that "perhaps Litvinov, who seems to be without any conscience whatever, is deceiving [Troianovskii] just as he deceived the
President and yourself when he was here and precisely as he has ignored
all of his promises in his conversations with you at Moscow."[49] Bullitt
could not have been very happy about being identified as a pawn in
Litvinov's chess game.

Despite his view of Litvinov's role, Bullitt believed that he could
either convert Litvinov, get around him, or go over his head. He told
FDR that, because he could not get anywhere with Litvinov, he merely

---

[48]I asked Frances Perkins if she knew of Bullitt's closeness to Moore and Missy
LeHand. She did not answer directly but said that it did not surprise her as Bullitt was
a very ingratiating fellow. Interview with Perkins.

[49]Bullitt, *For the President*, p. 92.

maintained cordial relations with him and had commenced "building
a backfire in the Kremlin by way of Voroshilov and (Lev) Karakhan."
Bullitt approached Voroshilov by importing polo equipment for the
Red Army cavalry and described the difficulties of teaching the more
refined points of the game, sans polo ponies:

> We play every other day on a broad plain. . . . All the ponies were
> sixteen-hand stallions who savaged each other and the riders when-
> ever they came to close quarters, and on the first day a Mongolian
> soldier with an undeveloped genius for the game carried the ball
> in a bee-line three miles cross country before he could be stopped!
> The polo has brought not only myself but our military men into
> the closest relations with the Red Army leaders and has been most
> useful.
>
> As you know, I have also started baseball here and that has
> helped to bring us into intimate relations with the Moscow Soviet.[50]

President Roosevelt wrote Bullitt in late August, indicating that
he had accepted Litvinov as the source of the obstruction: "I have not
seen Troyanovsky since you returned but everybody likes him at the
State Department and I am very certain terms could be arranged if
he had a more free hand."[51] In a letter of September 8, Bullitt explained
to FDR his current assessment for the cause of the impasse. He thought
that the Russians were feeling cocky thanks to their successes, which
included a good harvest, the alignment with France, and easing of
pressures in the Far East.[52] He was, however, still confident of the
future of American-Soviet relations. On the same date he wrote Moore,
suggesting that they should go ahead with plans for the embassy and
predicted that, "unless all signs are deceptive, Moscow will become
with each year an increasingly important point in international relations. Moreover, it is almost impossible to imagine a situation which
would cause us to have exceedingly bad relations with the Soviet Government for the simple reason that the two countries have no major
conflicting interests."[53]

Still undaunted, on October 6, 1934, Bullitt wrote Moore of yet
another approach to the debt question. This time the ambassador tried
to talk to Troianovskii while the latter was in Moscow. Bullitt related

---

[50]Bullitt to FDR, August 5, 1934, PSF, Russia. See also Edgar B. Nixon, ed., *Franklin
D. Roosevelt and Foreign Affairs*, 3 vols. (Cambridge, MA: Belknap Press of Harvard
University Press, 1969), 2:171. Charles Bohlen contended that his future brother-in-law
Charles Thayer was actually the one who introduced polo to the Russian cavalry. Charles
E. Bohlen, *Witness to History, 1929–1969* (New York: W W. Norton, 1973), pp. 23–24.

[51]Bullitt, *For the President*, p. 95.

[52]Ibid., p. 96.

[53]Ibid., p. 97.

a "rather amusing little incident" in a talk with Litvinov, during which he tried to convince the commissar to arrange a meeting with Troianovskii. Litvinov told Bullitt that the American ambassador would have to stay in Moscow for two or three weeks for the talks to be fruitful. Bullitt replied that he did not see why when all that was necessary to achieve agreement was for Litvinov to give up on the idea of a loan or an unrestricted credit. Litvinov continued to insist that two or three weeks would be necessary. However, Bullitt knew that Stalin was in the Caucasus and would not return until early November so he said: "What you mean is that the Government will be in the Caucasus for the remainder of the month." Litvinov grinned and nodded. Bullitt suggested to Moore that Litvinov underestimated the influence that the United States could have in preserving peace in the Far East and that the Russian therefore was not putting any energy into the work of achieving agreement. Bullitt thought that Voroshilov might still bear more influence in the matter than the commissar of Foreign Affairs.[54]

After some dispatches from Moscow at the end of 1934, which seemed to indicate that the Kremlin was going to settle the debt question, the disillusionment that followed a conversation between Bullitt, Hull, and Robert Kelley of the State Department and Troianovskii was shattering. Secretary Hull listened to the Soviet ambassador again hedge on a settlement and then told Troianovskii that he had sought in every way to cooperate with the Soviet government without much success. It was too bad, Hull noted, for a settlement of the outstanding questions would have furnished a basis for cooperation in important matters of world significance. The secretary regretfully concluded that, if the two governments could not deal in a statesmanlike way with what, after all, was a minor problem, there was little expectation of them being able to cooperate on larger issues.[55]

Troianovskii argued that the only holdup to a settlement was the American refusal to grant a $100 million loan so that the other nations could not afford to demand similar settlements. Hull replied that the United States had gone to the limit and had made considerable concessions. If the Soviet Union had no new proposals, in his opinion, the debt negotiations had come to an end. Troianovskii agreed simply because he had no more proposals.[56] The meeting occurred on January 31, 1935; Secretary Hull immediately announced to the press the general points of the discussion and its conclusions. The Soviets, he said, had rejected the latest American offer of compromise, and

---

[54]Ibid., pp. 98–99.
[55]*FRUS: Soviet Union*, p. 170.
[56]Ibid., pp. 170–71.

there would be no further proposals for settlement from the United States.[57]

By leaving the debt question largely in Bullitt's hands and by accepting Bullitt's explanation for the reason the negotiations were stalled, Roosevelt literally ensured that no resolution would follow. The president, however, contributed to the problem when he accepted the assurances that the stalemate could be resolved by hanging tightly to the position of no compromise on either the amount or the form of the debt. Litvinov and Troianovskii were not so adamant against payment as the Americans thought, and a concession to the bargainers in the Politburo on the amount of credits, even restricted ones, might have swung the day. As it happened, the negotiations became a matter of principle on both sides and, when the position hardened, compromise disappeared as a prospect. At the point where Bullitt and his staff in Moscow decided that perhaps concessions on the credit issue were in order, they found that Secretary Hull had taken the matter personally and would not give ground.

From the embassy in Moscow there were some dim forebodings about future collaboration, but the hope still prevailed that the Soviet Union was on a new course and that intransigence on the debt question was due to a lessening of Soviet fears about Japan. Charles Bohlen recalled in his memoirs that the Americans were not the only ones misled about the changing climate in Moscow. When the name of the OGPU, the secret police, was changed to the NKVD in 1934, Litvinov told Bohlen, in all sincerity Bohlen thought, "that this marked a definite step in the liberalization of the Soviet regime. It indicated, he said, that the Revolution had conquered and Soviet power was established." Litvinov confidently predicted that soon the NKVD would hold no more terror for Soviet citizens than the New York City Police Department did for Americans. Like many others in the Soviet hierarchy, Litvinov "was unaware of the dark recesses of Stalin's mind."[58] Those recesses soon caused the embassy personnel to begin to suspect every move the Russians made, including their intent to get along with the United States. In this, too, Bullitt played a role.

Ironically, the Russians and the Americans apparently realized that their objectives in securing the peace depended on moving beyond mere recognition and that success of any relationship depended on establishing economic connections. As Frederick C. Adams assessed the situation in his excellent survey of the subject, "To argue . . . that the Russians sought only recognition because this act itself provided

[57]"Debt Offer Rejected," *Literary Digest* 119 (February 9, 1935): 7.
[58]Bohlen, *Witness to History*, pp. 30–31.

them with the time necessary to construct a secure position in the Pacific is to fall wide of the mark."[59] Adams concluded that the Americans had more maneuvering room than did the Russians but clung too long to the belief that the Soviets so desperately needed U.S. support and credits that they had no choice but to accept whatever the Americans would offer.

Franklin Roosevelt was cautious in his approach to the Russians, but once recognition was assured he thought they were duty bound to live up to their "commitment" assumed during the debt negotiations because the Soviet Union was threatened by Japan on the east and by Germany on the west; no better solution was available than to cooperate with the Americans in opposing these joint threats to national security. William Bullitt's constant reassurance that the Soviet leadership had no alternative to American assistance made the president reluctant to surrender any points on the debt since he did not have to do so. Later the debt settlement became a stumbling block to further negotiations for mutual security arrangement because it symbolized a first step beyond which it was unwise to move unless some token of sincerity was offered by the Soviet leaders. Meanwhile, Litvinov tried to carry the promised cooperation to a next phase of exerting real pressure on the powers intending to disrupt the status quo, suggesting that, where the debt was concerned, the Americans could afford to be either forgiving or generous when larger matters were at stake. Litvinov was correct but misread how important the debt issue was to the Roosevelt administration. Roosevelt was angered and suspicious of Russian reluctance to reach a settlement, at least in part because he was afraid of the internal reaction that might lead to demands from the congressional isolationists to sever relations. If the pressure to break relations gained public credence, then FDR's scheme to block the aggressors would be minus an important ingredient when he could no longer use closer collaboration with the Russians as an implied threat against the powers intending to disrupt the world balance of power.

---

[59]Frederick C. Adams, *Economic Diplomacy: The Export-Import Bank and American Foreign Policy, 1934–1939* (Columbia: University of Missouri Press, 1976), p. 125.

III

President Roosevelt's Peace Policy and the Russians

FRANKLIN DELANO ROOSEVELT and Maxim Litvinov held a common view that blocking the aggressors was important for reasons other than simply for the sake of the peace. They perceived disarmament as essential to national economic recovery, which underlay national stability. In one sense, Roosevelt was more realistic than Litvinov for he saw the problem as global. If it were not solved everywhere by a cooperative solution, then any agreement would rest on a shaky foundation subject to disruption at the whim of some regional power. Roosevelt thought that there was an echo effect to international crises and that this had caused the World War. The shot at Sarajevo was heard in various capitals at different times, and there was no cooperative effort to keep it from creating a deafening roar that drowned out voices of moderation. Litvinov tried to provide both a universal disarmament plan and collective security that would possibly encourage the arming powers to agree to arms limitations when confronted by the choice of cooperating or facing a series of powers committed to collective security. In this fashion, he attempted to isolate the aggressors, or at least protect the Soviet Union from attack.

Litvinov may have been correct in deciding that the peace was not going to be preserved unless he could prove to the hungry powers, via his series of regional defense and nonaggression pacts, that they faced defeat. However, President Roosevelt did not think a fragmented solution was viable. He did not believe that piecemeal approaches would prevent the impending war. The tragedy of the situation was that they were both right. Practical politics dictated the need to appeal to baser instincts for survival, as Litvinov did. Practical domestic political realities told Roosevelt that, if he could not mobilize international public opinion to halt the developing arms race, he was not free to enter regional agreements.

Cordell Hull spoke to the disarmament question and FDR's position with fair accuracy: "The President and I had the same views. We knew there could be no peace without suitable . . . 'disarmament.' . . . We knew this was not possible except under a world policy strongly supported by universal public opinion."[1] The Russians spoke to the question by demanding either total disarmament with guarantees for periodic inspections with no loopholes, which they actually did not believe to be possible, or a continuous peace conference with the power to apply universal sanctions, both economic and moral, against an aggressor.

Litvinov presented the Soviet plan to the Geneva Disarmament Conference and defined aggressors as states that marched military units across another state's borders.[2] President Roosevelt agreed with the definition but would not approve sanctions. After Germany left the Geneva Conference, FDR tried to back away from Litvinov's proposals by identifying them as strictly European solutions on which the U.S. position was clear. He said that the United States "drew the line and distinction between European political adjustments and world disarmament."[3] In other words, without Germany what remained was a defensive alliance among the threatened powers.

Norman Davis, who chaired the American delegation at Geneva, at first tried to persuade the United States to abjure its neutral rights if an aggressor were named by a diplomatic consultative conference.[4] After first approving this, Hull backed down; the plan would require identifying a power breaking its pledge on arms limitations to be subject to sanctions, and he thought that public opinion would only approve action against a proven aggressor.[5] In essence, the United States would oppose taking the ax from an aggressor's hand while still in the air. It had first to descend upon the victim's neck before any attempt could be made to prevent the execution.

France was desperate to attract the Americans to a commitment at Geneva and appealed to FDR for support. Through his representative at the conference, the president vowed his wish to help France

---

[1]Cordell Hull, *The Memoirs of Cordell Hull*, 2 vols. (New York: Macmillan, 1948), 1:22.

[2]"On the General Commission of the Conference on Disarmament—A Speech by the People's Commissar of Foreign Affairs Com. M. M. Litvinov," *Pravda*, May 30, 1934.

[3]Press conferences, 3, No. 94, February 2, 1934, p. 126.

[4]*FRUS: General, British Commonwealth, 1933*, p. 166.

[5]*FRUS, Diplomatic Papers*, vol. 1, *General, British Commonwealth, 1934* (Washington, DC: Government Printing Office, 1951), p. 38.

find a solution by every means available but did not suggest the means. Instead, Davis asked the Europeans to promote a general accord on disarmament plus the requisite European regional agreements, while at the same time he warned the French: "American policy was cooperative, but it would not press anyone to accept any particular solution. . . . Let Europe make the first move, then the President would see what he could do. From his new post in Brussels, Paul Claudel blamed his countrymen as much as the Americans for degrading the intent of 'a great man.' He found the results 'enough to make one cry.' "[6]

Howard Payne related the sad realities that French and American statesmen confronted pertaining to "political impossibility" at home and the frustration of Claudel and others who suggested that any American gesture should be seized. After the French Council of Ministers refused to ask Parliament for a payment on the American debt, Claudel and André de Laboulaye thought the moment had passed for Franco-American cooperation. Even a token payment might have given Roosevelt the opportunity to do something for France later because it had shown good faith, but as a "dishonest debtor" it could expect little. Payne observed that "thereafter, Laboulaye's prediction of the previous year became an axiom in Paris: Roosevelt could risk international gestures 'of an entirely moral character'; but, Laboulaye was sure that he would never dare advocate any 'precise obligation for the future.' "[7]

British leaders faced the same problems as did the Americans, in the sense that they were highly conscious of the limitations placed on them by public opinion. When a safe Conservative seat in Parliament was lost to the Labour party on the disarmament issue eleven days after Germany withdrew from the Geneva Conference, the Conservatives "took this decisive defeat as an indication of the national mood and the dominance of pacifistic intentions in Labour circles." This in its turn "frightened the National Government and showed the political dangers of a firm policy which involved sanctions or British rearmament."[8]

Part of the difficulty at Geneva was that the British vacillated as much as the Americans. The British government knew that the wise course was to force arms limitations by adequate supervision and inspection of arms production and, if necessary, to impose an economic

[6]Howard C. Payne, Raymond Callahan, and Edward M. Bennett, *As the Storm Clouds Gathered: European Perceptions of American Foreign Policy in the 1930s* (Durham, NC: Moore, 1979), p. 29.

[7]Ibid., pp. 30–31.

[8]Stephen Edward Balzarini, "Britain, France, and the 'German Problem' at the World Disarmament Conference, 1932–1934" (Ph.D. diss., Washington State University, 1979), p. 338, n20.

blockade against violators. However, despite public support for disarmament, British opinion agreed with the American view that this
problem was worldwide and "England should not go into a treaty that
is essentially European."[9] Having been informed of this by Davis,
President Roosevelt knew that Britain woud not agree to any plan that
Germany and Japan would not accept, which only reinforced the timidity of the Americans.

France insisted on commitments that the United States was
unprepared to make, and Great Britain refused to deal with the question
except on a worldwide basis, which left disarmament in an all or nothing
situation. Viewed from this perspective, Litvinov had no chance of
gaining American support for regional agreements, even in the Far
East. Unless he wished to enter another Kellogg Pact—and one was
enough—the Soviet commissar could not expect much from the United
States, under the circumstances, and he and other Soviet leaders became
less concerned over what the Americans desired. This was the dilemma
Franklin Roosevelt faced in his peace policy as the honeymoon period
of American-Soviet relations ended. The Europeanization of the Geneva
Conference pushed Roosevelt to become less inclined to act in other
international areas, such as U.S. membership in the World Court, or
a discriminatory arms embargo bill, which he thought of proposing
but abandoned.[10]

President Roosevelt and Secretary Hull were honest in their dealings with most foreign powers. The secretary of state believed that
public opinion would not condone so-called political commitments to
Europe, and he did not desire to build false hopes on the part of
European statesmen. This was in line with the policy he outlined from
the beginning of his time in office:

> I made two rules, among others, in dealing with foreign ambas-
> sadors. One was to utter no threat unless we had the force and
> will to back it up. A threat without a backing of force was a bluff,
> and a bluff could be called with embarrassing results.
>
> The other rule was to make no promise that was not certain
> of fulfillment.[11]

Some examples have been cited in American dealings with Russia where
these rules were not followed to the letter, but in relation to the disarmament question they were adhered to consistently. If American
policy is open to criticism on the disarmament issue, it is not directed

---

[9]Nixon, *Roosevelt and Foreign Affairs*, 2:15.
[10]Dallek, *Roosevelt and American Foreign Policy*, pp. 69–71.
[11]Hull, *Memoirs*, 1:188.

toward what Roosevelt and government members did but rather what they failed to do. The pronouncements of the president, the secretary of state, and State Department officials indicated that the administration was not sure that the policy being pursued was the best one available. They seemed to feel, however, that the best policy would run into public opposition. Thus they followed the line of least resistance; the policymakers made no sustained effort to lead public opinion toward the acceptance of a plan more in line with the national interest.

President Roosevelt twice suggested proposals that were at least closer to the commitments which England, France, Russia, and other threatened powers in Europe hoped to obtain from the United States, but the fear of public opinion again provided the stumbling block and paralyzed any attempt at effective action. In the first of these proposals, FDR told Emile Francqui, head of the special Belgian mission to the United States to announce the accession to the throne of Leopold III (king of Belgium), that in relation to the disarmament conference he was willing that there should be a period of three years for gradual disarmament to become effective. During this time there should be automatic commissions of inspection. If Germany should refuse to take part, "sanctions should be applied in the nature of a boycott against the purchase of any German goods; while Germany should be permitted to buy as much as she pleased abroad; . . . any such concerted movement would quickly bring Germany to terms."[12] Francqui immediately asked the president if the American people would support such a move; FDR replied affirmatively.[13]

Roosevelt's conversation with Francqui occurred on May 16, 1934, and the president did not bring up the subject again until October 23. In the interim, Hull argued that public opinion would not tolerate sanctions against a violator of the disarmament agreement, and FDR altered the extent to which the United States would go in support of economic pressure. Ambassador Davis wrote on October 22 that he was skeptical about America continuing to fan the air much longer without a specific objective that contained the possibility of realization. Roosevelt then made his second proposal: the powers signing his suggested convention would agree, over a period of ten years, not to allow any armed forces to cross the frontier of any neighbor nation, or of any other nation, and that such an act would automatically be defined as the act of an aggressor. Under these circumstances every signatory power would agree that, "in the event of any act of aggression, as defined above, it will decline to trade in any manner shape or form

---

[12]*FRUS: General, British Commonwealth, 1934*, p. 70.
[13]Ibid.

with an aggressor. If any question should arise with regard to the act of an aggressor as, for example, two nations sending armies across the border simultaneously, each signatory power will agree not to trade with the aggressors."[14] To this the president added a provision that at the end of five years the League of Nations would call a conference to discuss arms limitations and the strengthening of the agreement itself. This plan was obviously one that Roosevelt deemed both advisable and necessary in view of the seriousness of the situation in Europe.

Undersecretary of State William Phillips sent the president's proposal to Chief of the Division of West European Affairs Jay Pierrepont Moffat for his examination and comments. Moffat attacked Roosevelt's plan as impractical. He had been opposed to so-called political commitments on disarmament from the beginning; his position had not changed.[15] He charged that the president was not familiar with the intricacies of European politics that affected the disarmament question.[16] Moffat suggested that Roosevelt's proposal would leave the way open for Germany to prepare for war without interference until it was ready to strike. This was true, but at the same time Moffat opposed any solution but a universal agreement lest the United States become involved in an entangling alliance through committing itself to non-aggression pacts with less than all the major powers. He also asserted that signing such a pact, as the president suggested, would follow a direct course to war because rigid economic sanctions outlined in the plan were a casus belli and inconsistent with the duties of neutrality. Moffat automatically assumed that the United States not only desired but also would be able to keep out of a European war; the president's plan would deny this possibility.[17] FDR again did not make any attempt to come forward with a realistic proposal for a settlement of the disarmament question, and the United States therefore resumed the role of the interested observer, willing to take the position of amicus curiae but not at the expense of involvement in European political problems.

With President Roosevelt's withdrawal from his peace initiative, the opportunity to lead in this area passed to the Soviet Union. Litvinov proposed that hard facts had to be faced: an effective disarmament convention could not be reached and a realistic alternative had to be sought. This came in the form of Litvinov's plan for a permanent peace conference, which was as firmly opposed by the United States as France's

---

[14]Ibid., p. 170.

[15]Nancy Harvison Hooker, ed., *The Moffat Papers: Selections from the Diplomatic Journals of Jay Pierrepont Moffat, 1919–1943* (Cambridge, MA: Harvard University Press, 1956), p. 105.

[16]Ibid., p. 93.

[17]Ibid., p. 170.

regional agreements. Litvinov's proposal received wide acclaim in France and from some members of the American press who considered the long-range threat to U.S. security emanating from an aggressive rearmed Germany.

Litvinov called upon the delegates to the disarmament conference to admit that existing circumstances had made further discussions futile, pointing out that some states had made their position so clear that they would not disarm that any more talks on the matter, without an alternative proposal, were a waste of time. Disarmament as a means of securing international peace required the agreement of every state, or at least all of the large ones. This being impossible, Litvinov suggested an alternative plan, one that could guarantee security without including all nations. His permanent peace conference required periodic meetings, during which the machinery could be perfected to respond to warnings of growing military dangers and call for aid to the endangered powers, thereby taking the form of moral, financial, economic, or any other needed assistance. The commissar conceded that probably it would be necessary to exclude the prospect of using military force to gain the support of some of the interested states, but he argued that this would not destroy the effectiveness of the plan if the sanctions involved were rigidly enforced.

For the benefit of the United States and Great Britain, Litvinov warned that to believe aggressive states, once they started on the road to conquest, would draw the line at certain borders was pure folly, for their appetites would know no bounds. For the benefit of the British and the Poles, he charged that those who thought that the nations wishing war would turn only in one direction were nourishing a vain hope. If the aggressors knocked Russia out of the war, they could leisurely turn their attention to the conquest of the democratic states. The Soviet commissar said that in view of these dangers "no single state in the interest of self-preservation can wash its hands of and refuse to participate in the common international cause of preventing this danger."[18]

At first Ambassador Davis reacted quite favorably to the Litvinov plan, writing to Hull that the commissar had furthered the solution to the problem of security.[19] By October 1934 the Americans viewed the plan with skepticism. Ambassador Hugh R. Wilson, the other U.S. representative to the Geneva Disarmament Conference, pointed out the difficulties involved in American participation in the permanent

---

[18]"On the General Commission of the Conference on Disarmament," *Pravda*, May 30, 1934.

[19]*FRUS: General, British Commonwealth, 1934*, p. 85.

peace conference. Wilson correctly surmised that part of Litvinov's intention was to set up an organization, of which the United States would be a member, so that Japan and Germany would be confronted by a combination of peace-minded states all on their guard and jointly and continuously scrutinizing the situation. The United States could have nothing to do with such a proposal because of the probability that "to ask the United States to join the 'permanent peace' organization would face our President with a political decision of high importance, this especially since no one could predict with what type of questions the peace organization would occupy itself."[20] Wilson feared the questions would involve purely European threats to the peace, with which the United States would not be concerned, such as the maintenance of Austrian independence, the Saar question, or the problem of the Polish Corridor.

Seeking support, Litvinov approached the Americans directly. He told Bullitt bluntly that war in Europe was inevitable unless his plan, or a similar one, succeeded in being accepted by the major powers interested in preserving the peace. According to Bullitt, there was a note of resignation and discouragement in Litvinov's tone,[21] part of which rested on the Russian's conviction that there was no government in Europe, even France, that was ready to act realistically to develop such a peace program. In view of this, he believed that the Soviet Union had no choice but to do whatever was necessary to strengthen the Red Army as a bulwark against the forces of aggression; everything, including the money owed the Americans, would have to be spent for tanks and guns.[22]

II

There were numerous efforts to drag the Americans into some form of commitment or force them to act in defense of the peace. Roosevelt reacted to these within the parameters he thought were available but was cautioned from all directions—public and congressional opinion, the media, his own advisers, and members of the administration—to hold back and avoid commitments. Bullitt, foreseeing Russian efforts to involve the United States and anticipating internal pressures to abandon isolationism, warned Roosevelt to beware. He wrote FDR in May 1935, asking him if he remembered the bet they had made concerning where the war would begin and reminding the president that

[20]Ibid., p. 153.
[21]*FRUS: Soviet Union*, p. 155; *FRUS: General, British Commonwealth, 1934*, p. 154.
[22]Ibid.

he had picked the Far East while Roosevelt had selected Europe; however, the ambassador changed his mind:

> I am beginning to be inclined to think that you will probably turn out to be right as usual. The Austrian situation seems to contain all the elements of a major explosion while the Far Eastern situation is momentarily quiet. The long range outlook everywhere is about as bad as can be and the worst of it is that we can do nothing whatever to stop the march of events.
>
> I see no way that we can achieve anything by attempting to stop the march of events—horrible as it is—except our own involvement in war and I hope that you will turn a very deaf ear to the songs of the sirens who must be keeping you awake nights with their music. I saw that Stimson had donned the mermaids tail and there must be a thousand others whose hearts are better than their heads.[23]

FDR responded on June 3 but gave Bullitt no clue as to his thoughts about the impending European conflict.

Bullitt was concerned lest the president succumb to the siren songs and not merely from Americans. John C. Wiley was chargé d'affaires ad interim in March when journalist Pavel L. Mikhailskii called on the American embassy in Moscow to talk with the chargé, a conversation that Wiley reported to both Bullitt and the State Department. Writing for the Soviet news agency TASS in the 1930s, Mikhailskii was one of the few Russians who knew America fairly well and thus was the logical choice to speak to the Americans because of his U.S. connections. He attacked the inconsistency in the attitude of the American government and told Wiley that when Litvinov was in Washington he had been promised political collaboration, which had not occurred. The chargé responded: "The fact that a large embassy was established in Moscow, at a time when the Soviet Union was apprehensive of Japanese aggression, was in itself effective political collaboration." Wiley also informed Mikhailskii that he thought him unusually optimistic if he believed that closer collaboration would come after the Soviets reneged on debts and claims. The chargé thought that Mikhailskii had been sent to see him under orders, reflecting the uneasiness of the Soviet government concerning relations with the United States.[24]

Wiley identified the source of Soviet concern. The Russians had desired recognition in the first place because they believed it would help forestall an attack from Japan. That threat had subsided, due to

---

[23]Bullitt to FDR, May 1, 1935, PSF, Box 15.
[24]Dispatch, Wiley to Hull, March 25, 1935, DSF 711.61/521.

Japanese insecurity over the extent of American-Soviet cooperation, and he thought this accounted for the declining interest in furthering relations with the United States. In 1935 the Kremlin's renewed readiness in establishing friendly ties with the Americans resulted from the need for political cooperation since "an acute fear of aggression from the West has arisen; that Germany was preparing to embark on a policy of conquest at the expense of the Soviet Union." Wiley also reported a conversation with the Chinese ambassador to the USSR who recently had discussed American-Soviet relations with Litvinov and had said that Litvinov charged that the strained relations with America resulted from "a deliberate change of policy on the part of the United States." This confirmed Wiley's impression that Litvinov was on the defensive.[25]

Bullitt was not alone in his efforts to make Roosevelt aware of the dangers inherent in too forward a policy. In a memorandum Secretary Hull relayed the forebodings of the Division of Far Eastern Affairs concerning the march of events to war in Asia and warned against an American tendency:

> One of the great weaknesses of the US in connection with the problem of foreign relations, as disclosed in the facts of our history, has lain in the fact that, in the conducting of our foreign relations, some if not the majority of our administrations have made their decisions on the basis merely of the circumstances and the superficially apparent need of the moment, according to the conceptions of parties in power or interests possessed of influence at the moment.[26]

The framers of the memorandum knew the basic ingredients of American foreign policy quite well, and they assumed that the cornerstone of U.S. policy was the intention to play the part of the good neighbor. In addition, they identified the greatest objective of this policy as peace with national security. Given these premises they asked what the United States could do to preserve the basics. The problem was that, "at the same time, it must be taken into consideration that the Japanese nation is engaged in a natural and inevitable course of expansion, . . . motivated by pressure and vitality from within Japan and the Japanese people. . . . The Philippines lie on one of the natural lines of Japanese advance."

---

[25]Ibid.

[26]Hull to FDR, March 5, 1935, PSF, No. II, Departmental Files, Box 20, State Department File, 1933–1937.

Having laid out this scenario and identified Japanese interests in Philippine raw materials and the oil in the Dutch and British possessions lying south of there, the memorandum pointedly gave President Roosevelt two alternatives: either abandon the islands or build an adequate defense, via an expanded navy, and bases for it. Retaining the Philippines would not in itself lead to war with Japan, but a piecemeal approach would. If the administration intended to promote the required security forces, then the authors of the memorandum advised that the islands should be retained. What needed deciding was what would contribute most toward promoting national and international stability, human welfare, political order, justice, and the greatest good for the greatest number, "conditions which are physically and psychologically tolerable and acceptable to the peoples most directly affected, conditions in line with the ideals of a 'new deal' in relation not alone to the people of the US but to all peoples."[27]

While this was a cautious admonishment, others were more blunt. One of the president's former supporters, who still followed his lead on some of the New Deal domestic issues, gave him advance notice that he would attack him on his request for discretionary powers on the neutrality issue. Raymond Moley, who become editor of *Today* magazine after his departure from the administration, wrote to FDR on November 30, 1935, advising him to break with the "international crowd" before they ruined everything he had gained in his domestic program. Moley's plea was typical of the progressive isolationist group. He expressed in bold terms his belief that Roosevelt was being duped into following false prophets who were not doing right by him, writing the president: "You hold views with which a vast majority of the country agrees, but with respect to which those through whom you are acting are intent upon making a quite different national policy prevail."[28]

Moley told Roosevelt that there were two extreme positions in regard to U.S. foreign policy, one advocating complete isolation and the other complete entanglement. FDR's most loyal following, Moley wrote, came primarily from the former group, which he believed also encompassed the vast majority of Americans. The Department of State, he continued, was leading the president down the primrose path. "No one knows better than you, I am sure," Moley cautioned, "how settled are the policies of the State Department and how they differ from your own progressive principles."[29] The former New Dealer maladroitly said Roosevelt did not understand the significance of a discriminatory arms

---

[27]Ibid.
[28]Moley to FDR, November 30, 1935, PPF 743, Raymond Moley Folder.
[29]Ibid.

embargo because his Department of State advisers had failed to inform him that such an embargo was actually a denial of neutrality. Moley's final touch was a patronizing lecture on the executive function: "Under our form of government Congress determines what national policies shall be and expresses its decisions in the laws it makes. The members of the executive branch have the duty of enforcing these laws. That is the meaning of their oath of office."[30]

Moley argued that the purpose of neutrality legislation should be to keep the United States absolutely aloof from contact with Europe. He contended that strict impartiality was the only moral course. Who might win the European struggle for power was of no concern to America.[31] This was one of several communications from Moley to FDR which moved the president, at a later date, to remark to Secretary of the Interior Harold L. Ickes that, while Moley said favorable things about him, he said them in such a way as to make it hurt.[32]

In his admonition, Moley was joined by Senator Key Pittman, chairman of the Senate Foreign Relations Committee, who announced in March that the United States was not concerned with Europe's crisis. Hitler's violation of the Versailles Treaty did not interest the United States in the least.[33] According to Pittman, the führer was a man of courage and zeal who had accomplished much for Germany, a man who was "a greater crusader than . . . a statesman and diplomat."[34] The chairman told reporters that Hitler provided no real threat to America unless the United States interfered in something that was really none of its business.[35] A member of the Daughters of the American Revolution wrote to congratulate the senator for his firm stand against being dragged into European entanglements.[36] He lashed out again in April 1935, declaring: "War! War! Threat of war! Why should we inject ourselves into this grave conflict? . . . What good could possibly be accomplished by our intervention? None whatever. . . . We must remain neutral."[37]

Senator Pittman wanted the administration to slight foreign affairs, and in this vein he wrote Roosevelt, criticizing him for not keeping his government departments from engaging too much in the international

[30]Ibid.

[31]Ibid.

[32]Harold L. Ickes, *The Secret Diary of Harold L. Ickes*, vol. 1, *The First Thousand Days, 1933–1936* (New York: Simon & Schuster, 1953), p. 692.

[33]*New York Post*, March 25, 1935.

[34]*New York Herald Tribune*, March 18, 1935.

[35]Ibid.

[36]Letter of March 29, 1935, Committee Papers, SEN 74A-F9 (123C), Correspondence M.

[37]*Washington Herald*, April 7, 1935.

arena. The president, Pittman complained, was not living up to his promise, made in a speech of July 4, 1933, to defer efforts on the international scene until domestic problems were settled.[38] When the Ethiopian crisis erupted, the senator said it was strictly a matter for the League of Nations and Benito Mussolini to settle. America's only concern was to ensure that the neutrality law was properly applied.[39]

Ironically it was Senator Pittman who, earlier in the year, had posed a pertinent question to FDR concerning the direction of American policy. In a querulous message he stated that "no one today knows what is the foreign policy of our government. Are we going to participate in European affairs, or are we going to keep out of them? Are we going to enforce treaties, or are we going to abandon them? . . . Now anybody can give away his own horse, but he cannot give away the horse of his master."[40] Pittman was concerned lest U.S. policy might be leading away from insularity, or that there might be no policy at all. In any event, the question he posed was a relevant one: Where was America going?

Senator Pittman's question was variously answered by administration spokesmen in the light of their own understanding of the president's policy, but the one person who could give the most direct answer seemed reluctant to do so definitively. President Roosevelt said, in his annual message to Congress in January 1935, that change was the order of the day both at home and abroad. Attempts to alter the status quo beyond American shores gave cause for apprehension concerning the armaments race and new struggles for power but did not, in FDR's opinion, give grounds for fears that the relations of the United States with other powers would be anything but peaceful.[41] He chose not to address the subject of possible shifts in U.S. policy and indicated in a letter to Ambassador William Dodd that he did not expect much in the way of improvement in foreign affairs: "We shall go through a period of noncooperation in everything I fear, for the next year or two."[42]

In particular situations, President Roosevelt avoided specific answers to questions relating to the direction of American policy. When a reporter once asked him to comment on the U.S. position concerning German rearmament, the president refused, saying that the United

---

[38]Pittman to FDR, February 19, 1935, Box 18, Key Pittman Papers, Library of Congress, Washington, DC.

[39]Press release, September 17, 1935, Box 39, Pittman Papers.

[40]Pittman to FDR, February 19, 1935, Box 81, ibid.

[41]Samuel I. Rosenman, ed., *Public Papers and Addresses of Franklin D. Roosevelt*, vol. 4, *The Court Disapproves, 1935* (New York: Random House, 1938), pp. 15ff.

[42]FDR to Dodd, February 2, 1935, PPF 1043.

States would adhere to the concept of the good neighbor and the hope that American principles would be extended to Europe where they would help lead the way to arms reduction.[43] Later, at another press conference in October 1935, the president was asked, in connection with the Ethiopian crisis, how much the United States was really concerned in Europe's problems. Roosevelt responded that "the government is determined not to become involved in the controversy."[44]

There was one area in which President Roosevelt and Secretary Hull believed they could act safely in foreign affairs; they could provide moral leadership and give object lessons. One of the president's confidants, Ray Stannard Baker, suggested that FDR could do this at home as well and wrote to the president, proposing that he might more effectively utilize his fireside chats and his access to newspapers to educate Americans regarding the needs of diplomacy and to identify what was right and wrong in the world. FDR answered:

> You are so absolutely right about the response that this country gives to vision and profound moral purposes that I can only assure you of my hearty concurrence and of my constant desire to make the appeal. At the same time . . . you will be sympathetic to the . . . view that the public psychology . . . cannot because of human weakness, be attuned for long . . . to a constant repetition of the highest note in the scale.[45]

Here was an example of FDR's reluctance to play Woodrow Wilson's game. Baker had helped Wilson as a speech writer and admired FDR's Democratic predecessor for his idealism and courage, but Roosevelt was determined not to hear the siren songs of the Wilsonians luring him toward public opposition.

Sometimes it is difficult to ascertain when Roosevelt spoke earnestly and when it was for effect. There were occasions, however, when his intent was perfectly clear. Such was the case when he telegraphed Hull, calling attention to a speech, given in California, in which the president had dealt with the objectives of American policy. He suggested that the secretary should circulate it to U.S. embassies abroad. In his speech Roosevelt said that, although the threat of domestic strife still existed in the United States, there was a greater one to the future of civilization in the form of a possible foreign war, and many Americans were concerned for the safety of their nation because another holocaust like World War I might mean that civilization could not

---

[43]Press Conferences, 5, No. 192, March 20, 1935, p. 168.
[44]Ibid., 6, No. 244, October 22, 1935, p. 226.
[45]FDR to Baker, March 20, 1935, PPF 1820.

wholly recover. President Roosevelt expressed his firm belief that a threat to the continuation of a world acceptable to the United States existed and outlined America's duty:

> In the face of this apprehension the American people can have but one concern and speak but one sentiment: despite what happens . . . overseas, the United States of America shall and must remain, as, long ago the Father of our Country prayed that it might remain—unentangled and free. . . . Our national determination to keep free of foreign wars and foreign entanglements cannot prevent us from feeling deep concern when ideals and principles that we have cherished are challenged.[46]

In an Armistice Day address at Arlington National Cemetery, FDR went a step further in defining what America was prepared to do to preserve its own security:

> While . . . we cannot and must not hide our concern for grave world dangers, and while, at the same time, we cannot build walls around ourselves and hide our heads in the sand, we must go forward with all our strength to stress and to strive for international peace. In this effort America must and will protect herself. Under no circumstances will this policy of self-protection go to lengths beyond self-protection.[47]

Roosevelt also responded in this address to the rumor that France and the Soviet Union were wooing the United States to an alliance or commitment to them in case of war. He quickly scotched this rumor with assurances that there would be no entangling alliances with anyone; America would fight only to defend itself—pure and simple.

III

While the president kept a wary eye on any threats to the peace in Europe and Asia, American-Soviet relations were becoming strained just when cooperation seemed most imperative. In August 1935 a bombshell dropped on the Roosevelt administration in the form of the speeches given at the Seventh Comintern Congress in Moscow by members of the American Communist party who advertised the progress of the Communist movement in the United States. The Comintern was the organization against which the propaganda and subversion pledge

---

[46]Telegram, FDR to Hull, October 1, 1935, OF 20, State Department Folder.
[47]Rosenman, *The Court Disapproves*, pp. 442ff.

in the recognition agreement had been aimed and was presumably the promotional agency for the world revolution. Roosevelt and Hull never really expected the Soviet Union to abandon the organization, but they hoped the Russians would restrain it from agitating in America and would prevent direct mention of the United States in its proceedings.

Because the world revolution was played down by Stalin during the drive for socialism in one country, no meeting was held between 1928 and 1935. While Litvinov tried to gain collaborators for the Soviet peace compaign, the Comintern kept a low profile. After much debate the Communist hierarchy decided to revive the Comintern in 1935 to act as the directing force for the Popular Front Movement, which was aimed at getting anti-Fascist governments in power wherever possible. The organization still gave lip service to the world revolution, but this ceased to be the prime reason for its existence. The congress was not in itself a surprise, nor was the appearance of the Americans William Z. Foster and Earl Browder. Their attacks on the United States were unexpected, however. In early July, Louis Fischer had called on Ambassador Bullitt to find out what the government's reaction would be to the appearance and speeches of the Americans at such a gathering on Soviet soil. Fischer was worried because his interpretation of the notes exchanged in November 1933 convinced him that the meeting would prove a definite violation of the Litvinov pledge on propaganda and internal subversion.[48] Fischer thought it was hardly the time to create friction between the United States and Russia, with the menace of Nazi Germany looming larger and larger, and he obviously hoped that the United States would ignore the presence of Foster and Browder. That friction came anyway, he blamed more on Ambassador Bullitt than on the Soviets. Fischer charged that Bullitt chose to make a break with Moscow when the Russians were taking a more moderate line in the Popular Front Movement in order to combat fascism.[49]

Bullitt let Litvinov know beforehand that American-Soviet relations would be gravely affected if the Comintern Congress dealt with anything which could be considered a violation of the pledge the commissar made in Washington. The ambassador reported to the State Department that his remarks had struck home as they had caused Litvinov, Voroshilov, and Molotov to protest vigorously to Stalin against holding the congress. There may have been some protest but certainly nothing on the scale Bullitt surmised. He closed his dispatch with an incredibly naive assumption: "I feel that the decision to hold the Congress may be reversed."[50]

---

[48]*FRUS: Soviet Union*, p. 223.
[49]Fischer, *Men and Politics*, pp. 305ff.
[50]*FRUS: Soviet Union*, p. 223.

On July 19 Bullitt forwarded to the State Department his conclusions regarding Soviet policy. When the Soviet leaders temporarily abandoned the world revolution, Bullitt thought it was permanent; the revival of the Comintern meetings made him decide that it had never been abandoned and that there could be no real collaboration with the Soviets because "diplomatic relations with friendly states are not regarded by the Soviet government as normal friendly relations but 'armistice' relations and it is the conviction of the leaders of the Soviet Union that this 'armistice' can not possibly be ended by a definitive peace but only by renewal of battle."[51] European diplomats were constantly amazed by the tendency of Americans to believe that true friendship of a lasting character was possible among states. Bullitt illustrated again this incredible expectation which, if unfulfilled, seemed to negate any possible "real" collaboration.

One remark by Mikhailskii, which Bullitt repeated in his dispatch, was far more significant than the ambassador could have known. Bullitt, by quoting the Russian journalist, defended his argument that the Soviets had not given up the Marxist-Leninist concept of the world revolution: "You must understand," the old Bolshevik told him, "that world revolution is our religion and there is not one of us who would not in the final analysis oppose even Stalin himself if we should feel that he was abandoning the cause of the world revolution."[52] Mikhailskii disappeared during the purge of June 1937[53]; his execution coincided with that of a number of others who continued to believe that the world revolution was, and had to remain, the primary objective of a Sovietized Russia.

Although Ambassador Bullitt's enthusiasm for the Soviet experiment waned, he did not let his newly acquired fear of Bolshevism carry him to the extreme of recommending the severance of diplomatic relations. On the contrary, he argued persuasively that such action would be detrimental to the best interests of the United States:

> If we should sever relations . . . we should almost certainly not
> be able to reestablish relations with the Soviet Union during this
> decade. In this decade the Soviet Union either will be the center
> of attack from Europe and the Far East or will develop rapidly
> into one of the greatest physical forces in the world. As the Soviet
> Union grows in strength . . . the maintenance of an organization
> in Moscow to measure and report on the . . . activities . . . of the
> Soviet Union seems definitely in the interest of the American
> people.[54]

---

[51]Ibid., pp. 224–25.
[52]Ibid., p. 225.
[53]Fischer, *Men and Politics*, p. 438.
[54]*FRUS: Soviet Union*, p. 245.

Bullitt said he was out of touch with the Americans' reaction to the Comintern Congress and therefore did not know what pressures there might be to withdraw recognition, but he hoped they could be resisted unless the provocations were extreme.

Ambassador Bullitt tried to frighten the Soviets into living up to Litvinov's pledge by "exuding gloom and expressing my personal opinion that the congress may produce the severance of diplomatic relations." He acknowledged to FDR that, at the very least, there would be a technical violation of the Litvinov pledge and cautioned:

> Some people in Washington will doubtless want to break relations . . . but I can hear you roar with laughter over the idea of breaking relations on the basis of a mere technical violation.
>
> If the violation should be not technical but gross and insulting, I suspect that you will feel obliged to break relations. If we should not, the Soviet Government would be convinced that it could break its pledges with impunity and would feel free to direct actively the American Communist movement.[55]

Bullitt obviously tried to play both sides against the middle. If Roosevelt were pressured into breaking relations, he wanted the president to know he understood the political necessity.

Bullitt made sure that Roosevelt knew what the consequences would be if the president withdrew recognition. He warned that, if relations were broken, five unfortunate results would occur: the Russians would drastically reduce purchases in the United States; there would be a long period without relations, for once having withdrawn on grounds the Russians did not keep their word how could the Americans say that the Russians were worth trusting again; the observation post in Russia would be gone; the chance that Japan would attack Russia would increase; and Russian influence and prestige would suffer. As Bullitt and the president had desired recognition to preserve the peace and still thought this important, the increased prospects for war made a break in relations undesirable. FDR avoided making a public issue of the Comintern Congress by simply not mentioning it in his press conferences.

Despite American protests the Comintern Congress not only took up the success of the American Communist movement and fulminated against U.S. capitalist exploitation, Foster and Browder were elected to its presidium. Roosevelt decided not to break relations, but he approved a note from Hull in extremely strong language. One sentence

---

[55]Bullitt to FDR, July 15, 1935, PSF, Russia.

from the message proved to be a focal point for comments by the American press:

> The Government of the United States would be lacking in candor if it failed to state frankly that it anticipates the most serious consequences if the Government of the Union of Soviet Socialist Republics is unwilling, or unable, to take appropriate measures to prevent further acts in disregard of the solemn pledge given by it to the Government of the United States.[56]

Reactions to the news of the Comintern Congress and the violations of the Litvinov pledge were politically predictable. The general mood reported in the nation's press and in the corridors of Washington was one of disappointment, disillusionment, or triumphant crowing.[57] Senator Lester J. Dickinson (R–IA) who had bitterly resented Roosevelt's resumption of relations with Russia, immediately issued a statement for publication, in which he piously proclaimed that it was "just another situation where, if you play with the devil, you're bound to wear some of his stains." He reminded the public that his prediction had come true: "There's no question that recognition was a mistake. Not only have we not gained any trade, but we have given them an opportunity to come in here and spread propaganda among our people without limit."[58] In the House of Representatives, George H. Tinkham (R–MA), who also had been a determined foe of recognition, said that "the President should sever diplomatic relations with the Union of Soviet Socialist Republics. He is acting too late and not with vigor enough for the protection of the United States and its institutions. The Union of Soviets is a union of homicidal terrorists."[59]

House Foreign Affairs Committee Chairman Samuel D. McReynolds, who had supported recognition, announced that he had been aware for some time that the note would be sent and called it "timely"; William Borah, who had been a Republican supporter of recognition, refused to comment.[60] The *New York Times* had greeted recognition with cool reserve in 1933 and let Roosevelt know that it had been right in its skepticism of the president's precipitate action in recognizing the untrustworthy Bolsheviks:

---

[56]*FRUS: Soviet Union*, p. 251.
[57]"Soviet Russia's 'Retort Contemptuous,' " *Literary Digest* 120 (September 7, 1935): 12.
[58]*New York Times*, August 26, 1935.
[59]Ibid.
[60]Ibid.

> The Administration was warned at the time that exactly this trick-
> ery would be practiced upon it, if the Soviets were true to their
> own professions of being always ready to break their word, when
> they could profit by so doing. All that is now water over the dam.
> In the present sensitiveness here regarding all kinds of Red pro-
> paganda and scheming, the Government is certain to have public
> backing in the firm front which it has shown to Moscow.[61]

On August 27 the *New York Times* reported the reaction of nearly everyone who had been important in opposing recognition and quoted them
in detail. The paper asserted that members of Congress had approved
the tough stand almost unanimously and with apparent glee reminded
its readers that Congress, after all, had never had the chance to pass
on recognition because it had been done by executive order.[62]

Ambassador Troianovskii took advantage of an interview to comment that he believed that agitation in America against Moscow was
just as much of an interference as threatening talk in Russia against
the United States. The *New York Times* reported the ambassador's comments and contested them on the grounds that, in the United States,
public meetings in which Russian questions were considered confined
themselves almost wholly to a defense of religious liberty and human
rights while "never proposing any methods except those of oral sua-
sion."[63] A check of the *Times*'s own morgue would have illustrated the
hyperbole employed by the writer. It had been less than three months
since Admiral Yates Stirling suggested a holy war against the Soviets.[64]
The editorial also erroneously asserted that the United States, in any
event, had not bound itself to prevent attacks on the Soviet Union from
U.S. soil. The editorial further contended that the agreement had been
binding on the Soviets only.[65]

Newsweek, despite a chauvinistic title for its first story on the
matter, gave a fairly objective coverage of what had taken place,[66]
although a second article was more slanted. It noted that the president's
action, "some theorists felt," might be aimed at forestalling charges of
undue sympathy with the Reds, or that the statement was intentionally
weak, "critics decided," because a break with Moscow would have

---

[61] Ibid.

[62] Ibid., August 27, 1935.

[63] Ibid., August 28, 1935.

[64] Telegram, Laura Packard Redman to FDR, June 8, 1935, OF 220-A. The telegram
reporting Stirling's remarks was read to FDR's recording secretary Henry M. Kanee
over the phone, and in turn he was ordered by the president to relay it to Admiral
Joseph K. Taussig, Stirling's immediate superior.

[65] *New York Times*, August 28, 1935.

[66] "Eagle Shows Bear Its Talons: Keep Out of My Nest!" *Newsweek* 6 (August 31,
1935): 16.

shown recognition was a mistake.[67] Ambassador Bullitt fared well at the hands of former skeptics when they viewed him in his new anti-Bolshevik role.[68]

Time magazine attributed the administration's action to the desire for domestic applause in the face of the criticism, which was sure to come when the proceedings of the Comintern Congress were made public. It reported that the problem was that the answer from the Soviets to the tough note was a blunt refusal to accept it, which effectively called the president's bluff. The administration's only out was to issue a public statement after the Soviet refusal, but this would not give the Russians a chance to reply and had the advantage both of satisfying the American demand for strong language and of postponing the entire matter indefinitely.[69] *Time* then took a parting shot at FDR's policy, observing that it was too bad that the Russian people would not have the opportunity to find out from the Soviet press that President Roosevelt had "withdrawn the moral approval which 165,000,000 Russians were happy to think he extended when he recognized the Soviet Union."[70]

Reactions in the United States to the meeting in Moscow were not a product of a newly acquired fear of international communism so much as they were a part of the growing desire to be disassociated again from the turmoil and strife of Europe. The sentiment was best characterized by a cartoon from the Memphis *Commercial Appeal*, which was reprinted in *Current History*. Facing toward the dark shore of Europe and urged on by John Q. Public to turn up his volume, Uncle Sam stood on the American shore and sang "The Yanks Aren't Coming."[71] As the Roosevelt administration increased its attention to foreign affairs, Americans responded by refusing to be led into any policy labeled foreign entanglement. Obviously FDR's plans to promote security by a more outgoing policy, or by working with the Soviets, were in deep trouble.

Whether the president looked West or East he found nothing but clouded horizons. Tenuous plans to promote arms limitations rested on acceptance of them by powers determined to arm, and the realistic approaches to curtailing them, which appealed to Roosevelt, were too often opposed in his own Department of State. Maxim Litvinov urged Roosevelt to stand firm and support sanctions as did France, but the

---

[67]"Moscow Declines the American Protest Against Propaganda," ibid. (September 7, 1935): 13.

[68]Ibid.; "An Ultimatum," *Time* 26 (September 2, 1935): 19.

[69]"In a Red Hole," ibid. (September 9, 1935): 11.

[70]Ibid., p. 12.

[71]*Current History* 42 (June 1935): 279.

Roosevelt administration's policy was based on fear of public opposition. Even in the Far East, where the Russians expected more forthright collaboration, timidity ruled U.S. policy. Holding the Comintern Congress simply acknowledged the failure of both American-Soviet cooperation and FDR's peace initiatives.

IV

Darkening Clouds: Concern Without Panic

SOVIET AND AMERICAN LEADERS, although suspicious of one another's intentions, still expected that realism eventually would push their opposites to cooperation on their own terms. However, they were also determined to do whatever was possible to ensure their international position by initiatives that were not dependent on American-Soviet cooperation until such time as the anticipated "realism" forced the expected collaboration. There were moments when each set of leaders considered some helpful prodding necessary to awaken the other side to mutual dangers. In truth, the Roosevelt administration could afford to be more patient because its policy was aimed toward distant threats, while the Russians looked nervously at aggressive neighbors.

One thing was certain. Although they were in no hurry to meet each other via compromises, President Roosevelt and the Russians were careful to avoid ruptures in their relationship. They were aware that conditions were such that potential allies would be badly needed as threats to the peace became more evident. How to cooperate without compromise and how to persuade the opposing leadership of the dire need for recognizing the mutual threats to their security became the preeminent concern in Roosevelt's approach to the Russians and Soviet policy initiatives toward the Americans. At this juncture, using one another in plans to thwart the aggressors was more important in American-Soviet relations than actual cooperation against Germany, Italy, and Japan.

More than anything Russia desired peace for its own internal development, but, if it could not have peace, it preferred that someone else should be embroiled in war. The Soviets believed that in all probability they would be involved, however, and tried to make sure that whoever started the war would face a Russia with nations willing to assist it on the East and West. As Ambassador Troianovskii told an American audience, the next war could not be localized or isolated. It would inevitably be a universal war; and, if all governments could not take action to guarantee a pacific outcome for the dangerous troubles that Europe faced, they could at least give pledges to refrain from helping aggressors.[1]

Soviet newspapers gave prominent attention to the American reaction to German rearmament. Arthur Krock was, according to *Pravda*, the Washington expert for the *New York Times*. He illustrated that just because no formal protest came from the Department of State concerning Germany's violation of the Versailles Treaty this did not mean that the problem had escaped Washington's attention. The United States chose rather to register its protest through an unofficial statement from Secretary Hull. Krock criticized this cautious approach, which created "the impression among National-Socialist and Japanese militarists that one can violate pacts with the United States with impunity."[2] The implication was accurate but the choice of words was poor, as the United States did not sign the Treaty of Versailles.

Amidst all the maneuverings for security agreements, Soviet diplomats and journalists in Europe continued to search for signs that the United States might still wake up to its danger and prove to be an effective partner in keeping its pressure on Japan. Occasions indicating such an awakening gave brief bursts of sunshine on the Soviet diplomatic horizon in 1935 only to be just as quickly submerged again in murky clouds of doubt about the nature of American policy. Even after Raymond Moley departed the administration, the Soviets imagined that he still exerted some influence on it and that he was included in the briefings on the twists in policy. Thus *Pravda* found an article by Moley in his weekly *Today* to be highly significant, as well it should have considering Moley's previously almost paranoid isolationism: "The United States should consider the advisability of a union with Great Britain, an improvement of Soviet-American relations, and a stronger U.S. position in the Far East."[3] *Pravda* noted that, although Moley no longer held an official position, he was a frequent adviser to President Roosevelt and often his articles seemed to anticipate the president's policy.[4]

Despite all the agitation and defensive posturing over the Comintern Congress, American and Soviet negotiators concluded a trade agreement in 1935, illustrating that neither side expected a complete

[1]*New York Times*, March 23, 1935.
[2]"German Rearmament and the Position of the USA," *Pravda*, April 27, 1935.
[3]"The Foreign Policy of the USA," ibid., May 30, 1935.
[4]Ibid.

rupture in relations. The Comintern did not meet until after the trade agreement was signed by Bullitt and Litvinov on July 13; however, the American government was determined to conclude the pact despite foreknowledge of the Comintern meeting and the possibility that the United States would be a subject of comment. Bullitt specifically recommended on July 9 that "the possibility that the Congress may be held should not make us hesitate to sign at once the notes with respect to trade."[5]

Negotiations on the trade agreement had proceeded tediously from April to July, accompanied by maneuvering over whether the Soviets would guarantee how much they would spend in the United States in return for most-favored-nation treatment similar to that specified in a treaty between the United States and Belgium on February 27, 1935. The Americans desired a commitment to expend $30 million by the Russians, while Litvinov held out for a general statement, thus obligating the Soviets to buy considerably more than they had the previous year. The Americans won the point, and the USSR guaranteed a minimum $30 million purchase by one year from the date of the agreement.[6]

Political connotations interlaced the willingness of the Americans and the Soviets to sign the 1935 trade agreement. The Roosevelt administration desired success in its Soviet policy in order to offset the breakdown of the debt negotiations and the Comintern meeting. A doubling of Soviet purchases over the preceding year's figures would satisfy critics, but the Russians wanted some proof to show their potential enemies that American-Soviet relations had not gone sour.[7]

When the trade agreement was signed in July, the Russians cited American newspapers to prove that the pact heralded a tremendous improvement in general relations between the two countries.[8] In a speech delivered in Washington, Ambassador Troianovskii pleaded the Russian case for improved relations, via an appeal for Americans to examine the record of Soviet diplomacy and its support of the peace. He asked if peace could be maintained without the collaboration of the major powers and then answered no. The speech was couched in language explaining Soviet policy but sounded very much like an appeal to American realism.[9] When the press in the United States broke out in a rash of tirades against the Soviet Union after the Comintern

[5]*FRUS: Soviet Union*, p. 223.
[6]*Press Releases*, July 13, 1935, p. 45.
[7]*FRUS: Soviet Union*, pp. 193–94, 200, 204.
[8]"In the USA They Salute the Soviet-American Agreement," *Pravda*, April 27, 1935.
[9]A. A. Troianovskii, "The Foreign Policy of Soviet Russia," *Vital Speeches* 1 (August 12, 1935): 727–31.

Congress, the Soviet press virtually ignored the American reaction, partly because the Soviets were sure that the Comintern was not the real cause of tension.[10] By this juncture, the Russians were beginning to wonder whether the testy U.S. response to the Comintern meeting was not simply a way for the Americans to claim legitimate grounds for not following through on the political cooperation promised during Litvinov's conversations with Roosevelt.

Soviet assessments of the U.S. neutrality law shortly after it passed provided another indication of Russian hopes for Roosevelt's leadership to prod the Americans out of isolation. The Russians visualized FDR taking a firmer hand in attempting to deal with the international crisis. *Pravda* announced passage of the new legislation, commented on the short duration of the law, and concluded: "At the same time Roosevelt proclaimed that when the next session of Congress opens, he will insist that Congress review the resolution and grant the President freedom of action and the possibility of supporting one warring power against another."[11] The Russians expected the legislation to provide a means for FDR to exert pressure on an aggressor; when it became obvious the intent was to avoid involvement, the Russians were less concerned about what the Americans did. *Pravda* quoted Hull on the purpose of neutrality legislation, without comment: "The United States has no aggressive pretensions. We are prepared only to defend our security and welfare from any threat. . . . We are firmly convinced not to take part in armed conflicts which might arise between other countries and adhere to the policy which is needed to avoid such a risk."[12]

When President Roosevelt and Secretary Hull gave evidence that internal politics were influencing their conduct of foreign policy, the Russians demonstrated that they were no longer interested in games of pretense without definite collaborative objectives. Litvinov explained to the Chinese ambassador why the Kremlin no longer wooed the Americans: "The feelings of the United States with regard to any international question at the present time [are] unimportant, [it is] impossible to get the United States to involve itself in any effective way in international affairs either in Europe or the Far East."[13] Litvinov also commented that there was little use in making special efforts to be cordial to the United States, which moved Bullitt to conclude that there was not much hope for improvement in American-Soviet relations

---

[10]Walter Duranty, "Press in Russia Ignores Protests by U.S.," *New York Times*, August 27, 1935.

[11]"Law on Neutrality in the USA," *Pravda*, September 2, 1935.

[12]"An Appearance by Hull," ibid., October 17, 1935.

[13]Dispatch, American embassy in Moscow to Hull, October 26, 1935, DSF 711.61/574.

until the Soviet government became acutely afraid of an attack by Germany or Japan.[14] In late November Troianovskii added his warning that, although the Soviet Union desired closer relations, there seemed to be a lack of enthusiasm for such ties by America. The Russian ambassador said he was especially concerned over improving collaborative efforts, but in Moscow "the chief difficulty he was encountering was the conviction that the United States was so determined to remain aloof from foreign affairs that it was relatively unimportant to maintain good relations with the United States."[15]

Just before Christmas the Russians joyfully received a present from Senator Key Pittman who delivered an address so bellicose it required no elaboration by *Pravda*. Quoting the United Press, the Russian paper emphasized his announcement that, if the current Japanese government remained in power, the United States would invariably be forced to conduct a defensive war in the Pacific Ocean. The senator compared Japan's aims with those of the kaiser in 1914; the capture of China was merely the first step in Japan's imperialist program. The Japanese, he stressed, dreamed of capturing the western shore of the United States, Mexico, and South America. Pittman was tired of the cautious terms used when speaking about Japan, especially after the announcement of the Japanese representative at the London Naval Conference that Japan needed a navy larger than that of the United States because it feared war with America in the Pacific.

Japan, Pittman averred, feared two things: the English navy and the U.S. Navy; if both of them held maneuvers off Japan at the same time, perhaps the Japanese might listen to reason. "I am not a panicker," he asserted, "but the time has come for someone to tell the American people of the danger. If Japan should possess all of China, then she would be the most powerful country in the world and might realize her dreams of conquest. England understands this and therefore is trying to extricate herself from the Abyssinian conflict."[16] Britain could not let go of Mussolini because it would be like letting a thief get away with the loot. He concluded by saying, "I am a proponent of peace and neutrality, but in the present world situation we must decide to take a firm position."[17] Given the isolationist climate the Russians had observed during 1935, they were as perplexed by the senator's speech as Roosevelt had been. Surely it was a sign of a new departure; after all, Pittman was a major foreign policy spokesman for

---

[14]Ibid.

[15]Dispatch, of November 23, 1935, DSF 711.61/577.

[16]"Japanese Aggression Threatens the USA: Statement by Senate Foreign Relations Committee Chairman," *Pravda*, December 22, 1935.

[17]Ibid.

the Roosevelt administration in Congress. This was one of many occasions when the Russians seized on a statement made by an American who they believed spoke for the administration and touted the development of the long-awaited Roosevelt realism.

II

Ironically, at the time that the Soviets questioned whether there was anything more to be gained by serious consideration of political arrangements with the United States, Roosevelt became more aware of the seriousness of the international crisis. An exchange of communications with Ambassador Dodd bore witness to this, and it was important enough in the president's mind to bring to the cabinet's attention. The ambassador related the chaotic crumbling of European relations and warned the president of the bungled job the British were making of the Italian conflict in Ethiopia. He said that, if the British did not put the clamps on Italy, most of the small countries believed that the peace was done for and would abandon the League of Nations, leading to an "intense fear of war" and possible loss of independence. Dodd reported a forbidding prediction from a knowledgeable European concerning Hitler's intent. Supposedly the führer had made a blunt assertion that "we must go to war on the Soviets, and talked excitedly for minutes on the necessity, therefore, of the immense armaments here." He urged the United States to avoid a break with Russia because, "with Japan attacking Vladivostok, Germany breaking into Leningrad, we should have such horrors that one can hardly imagine the consequences."[18]

To Roosevelt, Dodd's communication was positively the most pessimistic letter he had ever read. European civilization was on the brink of the precipice, according to the ambassador, and nothing could restrain Hitler. The president said that, even allowing for Dodd's intense prejudice against Hitler, nonetheless the international situation was grave indeed. Secretary of the Interior Ickes recalled the disquieting news that FDR gave the cabinet: "Information in possession of the President is to the effect that there is an understanding between Germany and Japan which may result in a squeeze play against Russia."[19]

President Roosevelt began to express deep concern over the worsening situation abroad. Looking back on the events of 1935, he sounded an alarm in his annual address to Congress on January 3, 1936, recalling that in his inaugural he had devoted only one paragraph to foreign

---

[18]Nixon, *Roosevelt and Foreign Affairs*, 3:121–22.
[19]Ickes, *The First Thousand Days*, p. 494.

affairs, and that he had focused on the policy of the good neighbor in relations with Latin America. He said this policy had succeeded in the interim and that the Western Hemisphere might wish, 250 million strong, that the rest of the world would follow suit:

> Were I today to deliver an Inaugural Address to the people of the United States, I could not limit my comments on world affairs to one paragraph. With much regret I should be compelled to devote the greater part to world affairs. Since the summer of that same year of 1933, the temper and purposes of the rulers of many of the great populations in Europe and Asia have not pointed the way either to peace or to good-will among men. . . . A point has been reached where the people of the Americas must take cognizance of growing ill-will, of marked trends towards aggression, of increasing armaments, of shortening tempers—a situation which has in it many of the elements that lead to the tragedy of general war.[20]

President Roosevelt bore down hard on the deteriorating conditions that caused him alarm, warning Congress that the aggressively inclined nations did not apparently care that they threatened the peace and had resorted to the law of the sword. He spoke of their misguided messianism and assured Congress that his words might not be popular in such countries but so be it. Their obstinate determination to readjust the world to their liking had defeated the will of the majority of the world to promote disarmament; therefore, the United States had no recourse. "I realize," said the president, "that I have emphasized to you the gravity of the situation which confronts the people of the world. This emphasis is justified because of its importance to civilization and therefore to the United States. Peace is jeopardized by the few and not by the many. Peace is threatened by those who seek selfish power."[21] He further cautioned that, during the mad scrambles of kings and emperors for booty and empire, the world had faced such periods before, but Americans hoped they were not on the threshold of another such time:

> But if face it we must, then the United States and the rest of the Americas can play but one role: through a well-ordered neutrality to do naught to encourage the contest, through adequate defense

---

[20]Nixon, *Roosevelt and Foreign Affairs*, 3:153.
[21]Ibid., p. 154.

to save ourselves from embroilment and attack, and through example and all legitimate encouragement and assistance to persuade
other nations to return to the days of peace and good-will.[22]

After his warning, FDR wrote to Norman Davis, observing that
his message perhaps had been too bold: "I was a little afraid that my
message to Congress might cause a great deal of bitterness in Japan,
Germany, and Italy, but apparently it was taken very calmly. In any
event what I said had to be said not only for the record but in order
to solidify the forces of non-aggression."[23] Roosevelt was perplexed, if
not dismayed, when his speech failed to evoke more than moderate
vituperation within the German press and was scarcely noted by Nazi
and Japanese officials. Ambassador Dodd, like the president, thought
the address was really meaningful and had congratulated him:

> It is a marvelous but very shrewd indictment of all dictatorships,
> of all nations which persist in organizing great armies and pre-
> tending they have a right to annex smaller nations' territory. No
> German official can read this address without serious concern. It
> tells the whole world about the suppression of freedom here [Ger-
> many] and the complete subordination of the people.[24]

Soviet observers read the speech shrewdly. An *Izvestiia* writer
chose to quote the *New York Herald Tribune*, which emphasized Roosevelt's success in satisfying those elements of Congress which insisted
on international cooperation as well as the supporters of isolation. This
trick was accomplished, according to *Izvestiia*, by accurately appraising
and deploring the world situation as it stood, while declaring America's
intent not to become involved.[25] Writing in *Pravda*, a Soviet analyst
noted that the speech gave the basic outlines of American foreign policy
and deserved great attention because it showed "possible shifts in the
position of the USA on many questions, of significance not only for
the American continent but also for the entire world."[26] Focusing on

---

[22]Ibid., pp. 155–56. This transcript was the one the president used to address both
Congress and the nation via a broadcast over the radio. In other words, Roosevelt chose
to issue this warning to a listening audience to alert the country to the dangerous
disintegration of the world order.

[23]Elliott Roosevelt, ed., *The Roosevelt Letters*, 3 vols. (London: George G. Harrap,
1952), 3:166.

[24]William E. Dodd, Jr., and Martha Dodd, eds., *Ambassador Dodd's Diary, 1933–1938*
(New York: Harcourt, 1941), p. 293.

[25]V. Romm, "Comment on the Message by Roosevelt: The Frame of Mind in the
USA," *Izvestiia*, January 6, 1936.

[26]"International Review—Roosevelt's Message," *Pravda*, January 6, 1936.

the president's sharp criticism of German, Japanese, and Italian policy, he cautioned that it was still difficult to determine from Roosevelt's message how far the United States would go to join the efforts of states which were proponents of collective security. However, he judged that the signs were encouraging: "Neutrality . . . might have a broad meaning. . . . Both [the president's message and the neutrality bill] show that the government of the USA has taken some steps toward cooperation with those European countries which support the collective system."[27] To the analyst, Roosevelt would not have been so bold unless there were elements in influential circles of the government which were committed to the principle, strongly supported by Soviet policy, that the peace was indivisible in the struggle against aggressors. In conclusion, the writer suggested that Roosevelt had outlined a real change in American policy. In cautious language the assessment promised that at minimum Roosevelt's message strengthened the opposition to a new world war. By emphasizing that this was the least to be expected of the United States, it implied further forceful policy was to be anticipated.[28]

FDR was constantly corresponding with friends and State Department officers, voicing his concern over the disintegration of the peace. On January 25 he wrote to Leland Harrison at the American legation in Bucharest, expressing again that the crisis in Europe was getting out of control. The president told Harrison that "the situation changes so fast from day to day that it is hard to do more than make wild guesses in regard to the European future. Even though we can maintain a fairly stable and permanent course the general danger of the external situation continues disturbing."[29] To Ambassador Breckinridge Long in Italy, he wrote: "We watch the daily news from Europe with, I think, the feeling each day that the next will bring a major explosion."[30]

Precisely because he realized how desperate the situation might be in the near future, Roosevelt knew that something had to be done to block the aggressors. In March he wrote to Ambassador Dodd in Berlin that all the experts in Washington and elsewhere were saying that there would be no war, but, he continued, "They said the same thing all through July, 1914. . . . In those days I believed the experts. Today I have my tongue in my cheek. This does not mean that I am become cynical; but as President I have to be ready just like a Fire

---

[27] Ibid.
[28] Ibid.
[29] FDR to Harrison, January 25, 1936, PSF, No. II, Departmental Files, Box 20, State Department File.
[30] Roosevelt, *Roosevelt Letters*, 3:170.

Department."[31] The analogy was a good one; he was like a fire chief trying to gauge how much equipment was required to fight fires that already had been set.

One reason for the president's growing concern over the prospects of war was the increasing alarm conveyed to him in dispatches from the Department of State. Ambassador John Cudahy, for instance, had complacently announced in 1934 that the Nazi SS, SA, and other such organizations in Germany could be compared to the Elks but changed his mind in 1936, reporting from Warsaw in April that the repudiation of Locarno could mean only one thing: it would take a miracle to prevent war. It might not start for two or even five years, but, unless Hitler were overthrown, war was inevitable.[32]

President Roosevelt asked the new minister to Latvia, Arthur Bliss Lane, to report his observations on the Soviet-German struggle for dominance in the Baltic states. On October 8, 1936, Lane wrote that "these countries count on the private statements which Hitler has made . . . that he desires the integrity of the Baltic States as 'bulwarks against Bolshevism.' "[33] More significantly, he relayed information from well-informed quarters which contradicted the assertions of Nazi anti-Bolshevism. According to these sources, Germany would seek a rapprochement with the Soviet Union in order to deal with France, and Lane implied that for reasons of security such an arrangement might not be repugnant to the Soviets.[34] Later he decided that whatever the United States could do to avert this had to be done, including getting rid of Robert Kelley's influence in the State Department.

Career Foreign Service officer George S. Messersmith wrote from Vienna to Secretary Hull, warning of a Nazi attempt to camouflage German aggression under the guise of an anti-Communist crusade. The Nazi menace, he believed, was worse than the Bolshevik one and not greatly different. R. Walton Moore passed Messersmith's conclusions along to the president.[35] By this juncture, FDR was anti-Nazi and fearful of German aggression. If Germany was bent on picking on the Russians, the Soviets had the automatic sympathy of Franklin Roosevelt.

In late April the president illustrated what he thought he could do to prepare to meet the prospects for war, announcing at a press

---

[31]FDR to Dodd, March 16, 1936, OF 1561, Neutrality Folder, Box 1.

[32]Roosevelt, *Roosevelt Letters*, 3:176.

[33]Lane to FDR, October 8, 1936, PSF, No. II, Departmental Files, Box 20, State Department File.

[34]Ibid.

[35]Memorandum, Moore to FDR, November 6, 1936, PSF, No. II, Departmental Files, Box 24, State Department File, R. Walton Moore Folder.

conference his determination to secure more naval vessels in the battleship class if "other nations started battleships ahead of us . . . making our construction wholly dependent on what the other people do."[36] Roosevelt tried a little personal diplomacy to turn the trick in favor of peace. He queried Ambassador Dodd concerning what would happen if he personally and secretly asked Hitler to outline the limits of German objectives during a ten-year period and whether he would sympathize with a general limitation of armaments proposal. What the president hoped to accomplish by this was not clear, but it indicated his rising optimism over the pessimistic facts. Hitler's response, however, shattered any hope for a conference; he demanded advance guarantees that Italian and German colonies would be restored and that Russia would be condemned.[37] This provided further evidence to FDR of Hitler's determined anti-Soviet posture and reinforced the president's belief that the Russians had to move to the side of the Americans if they hoped to have friends who would help avert the aggressive designs of Germany and Japan. In other words, it proved that Germany was as much a foe of Russia as was Japan, and that the Soviets were desperately in need of allies.

Roosevelt continued voluntarily to foreswear American involvement in European political affairs, but he began to imply that the choice might not be left up to the United States. In a speech at Chautauqua, New York, on August 14, 1936, the president declared his concern over the disintegrating peace structure. Subtly, Roosevelt inserted the rampant conditions leading to another world war: "There are ancient hatreds, turbulent frontiers, the 'legacy of old, forgotten, far off things, and battles long ago.' There are new fanaticisms, convictions on the part of certain peoples that they have become the unique depositories of ultimate truth and right." He foretold the grab for profits which would move people to take sides in a new global conflict and thus break down American neutrality. The president inferred that in 1917 the government had paid insufficient attention to the little events that led to American involvement, and swore that he would not make that same mistake. He cautioned, however, that "we must remember that so long as war exists on earth there will be some danger that even the Nation which most ardently desires peace may be drawn into war."[38] FDR spoiled the oblique warning by rapid backpedaling when he asserted that the United States was prepared to defend only itself and its neighborhood against those who might wish America harm.

---

[36]Press Conferences, 7, No. 290, April 26, 1936, p. 227.

[37]Roosevelt, *Roosevelt Letters*, 3:183.

[38]Samuel I. Rosenman, ed., *The Public Papers and Addresses of Franklin D. Roosevelt*, vol. 5, *The People Approve, 1936* (New York: Random House, 1938), pp. 288–92.

Edwin L. James of the *New York Times* noted that Roosevelt's concern was genuine, necessary, and nearly useless, given the framework of U.S. foreign policy. In a penetrating, perceptive, and accurate analysis of the past, present, and future of American foreign relations, James pinpointed the fallacy of building false hopes on an unworkable foreign policy based on a belief in the innate goodness of men and nations. With cold rationality, he urged his readers to face the fact that security founded on wishful thinking did not work. America was only fooling itself if it did not recognize reality; the world was arming as never before despite proclamations that the whole world loved peace. America was also engaged in self-deception if it did not acknowledge the need to protect itself, but James wondered if this were truly possible and questioned the value of moral sanctions:

> The Church has never removed the need of the police station. . . . The pulpit has never emptied the jails. Signatures of statesmen on a parchment filled with declarations of brotherly love have never stopped wars.
>
> And so, here we are, planning on what we shall do when the next one starts. And we shall probably do nothing of what we are planning.[39]

Like most of the other realists of his day, James believed that the situation was nearly hopeless. He thought Hull and Roosevelt should be more alert to reality in their appraisals of what the national interest demanded; yet, he did not blame them for not following the logical course. Public opinion would not tolerate it.

President Roosevelt closed the year as he had begun it, on a note of concern over foreign affairs. Writing to former Democratic presidential nominee James M. Cox, he said: "I am still most pessimistic about Europe and there seems to be no step that we can take to improve that situation. Therefore until there is something I can hang my hat on, I must keep away from anything that might result in a rebuff of an offer to help."[40]

III

Roosevelt was reluctant to do anything in 1936 that openly hinted at a favorable attitude toward the Soviet Union, and certainly with Bullitt as his representative there he was not likely to receive much encouragement to explore new avenues to approach the Soviets on the peace

---

[39] Edwin L. James, "Again We Sermonize on Brotherly Love," *New York Times*, September 20, 1936.

[40] FDR to Cox, December 9, 1936, PPF 53, James M. Cox Folder.

question. Despite this American coolness toward Russia, there was no reciprocal reaction; that is, the Soviets did not strike out against the Americans as they did other nations that disappointed them. Partly this was because they judged the Americans still to be on their side by necessity. Russians might talk of capitalist plots and pseudoaltruism on the part of the Americans, but this attitude did not determine their policy. Molotov delineated the Soviet posture toward America in an address to the second session of the All-Union Central Executive Committee, in which he referred to the relations of the United States and the Soviet Union as having developed normally during the preceding year. He said that this happened despite the attempts of "certain reactionary and fascist inclined circles" to develop anti-Soviet campaigns in some parts of the American press, "with the purpose of disrupting the policy of rapprochement between the USSR and the United States of America which had enormous significance from the point of view of the preservation of the general peace."[41]

Loy W. Henderson, chargé of the American embassy in Moscow, evaluated the speech and emphasized Molotov's assurance to his audience that Japan's aims in the Far East still included a portion of Russian territory. Henderson thought that this Far Eastern threat, combined with a fear of Germany, accounted for increased defense appropriations in Russia.[42] In a separate report the chargé focused on Molotov's statement concerning the American-Soviet rapprochement "from the point of view of the preservation of peace." He considered this to be highly significant, in view of Litvinov's remarks to Ambassador Bullitt on November 9, 1935 when he said that, if the truth were known, the United States actually desired to remain aloof from all active interest in international affairs and implied that really friendly relations with the United States were of small importance to the Soviet Union. Henderson thought there had been an obvious change of heart since November 1935. He relayed the contents of a conversation with Troianovskii, who was home on leave. The Russian optimistically reported his progress in attempting to offset tendencies in certain Soviet circles to belittle the importance of the United States as a factor in world affairs. He also told Henderson that he was hampered in his efforts by developments in American neutrality policies which tended to further curtail the influence of the United States in international politics. "Molotov's words," Henderson concluded, "seem to indicate that the efforts of Troianovskii and others who hold his views had not been without

---

[41]"The Address of Comrade Molotov to the Second Session of the All-Union Central Executive Committee," *Pravda*, January 11, 1936.

[42]Dispatch, Henderson to Hull, January 11, 1936, DSF 711.61/589.

success. It is probable that the President's message and particularly his condemnation of autocracy and aggression played an important part in this development."[43]

More likely as a cause for the Soviets' soft-pedaling of their problems with the United States was their determination not to alienate unnecessarily anyone who might be of the slightest help at a time when Litvinov's three years of hard work building the collective security system seemed to be crashing down around him. The American chargé also told the State Department of a conversation from the Kremlin with the embassy's "usual emissary," who reported on January 16 the government's conviction that it could not rely on French military assistance unless France were actually attacked. As Henderson concluded, "While the Soviet Government will continue to push the program of collective security the Kremlin in the future will place little dependence on the success of that program in making decisions of a military or international political character."[44]

Shortly after Henderson's surmise that the Soviets were not going to bank on collective security to defend themselves from Germany, the Russians began lumping the Finns with their other threatening enemies. Marshal Mikhail Nikolaievich Tukhachevskii, assistant commissar of defense, mentioned Finland in company with Germany and Japan, noting, along with the hostile buildup of Germany and Japan, that the system of landing fields in Finland was far greater than necessary for Finnish aviation.[45] This was the first step in the Soviets' plan to enhance their security by expanding Russia's defensive border. Later Soviet Baltic policy had its origin as an alternative to collective security.

Because American interests in Europe were limited, the Russians never really expected much more than moral support from the United States against German machinations. However, there was a brief period when Moscow believed the neutrality legislation might allow President Roosevelt some latitude in pressuring Germany if it attacked Russia. When Hull and FDR made it clear that their options were restricted in applying the neutrality law, Soviet leaders considered American assistance to be restricted primarily to the Far East. Commissar Litvinov tried to convince Bullitt that Russia was no longer fearful of a Japanese attack in the near future, assuring the ambassador that Japan knew it could not fight Russia without German assistance and that such a combination was unlikely. Soviet policy ensured that Germany had to worry about the mutual assistance pact, which Litvinov had

---

[43]*FRUS: Soviet Union*, pp. 284–85.
[44]Ibid., p. 286.
[45]Ibid., p. 287.

signed with France, and growing friendly relations between England and Russia. Because of the various East European treaties with Russia, only Poland remained as a route of attack.[46] Litvinov was more confident that, if war broke out in the West, France would be Germany's victim. Under such circumstances the British, despite a more restrictive policy regarding commitments to France and the Continent than those that had prevailed in 1914, when faced by the fact of German aggression, would take their stand and make war.[47]

The Soviets actually were not as worried about the immediate threat of war as they had been in 1935, otherwise they would not have flung down the gauntlet to Japan in a dispute over Outer Mongolia. The Russians decided to impress the Japanese with their determination to protect Russia's vital interests. The threat to the USSR through Outer Mongolia was indirect but nonetheless real, a fact noted early in 1936 by American observer Edgar S. Furniss, who identified Japan's interest, expressed through Manchukuo, in acquiring Outer Mongolia. Russia intended to incorporate the area into its borders to ensure a buffer against expanding Japanese power.[48]

Russia made Outer Mongolia an open issue in 1936 when the Commissariat of Foreign Affairs informed Japan privately through diplomatic channels that the Soviet Union, without hesitation, would come to the aid of the Mongolian People's Republic if it were attacked.[49] Stalin granted an interview to Roy Howard of the Scripps-Howard newspaper chain and used him as an instrument to announce Soviet policy to the world. Stalin told Howard that the USSR would fight to defend Outer Mongolia from Japanese encroachment. Japan, he said, was for the moment the primary threat to the peace, although Germany might assume that role at any time. He also assured Howard that the Soviet Union did not intend to foment revolution in the United States; it was possible and desirable for the Soviet and American systems to coexist in the world.[50]

Japanese leaders contended that Stalin was bluffing, taking advantage of internal disturbances in Japan[51] in order to get Japan to withdraw support from Manchukuo in its efforts to establish control in Outer Mongolia. The Japanese Foreign Office spokesman said of

---

[46]Dispatch of February 17, 1936, DSF 711.61/594.

[47]Ibid.

[48]Edgar S. Furniss, "War Fear in the Soviet Union," *Current History* 43 (January 8, 1936): 435–38.

[49]Memorandum of March 5, 1936, DSF 711.67/597.

[50]*New York Times*, March 5, 1936.

[51]This refers to the assassinations that plagued Japan in 1936, requiring the government to establish martial law.

Stalin's announcement: "We are not able to take his statement seriously."[52] Military authorities outside of Japan thought otherwise and concluded that Stalin's statement would undoubtedly cause Japan to alleviate its pressure on the Mongolian frontier. They thought Japan's purpose in these skirmishes had been to see how far the Russians would go to protect their interests in Mongolia, and Stalin's answer was unquestionably clear.[53]

Outside of Germany and Japan the world reaction to Stalin's statements in Howard's interview was generally favorable. Most of the world's press believed Stalin struck a note for peace, at least temporarily, and served Russian security interests by letting Japan know how far it could go before being confronted by military force.[54] According to Harold Denny of the *New York Times*, the Japanese had put the Soviets' determination to oppose Japan to a small test. In three days of border clashes, at a time when the Soviets were apparently concentrating all their efforts on European affairs, the Russians shot down Manchukuoan cavalrymen who allegedly crossed into Siberian territory at some point on the River Argun.[55] Such clashes became more frequent before Japan could be convinced that Russia was not only serious in its intent but also militarily able to carry out its promise to defend every inch of Soviet territory, disputed or otherwise.[56]

IV

Despite comments by Litvinov and Troianovskii that the United States was only concerned with its interests in the Far East, the Soviets continued to report the possibility that America wished to preserve the peace in both Europe and Asia. Various statements by Roosevelt and the U.S. press caused the Russians to believe that perhaps the attitude of the Americans might be stiffening toward those powers that threatened their interests in both regions. At least the Russians took pains to advertise the possibility even if they were not wholly convinced that it was true. Thus, after President Roosevelt's annual message to Congress in January, in which he criticized Japan, the Soviet press called attention to the 500 military vessels and 400 aircraft concentrated in southern California and prepared for secret maneuvers in the Pacific.[57]

---

[52]*New York Times*, March 5, 1936.

[53]Ibid.

[54]"The World Press on Stalin's Talk with Roy Howard," *Pravda*, March 6, 1936.

[55]Harold Denny, "Three Japanese Killed in Frontier Clash," *New York Times*, March 28, 1936.

[56]Harriett L. Moore, *Soviet Far Eastern Policy, 1931–1945* (Princeton: Princeton University Press, 1945), pp. 56ff.

[57]"Large Scale Maneuvers of the American Fleet," *Pravda*, January 7, 1936.

Another indication of Soviet intent to announce a more determined American policy appeared in an *Izvestiia* cartoon of January 9,
which showed a German, an Italian, and a Japanese looking at a
bulletin board labeled "Statement by Roosevelt," on which stood out
in bold print: "Warning to countries threatening the peace." The three
figures in unison wondered, "Is that some kind of hint?"[58] Further
substantiation of a shift in American policy presumably came from
Senator Pittman who advocated stronger defense measures and
demanded the construction of a fleet that would stand four U.S. ships
to one for Japan.[59] *Pravda* credited Secretary Hull with a tougher posture
toward Japan when it reported a statement by him to a congressional
budget committee of his desire to urge more attention to protecting
American citizens and interests in Japan. Hull's statement referred
strictly to commercial activity, but *Pravda* made it appear to be almost
an ultimatum.[60]

An article by Walter Lippmann on world conditions excited the
Russians, who evaluated it as an indication of a new awareness of
external threats. The Soviets still believed Lippmann spoke semioffi-
cially for the American government, thus lending special importance
to his observations. He wrote that the United States was affected by
the dilemma of Europe because the maintenance of peace and order
definitely served America's interest. The United States, he warned,
should not lead the world into error by giving half promises that it did
not intend to fulfill; it could not afford to make collective security
difficult by its position.[61]

Lippmann's article appeared three weeks after Roosevelt's message, and it could not have seemed more natural as a followup to the
president's warnings delivered to Congress. In the Soviet assessment
of American policy, if a "spokesman" for the administration made a
public declaration, it foreshadowed U.S. policy. When other American
newsmen supported an increase in the defensive capacity of the USSR,
demanded a lessening of American isolationism imposed by selfish
minorities, and criticized French officials for allowing Germany a free
hand in Eastern Europe, the Russians visualized a distinct and encouraging pattern for American policy in opposition to the aggressors.[62]

The first sign that Soviet peace plans were going sour came early
in the year. German reoccupation of the Rhineland in March 1936

---

[58]"The Outraged Innocents," *Izvestiia*, January 9, 1936.
[59]"Four American Ships to One for Japan," *Pravda*, February 14, 1936.
[60]"The Policy of the USA in the Far East—Statement by Hull," ibid., April 2, 1936.
[61]"The USA and Collective Security," ibid., January 26, 1936.
[62]"Japanese-German Plans of Aggression—The American Press Welcomes the
Increase in the Defensive Capacity of the USSR," ibid., February 5, 1936.

provided the most crucial test of the 1930s for the European security system. Hitler challenged the European status quo, and only the Russians responded directly. This may have been partly due to the Soviets' belief that a determined challenge would not result in a fight. They knew there was opposition from high members of the German general staff to the remilitarization of the Rhineland, based on the German officers' conviction that the Rhineland project would drain too much away from other military preparations.[63] Whatever his motivation, Litvinov was furious; he searched for support of collective security and found none. The British said that, in relation to the Rhineland, there had to be some new way to guarantee the borders of Belgium and France, with the rupture of Locarno and the abandonment of the Versailles Treaty. Litvinov argued that there was no better solution than to act on the basis of the existing agreements and stop Germany while it could be stopped. The Soviet commissar, after a stormy session with Pierre Étienne Flandin, the French foreign minister, reproached him for weakening in France's defense of league principles. Litvinov announced that "Germany cannot be allowed to return to the League by way of a treaty violation. France may accept this humiliation, but Russia never will."[64] The Soviets took some solace from American support for their position, which recognized its essential good sense and correctness.[65] This was small consolation, however.

Litvinov appeared before the League of Nations and pleaded his view that the whole peace structure rested on the action which that body decided to take in regard to the German violations of Versailles and Locarno. If anyone doubted the intention of the Nazis, he said, it was not necessary to take time out to cite appropriate quotations from German periodicals, textbooks, scientific works, or songbooks; it was only necessary to look at *Mein Kampf*. Hitler's testament made it quite clear that the remilitarization of the Rhineland was the first step in subduing the continent of Europe to German dominance.[66] Peace in Europe hung on the outcome of Litvinov's appeal and, when there was no firm response, the gates swung shut on any hope to avoid war. There may have been other points where Hitler could have been stopped but none so easily or so surely. Litvinov's motives may have been selfish, but his objectives were in the best interest of every state opposed to Fascist aggression and for the future security of Europe and the world.

---

[63]Dispatch of February 17, 1936, DSF 711.61/594.

[64]Augur [Vladimir Poliakov], "Locarno Powers Firm Against War," *New York Times*, March 14, 1936.

[65]"Comments on the Remilitarization of the Rhineland Zone—The Opinion of the American Press," *Izvestiia*, March 10, 1936.

[66]*New York Times*, March 18, 1936.

Not only were significant American sources speaking well of Soviet peace efforts in 1936 and providing hope of an aroused America, but the Russians also expected improved relations when the U.S. government withdrew William Bullitt as ambassador to the Soviet Union. Great expectations provided little results as Bullitt's long-cherished dream of an American-Soviet relationship of close harmony, aided by the ambassador's astute diplomacy, ended in a fizzle. He was embittered and conscious of his failure as he prepared to surrender his ambassadorship in Moscow where he had become persona non grata. The first rumor of Bullitt's departure circulated in May,[67] but he did not leave until three months later. When he returned to the United States, he took a temporary position as a consultant to Secretary Hull, without resigning his ambassadorship.[68] In Washington he awaited word from the president as to a new and appropriate assignment.[69] Finally, on August 25, FDR announced that Bullitt would replace the ailing U.S. ambassador to France, Jesse Straus. Roosevelt did not immediately replace Bullitt in Moscow, saying he had no one in mind and Bullitt would officially remain the ambassador to Russia until he took over his new duties in Paris.[70]

Bullitt, who left the Soviet Union under a hail of vituperation from Soviet newspapers,[71] was greeted by a similar barrage from the right-wing press in France on his arrival there. The pro-Fascist *Action Française* charged the new American ambassador with subversive intent. According to this account, Bullitt was sent to Paris as a Soviet agent to foment a Franco-German war. The ridiculousness of the assertion was heightened by the inclusion of Bernard M. Baruch as a coconspirator.[72]

Bullitt's successor in Russia was not chosen until November 21 when Joseph E. Davies, a wealthy Washington corporation lawyer, was named to the post. The appointment of Davies quelled rumors that Roosevelt would leave Russia without an American ambassador until the Soviets paid their debts. Despite FDR's disappointment over the Soviets' refusal to pay their indebtedness and to work toward friendly relations, some newsmen believed the assignment of Davies to Russia served to emphasize the importance Roosevelt attached to the Soviet Union. According to the conjectures enumerated in the *New York Times*,

---

[67] Ibid., May 13, 1936.
[68] Ibid., August 9, 1936.
[69] FDR to Bullitt, April 21, 1936, PSF, Box 15.
[70] "Nomination of Bullitt as Ambassador of the USA to France," *Pravda*, August 27, 1936.
[71] Memorandum, FDR to Bullitt, December 3, 1936, DSF 711.61/609.
[72] *New York Times*, September 15, 1936.

the president thought it highly important to have an able ambassador in Moscow, in view of the Soviet connection with the Spanish civil war and the possible reactions to the announced agreement between Japan and Germany, which was understood in Europe to be aimed against Russia.[73]

Indeed, the president attached considerable importance to the Soviet Union and had no intention of leaving the position vacant, and in this Ambassador Bullitt played a significant role. He intended to make sure Roosevelt and Hull understood there could be no thought of abandoning the Moscow listening post. Despite his disenchantment with the Russians and his developing anticommunism, Bullitt perceived Russia as an extremely important balance wheel in whatever crises might arise in the future. In a series of final dispatches from Moscow, Bullitt proved that he had learned an important lesson about Russia and its role in world affairs, which he passed on to Hull and Roosevelt.

As Bullitt expressed it in his reports to the president and Secretary Hull, the problems confronted in the USSR were not Communist ones alone; they were Russian. He quoted at length from the dispatches of the Honorable Neil S. Brown of Tennessee, the American minister to Russia in the 1850s. Bullitt prefaced his quotations from Brown's communiqués with the French adage, "plus ça change, plus c'est la même chose," by which he conveyed his impression that the Russian attitude was the result of cultural, ethnic, and historical continuity which would not necessarily change with a new government or a new system. He thought Brown's observations presented "an accurate picture of life in Russia in the year 1936." Brown complained of the many things in Russia which tried an American's patience, the most irritating of which were the secrecy with which everything was done and the degree to which one could be constantly sure that every move made was followed by unseen and prying eyes. Government officials, Brown found, were the most distrustful of a race of suspicious people. Bullitt also stressed his predecessor's observations on the police state mentality that prevailed and the sharp cut of the censor's knife, which, for political purpose, distorted all news from the external world.[74]

In a perverse way Bullitt must have felt great satisfaction at being able to find the sufferings of a kindred spirit almost a century earlier identical to his own. More than once he emphasized that it was not due to communism that these conditions prevailed; rather, they were a part of the Russian experience with roots centuries deep in its history.

---

[73]Ibid., November 21, 1936. The German-Japanese agreement referred to in the article was the Anti-Comintern Pact, which had become common knowledge at this point although it was not signed until November 26.

[74]*FRUS: Soviet Union*, pp. 289–90.

He could have been quoting one of his own complaints sent to Washington, as he cited Brown's observation:

> During the last year it has been evident, that the policy of Russia towards foreigners, and their entrance into the country, was becoming more and more stringent. I heard of several Americans during the past summer who were unable to procure visas from the Russian legations at different points, and were therefore compelled to abandon their journey. This arises mainly from political considerations, and a fear of foreign influence upon the popular mind.[75]

In his final dispatch, Bullitt suggested what should be done to counteract the antagonisms and calculated or incidental insults one encountered from the Kremlin. His answer was—nothing. It was best, he suggested, simply to maintain diplomatic relations because Russia "is now one of the Greatest Powers and its relations with Europe, China, and Japan are so important that we cannot conduct our foreign relations intelligently if we do not know what is happening in Moscow." Also, he argued that it was possible, despite efforts at secrecy, to discover considerable information in the Russian capital about Soviet political ambitions directed through the world Communist movement. American influence could be used, he thought, to oppose war in the Far East, not because of moral opposition but because, if there were a war, someone might win it:

> In case the Soviet Union should win, a Communist China would be inevitable. In case Japan should win, China would be completely subjected to Japan. If war comes between Japan and the Soviet Union, we should not intervene but should use our influence and power toward the end of the war to see to it that it ends without victory, that the balance between the Soviet Union and Japan in the Far East is not destroyed, and that China continues to have at least some opportunity for independent development.[76]

In dealing with the Soviets, Bullitt suggested the keynote for success was the ability to be calm and imperturbable in the face of adversity. It irritated him that lying was normal in Foreign Office statements, and he was insulted by the assumption that the lie was believed. "But patience and diplomats," he noted, "exist for just that sort of difficulty." Bullitt was concerned that the American eagerness

---

[75]Ibid., p. 290.
[76]Ibid., p. 294.

to settle problems quickly might be responsible for hasty decisions that could injure the U.S. position:

> We should neither expect too much nor despair of getting anything at all. . . . We should take what we can get when the atmosphere is favorable and do our best to hold on to it when the wind blows the other way. . . . We should make the weight of our influence felt steadily over a long period of time in directions which best suit our interest. We should never threaten. We should act and allow the Bolsheviks to draw their own conclusions as to the causes of our acts.[77]

That most of this advice might have been better heeded in subsequent relations with Russia is apparent. However, the essential point was that, after early false hopes concerning what might be gained from establishing relations with Russia, Bullitt narrowed his focus to the real importance of American-Soviet relations: the overriding fact that one large nation simply cannot afford to be without access to another highly significant one. The Russians might be reprehensible in their politics and economics, but this did not change their weight in international affairs. In his statement about the efficacy of long-term pressures consistently applied and the importance of maintaining contacts, Bullitt made implicit the prospect of a change in the pattern of Soviet life and the possibility for a better, if not wholly satisfactory, relationship. Once again Roosevelt was assured that the Soviet Union, as a threatened power, had to be on the side of the democratic states.

These final dispatches were only partly Bullitt's observations. They were also composites of the views of Foreign Service officers in the embassy who generally stressed the calm, dispassionate approach to an American-Soviet relationship in their assessments of proper diplomatic conduct. The dispatches that flowed from Russia, under the pen of Loy Henderson when he took over the embassy as chargé d'affaires, included the observations of his colleagues and were both factual and analytical. He saw Stalin moving in new directions and emphasized the developing purges as an illustration of the Russian leader's determination to rid internal opposition in preparation for the possible necessity to deal with external problems. The embassy personnel were shocked by the brutality of the purges and reacted with abhorrence. Henderson was repulsed by the process but reported accurately what Stalin sought to achieve.

---

[77]Ibid., pp. 295–96.

V

Maxim Litvinov marked Bullitt's departure with relief and hope for a better and more profitable American-Soviet relationship:

> I am glad that Washington decided to send us Davies. Troy-anovsky has supplied a full account of his talk with Davies at a lunch at our Embassy. . . . He affirms that Davies understands nothing about our affairs but that he is full of the most sincere desire to work with us in complete co-operation and to carry out strictly Roosevelt's instructions.
> I have always regarded Bullitt as our bitter enemy.[78]

Litvinov's desire to improve relations with the Americans rested in part on perceived necessity, for once again he saw the importance of the United States to Soviet plans to stop an impending war. For the Russians, the diplomatic events of 1936 closed on a note of concern, triggered by Hitler's Nuremberg speech in which he made an open threat to Russian territorial sovereignty.[79] Litvinov, who had been so confident earlier in the year that Germany was being isolated, was backed into a corner and found himself standing alone against a tide of appeasement which surely must have seemed to the Russians to be developing at the expense of their territorial integrity. The Soviet commissar took the opportunity to state his case at Geneva, where he demanded that German membership in the League of Nations be declared incompatible with league principles and called for immediate action in reforming the league to strengthen its coercive machinery. Litvinov's reply to Hitler's challenge, Clarence Streit stated in the *New York Times*, "was to pose, for all practical purposes, Russia's candidacy for the role of leader and protector of the Slavic countries of Central and Eastern Europe . . . who fear they are being abandoned now to Germany and Italy." The only way to deal with Hitler, Litvinov concluded, was "with a policy no less firm than his own and cold calculation of the relative strength of forces."[80]

Another blow that caused the Soviets concern was the German-Japanese Anti-Comintern Treaty of November 26, which was judged immediately to include a secret military alliance partly because the negotiations were conducted through Major General Oshima Hiroshi, Japanese military attaché in Berlin, without the knowledge of the Foreign Office in Tokyo and "very likely without the knowledge of the

---

[78]Litvinov, *Notes for a Journal*, pp. 243–44.

[79]"Speech of Hitler—Threat of a Madman," *Pravda*, September 18, 1936.

[80]Clarence K. Streit, "Speedy Reform Urged on League," *New York Times*, September 29, 1936.

German Foreign Office."[81] The Soviets instantly assessed the pact as the next step toward war.[82] Litvinov told the Central Executive Committee that the basis of Soviet foreign policy remained unchanged, but he could not say the same for other powers that had something to fear from the aggressor states. While the USSR still urged collective security and military preparedness for all who opposed aggression, others had deserted the policy. Furthermore, he said some had argued that the collective security system was bankrupt, but he did not see how this was possible when the policy had yet to be in effect. Some governments, Litvinov feared, believed that aggressors could be appeased, but they were learning the hard way that it was not possible. They understood, too late perhaps, that their freedom of choice in avoiding war was being severely restricted. In fact, the choices had been reduced to two:

> One leads to the collective security system advanced by the Soviet Union. . . . The other . . . is the . . . so-called *rapprochement* with the aggressors, the *rapprochement* of the crab with the shark in the hope that perhaps the shark will not gobble him up entirely, but just taste only one little bite.[83]

Litvinov assured his audience that the Soviet Union could afford to wait because it had prepared for any eventuality by readying to meet force with force if necessary. In such circumstances Russia was in the driver's seat. According to the commissar, "If the other nations really want to organize peace, to guarantee collective security, and oppose the forces of aggression they cannot do it without the Soviet Union."[84] Preparedness for any contingency was an essential ingredient of Soviet foreign policy. In meeting the needs of national interest, the Russians were not the least aggressive nation among the great powers. Toward the end of 1936, Henderson made a prophetic observation in this respect:

> In my opinion, the aggressive characteristics of Soviet foreign policy are largely due to the fact that that policy, to a greater extent than the foreign policies of most other powers, has before it a series of definite objectives, and that the work of Soviet officials responsible for the conduct of that policy is judged by the progress

---

[81] Joseph C. Grew, *Ten Years in Japan* (New York: Simon & Schuster, 1944), p. 191. Grew's conjecture was accurate. See also Lee Farnsworth, "Hirota Kōki," in Richard Dean Burns and Edward M. Bennett, eds., *Diplomats in Crisis: U.S.-Chinese-Japanese Relations, 1919–1941* (Santa Barbara: ABC-Clio, 1974), pp. 240–41.

[82] "The Japanese-German Alliance—A New Link in the Preparation for World War," *Pravda*, November 28, 1936.

[83] "Litvinov's Speech to the Central Executive Committee," *Izvestiia*, November 11, 1936.

[84] Ibid.

which those officials are able to make in the direction of these objectives.[85]

Foremost among the immediate objectives, Henderson believed, was the creation of a system of collective security which included "pacts of mutual military assistance aimed at discouraging acts of armed aggression on the part of the Powers, particularly Germany and Japan, which [the Russians believe] are most likely to attack the Soviet Union." It would not be enough, he informed the State Department, for the United States to take the first step, which the Soviets preferred, to assist in preserving Soviet security. Such an initiative would require the United States to make it known that it sympathized with the Soviet efforts at thwarting the designs of the aggressive powers. Beyond this, the chargé concluded, many Soviet officials would then urge that the United States

> give the 'aggressive powers' to understand that in case of an act of aggression the American government would favor the injured party by furnishing financial and technical assistance and military and other supplies. It would, of course, be preferable . . . if the United States were to enter at once into definite treaties of mutual military assistance . . . [strengthening] the whole collective security structure. They admit, however, that it would probably be necessary for a considerable amount of preparatory education work . . . before American public opinion would tolerate the assumption of obligations of so serious a nature.[86]

Henderson clearly stated the Soviet objectives. Russian leaders might still carry the world revolution in the back of their minds, but, since immediate problems were far more pressing, pushing the revolution was not in their best interests. The chargé thought Stalin and other Russian leaders had another and, to them, equally important problem. They feared losing control of revolutionary forces that would then turn against them. Henderson considered this to be well demonstrated by the fact that such revolutionary groups as those referred to by the Soviets as Trotskiists no longer looked to Moscow for inspiration. To these revolutionaries, the USSR had become "a nationalistic reactionary state in which the workers are being exploited for the benefit of the bureaucracy and a new *bourgeoisie*." Henderson thought that the Soviet Union eventually might move to a nationalistic chauvinism, but it made no difference at the moment. What counted were the current Soviet aims that the United States could not afford to support.[87]

---

[85]*FRUS: Soviet Union*, pp. 310–11.
[86]Ibid., pp. 311–13.
[87]Ibid., p. 313.

Despite rebuffs and disappointments in their expectations of American action in the interest of collective security, the Russians returned like moths to a flame at each new pronouncement from the United States which seemed to indicate an awakening. Thus, in the waning days of 1936, *Pravda* and *Izvestiia* again recorded hopeful words from Franklin Delano Roosevelt. *Pravda* reported on December 1 a *Washington Post* article on Roosevelt's speech at Rio de Janeiro. The *Post* suggested that the president had in mind a policy of collective security against aggression which the League of Nations should welcome. According to the *Post*, saving civilization had become the concern of the Western Hemisphere, which could no longer afford to ignore the events taking place in Europe.[88] On December 8 *Izvestiia* reported a Chicago *Daily News* conjecture that President Roosevelt clearly spoke out against fascism at the Pan-American Conference.[89] He had acknowledged the existence of a threat and had dramatized the departure in U.S. foreign policy by attending the Rio Conference in person. It was a beginning; in fact, the Russians accurately surmised a new policy toward them on Roosevelt's part, one that he began to implement in late 1936 and early 1937.

---

[88]"The Germano-Japanese Agreement—Roosevelt on Collective Action Against Aggressors," *Pravda*, December 1, 1936.

[89]"The American Press on Roosevelt's Speech," *Izvestiia*, December 8, 1936.

V

Arouse and Beware

IN ANOTHER TIME and context the seventeenth-century English poet Robert Herrick expressed perfectly Franklin D. Roosevelt's approach to the international crisis of the late 1930s: "None pities him that's in the snare, who warned before, would not beware."[1] When asked at what point FDR began to work toward preparing the American people for possible involvement in war, Frances Perkins replied:

> The President began to bring up the serious threats to the peace in the Cabinet regularly in 1935; in 1936 he began nagging us about it; in 1937 he nagged us on the subject all the time. It is a technique he may have gotten from me; I nagged the Cabinet quite often on things I thought they and the President should do something about. Nagging, you know, is another name for educating. By 1937 he was determined to educate us and the American people on the seriousness of the threat that Hitler and the Japanese posed to democracy. Yes, 1937 was the year he decided we really could not afford to bury our heads in the sand any longer.[2]

Certainly the evidence bears out Perkins's evaluation. Roosevelt resolved that he had no choice but to accentuate his program of education on the perils to the peace and to probe for possible ways to divert the aggressions arising around the world. As he admonished Americans to arouse and beware, he began a military preparedness campaign and reorganized the State Department, tried to promote a peace conference, gathered the Far Eastern powers at Brussels to help curb Japan, and

---

[1] Tryon Edwards et al., *The New Dictionary of Thoughts* (New York: Standard Books, 1949), p. 64.
[2] Interview with Perkins.

determined to use the Russians in some fashion to develop pressure on the arming nations. The president chose Joseph Davies and Treasury Secretary Henry Morgenthau, Jr., as his agents in approaching the Russians. Part of his effort to involve the Soviets in his peace plans included an attempt to bother Japan by providing the Russians with a warship.

With President Roosevelt's awareness of danger becoming more intense in 1937, it was almost inevitable that he would try a public appeal in order to create concern for American security. As in the case of Russian recognition, however, it was not likely that FDR would plunge into a bold declaration that America had to sharpen its perception to the threats surrounding it without some assurance that such a move would receive public support. Thus a portion of 1937 was spent in feeling the public pulse. Accordingly, Roosevelt wrote a letter to be read at the opening session of the University of Virginia's Institute of Public Affairs. In it he announced:

> As Americans, it must be clear to us that a continuation of the existing uncertainties in the international sphere is highly prejudicial to the well being of the United States . . . and to the well being of the man in the street, in common with plain citizens everywhere.
>
> The problem before every thinking man and woman, then, is how to avert this threatened disaster. . . . The more squarely and honestly this problem is faced by leaders in all walks of life, . . . the sooner will an effective solution be found.[3]

The *New York Times* acknowledged the letter as a grave warning that the outbreak of war would strike at the welfare of the United States, requiring leaders to meet the problem squarely and honestly, and the sooner the better.[4]

A letter to Roosevelt from Harrison J. Conant, an old classmate at Columbia Law School, evoked a revealing response. He wrote that the foreign situation was a result of a paralysis of fear which gripped the peace- and liberty-loving peoples of the world, making any price seem preferable to risking an attack from modern weapons of war. Such fear, Conant judged, would lead to the war which it so desperately sought to avert. "Those who wish for peace must be ready to fight for it," he continued. "We have treaty rights, human rights that are being

---

[3]Samuel I. Rosenman, ed., *The Public Papers and Addresses of Franklin D. Roosevelt*, vol. 6, *The Constitution Prevails, 1937* (New York: Macmillan, 1941), p. 284.

[4]Winfred Mallon, "Roosevelt Warns We Would Suffer from War Abroad," *New York Times*, July 6, 1937.

violated. If we don't resist, it will not be long before we wont [*sic*] enjoy any rights."[5] In response, Roosevelt told him that "I am grateful to you for your letter, and I fully agree with you in regard to the real perils of the international situation. I am disturbed by it and by its daily changing events. Soon I think the Nation will begin to appreciate the ultimate dangers of isolating ourselves completely from all joint efforts toward peace."[6]

During the latter part of September and early October, the president, in a swing across the country by rail, tested public response via a whole series of platform speeches. He delivered a sequence of parries on the need to ensure the future of the nation and its children and remarked on the necessity to protect the democratic form of government; the responses were positive.[7] He climaxed his tour on October 5 with a bridge dedication at Chicago, where he pulled together all of the hints he had made over the preceding few months, and the bridge-head he spoke of had very little to do with engineering design. It was another far more serious kind of support he discussed: a foundation for the security of the nation by its citizens in an appeal to stand against aggression before it raged out of control like an epidemic disease.

Roosevelt's Chicago speech was triggered by developments in the Far East and by the failure of any satisfactory conclusion to the China crisis. The president, as suggested by the Navy Department, had refused to make a direct assault on Japan while it was still engaged in North China but decided instead on a less aggressive course of action.[8] Harold Ickes told FDR that the president was the only one who could mold or guide world public opinion for the democratic ideal. The secretary of the interior, in fact, thought it was the president's duty to lead in this respect, and he argued that such a move would receive favorable public reaction.[9] Ickes was not solely responsible for promoting the speech; Secretary Hull and Norman Davis also urged Roosevelt to address the nation in some large city where the idea of isolationism was entrenched. As he often did, Roosevelt bounced the proposed speech off someone else before going to Ickes. On July 8 he tested the idea on Clark M. Eichelberger, director of the League of Nations Association, asking what he thought of the president making a dramatic statement to draw attention to the international crisis and possibly getting Americans to support "denial of trade to the aggressor."[10]

---

[5]Conant to FDR, September 27, 1937, PPF 4896.
[6]FDR to Conant, October 2, 1937, ibid.
[7]Rosenman, *The Constitution Prevails*, pp. 376–406.
[8]Ickes, *The Inside Struggle*, p. 211.
[9]Ibid., p. 213.
[10]Dallek, *Roosevelt and American Foreign Policy*, p. 148.

Eichelberger hedged his answer with numerous ifs, but in general he encouraged Roosevelt, saying that the public, without hesitation, had received FDR's proposals at Buenos Aires for consultation under the Pact of Paris and would not object to extending it to the rest of the world. "Once the world has accepted your principles, the denial of trade to the aggressor would be accepted by the American people."[11]

However the speech came to be tested, its most famous phrase apparently originated with Ickes.[12] In a conversation with Ickes, FDR told him he thought that, in establishing the direction of foreign policy, it was time to "take the ball away from Hull." Pursuing the subject further, Ickes recalled on October 9: "I said that it was just like a case of a contagious disease in a community. . . . The neighbors had a right to quarantine themselves against a contagious disease. The President said, 'That is a good line; I will write it down,' which he proceeded to do."[13]

At Chicago the president, after a long period of attempting various courses to create a foundation for U.S. security in a changing world, decided to try his case before the American people, with a stronger statement of both the menace and the possible remedy than he had previously made public:

> If [another major war] comes . . . in other parts of the world, let no one imagine that America will escape, that America may expect mercy, that this Western Hemisphere will not be attacked and that it will continue tranquilly and peacefully to carry on the ethics and the arts of civilization.
>
> It seems to be unfortunately true that the epidemic of world lawlessness is spreading.
>
> When an epidemic of physical disease starts to spread, the community approves and joins in a quarantine of the patients in order to protect the health of the community against the spread of the disease.
>
> War is contagious. . . . There must be positive endeavors to preserve peace.
>
> America hates war. America hopes for peace. Therefore, America actively engages in the search for peace.[14]

---

[11]Eichelberger to FDR, July 17, 1937, PPF 3833, Clark M. Eichelberger Folder.

[12]There is some controversy concerning the origin of the term "quarantine," but the evidence seems to indicate that Ickes was the originator. Dorothy Borg, "Notes on Roosevelt's 'Quarantine' Speech," *Political Science Quarterly* 72 (September 1957): 425–26.

[13]Ickes, *The Inside Struggle*, p. 222.

[14]Rosenman, *The Constitution Prevails*, pp. 407–11.

Except for the most extreme antiadministration papers, press reaction across the country was favorable, even in solidly Republican newspapers. The editorial comments of sixteen major dailies overwhelmingly approved the "quarantine" speech 13 to 3.[15] A *Literary Digest* survey taken on October 30 still indicated that most of the major news journals were in favor of the president's stand, although more of them were beginning to wonder what Roosevelt proposed to do to follow up his warning.[16] Had FDR acted more positively after the speech, he might have gained major press and public support for a move to interdict the aggressors.

In the Soviet Union, *Pravda* repeated nearly the entire speech and quoted the United Press commentary, identifying it as a definite call for concrete action against Japan. But *Pravda* also reported that influential diplomatic circles said Roosevelt never intended to display any diplomatic initiative.[17] *Izvestiia*, on the other hand, quoted the speech in full and resisted editorial comment, save for citing the same United Press assessment that appeared in *Pravda*. However, when in an October 6 memorandum the Department of State came out against Japanese moves in the Far East,[18] the Russians decided that there was more than rhetoric to Roosevelt's assertions. Two days later *Pravda* reported that Roosevelt's speech, taken together with the department's announcement, made it apparent that the Chicago address was part of a general policy activated by the United States to meet the threat from Japanese aggression.[19] *Izvestiia*, while assessing foreign press evaluations, surmised that formerly Japan had believed the United States would not interfere in its expansionist goals in China, but Roosevelt's speech had "burst that bubble."[20] In December *Pravda* noted that public opinion in the United States favored collective action against the aggressors. According to this account, a portion of the American press thought Roosevelt had recognized, in his speech, that the peace was indivisible.[21]

In his personal correspondence, Roosevelt indicated that he was not exactly sure what public reaction had been to his speech. He complained, in a letter to his old Groton schoolmaster Endicott Peabody, that he was fighting an uphill battle against "a public psychology of

---

[15]*New York Times*, October 6, 1937.

[16]"Was the President's Chicago Speech a Move Toward Peace?" *Literary Digest* 124 (October 30, 1937): 12.

[17]"Roosevelt on the International Situation," *Pravda*, October 6, 1937.

[18]*FRUS: Diplomatic Papers*, vol. 4, *The Far East, 1937* (Washington, DC: Government Printing Office, 1954), p. 62.

[19]"Statement by the State Department of the USA," *Pravda*, October 8, 1937.

[20]"Reactions to Roosevelt's Address," *Izvestiia*, October 8, 1937.

[21]"Public Opinion in the USA—On Collective Action Against Aggressors," *Pravda*, December 15, 1937.

long standing—a psychology which comes very close to saying 'Peace at any price.' "[22] On October 19 the president wrote to Colonel Edward M. House, expressing confidence in the public's acceptance of his message: "I thought, frankly, that there would be more criticism and I verily believe that as time goes on we can slowly but surely make people realize that war will be a greater danger to us if we close all the doors and windows than if we go in the street and use our influence to curb the riot."[23] The problem seemed to be that, once he set people thinking, the president believed they should drift toward reality on their own.

Roosevelt made a show of disregarding opinions of the press, but his protest was too loud. In a memorandum to Sumner Welles, he wrote:

> I have read your [dispatch] to Davis, quoting [the] Baltimore Sun, Washington Post and New York Sun. Frankly I do not believe that these newspapers carry any particular weight as expressions of public opinion, nor do I believe that any editorial writer—I repeat 'any'—has the knowledge of facts and circumstances open to the Administration; therefore, instead of quoting a newspaper you are merely quoting one member of the staff or the opinion of an individual owner.[24]

As a reminder that the press was not infallible, Roosevelt recalled for Welles how inaccurate the newspapers had been in their predictions of the outcome of the 1936 election.

Despite the president's cavalier dismissal of the newspapers' role as the agent of public opinion, he observed it closely and felt it keenly.[25] The "quarantine" speech had been attacked, but the assaults came from quarters that should have been expected to attack—William Randolph Hearst, Colonel Robert R. McCormick, and the prominent isolationists for whom no amount of reason would have converted. Even evidence in the president's own correspondence file is so substantially in favor of the speech that there can be no doubt that he at least must have had this brought to his attention. Yet he ignored it. In the final analysis, the primary reason for this must be adjudged to the lack of a follow-up plan by Roosevelt. The charge that he was too far out in front of public opinion was erroneous. However, the most significant

---

[22]FDR to Peabody, October 16, 1937, PPF 398, Groton School Folder.

[23]FDR to Colonel House, October 19, 1937, PPF 222, Colonel Edward M. House Folder.

[24]FDR to Welles, November 12, 1937, PSF, No. II, Departmental Files, Box 20, State Department File.

[25]Borg, "Notes on Roosevelt's 'Quarantine' Speech," p. 430.

reason for his failure to pursue the quarantine idea was his determination to make haste slowly. He had a rough idea in mind of how far he thought he could go, how much power he had available to threaten the aggressors, and what he might try as augmentary problem solving by peaceful means. A nagger seldom expects immediate results; the objective is to wear down resistance, and sometimes this is by a shock effect that will scare those needing education. This was the sum and essence of Roosevelt's quarantine message: to get the public's attention.

II

National defense was one area in which Roosevelt felt obliged to lead, and he warned Congress that the totalitarian powers threatened the very existence of democracy.[26] In the face of this danger, disarmament was no longer possible, for two days after his address to Congress he directed the Navy Department to construct two replacement vessels. "If we are not to reduce our Navy by obsolescence," FDR cautioned, "the replacement of capital ships can no longer be deferred."[27] He visualized the future of naval warfare as far more complicated than in preceding years and cautioned Secretary Hull concerning a suggestion on naval limitations that Hull had previously forwarded to the president: "The memorandum involves Naval problems and is based on much too simple a conception of what future Naval war may involve. Submarine attack, submarine defense, convoys, aircraft in the next war will bring about new problems which no one has hitherto visualized. It is therefore best not to tie our hands in any way."[28]

Throughout the year Roosevelt's pronouncements to the press emphasized his desire to increase naval strength as rapidly as possible.[29] At the end of 1937 the president wrote Edward T. Taylor, chairman of the House Appropriations Committee, anticipating the need for additional warships:

> World events have caused me growing concern. I do not refer to any specific nation or to any specific threats against the United States. The fact is that in the world as a whole many nations are . . . enlarging their armaments programs. I have used every conceivable effort to stop this trend, and to work toward a decrease

---

[26]Franklin D. Roosevelt, *Roosevelt's Foreign Policy: Franklin D. Roosevelt's Unedited Speeches and Messages* (New York: Harper, 1942), p. 118.

[27]Ibid.

[28]FDR to Hull, February 8, 1937, OF 20, State Department Folder.

[29]Press Conferences, 10, No. 383, July 23, 1937, pp. 367ff.

of armaments. Facts, nevertheless, are facts, and the United States must recognize them.[30]

Despite FDR's determination to expand the defense capacity, the United States was inadequately prepared to confront the armed powers. The defense budget was only large when viewed against U.S. expenditures between 1921 and 1937; if compared to military budgets in the aggressor nations and the USSR, it was pitifully small. Except for the navy, in fact, the United States would have ranked militarily as a third-rate power.[31] It remained for the president to arouse real public awareness if there were to be adequate preparation to promote American security. Also, it was obvious that the United States could not stand alone against the powers better prepared for war. Thus FDR tried to divert the crisis by diplomacy and to win the one available armed nation, the USSR, to the side of the democracies.

Part of Roosevelt's plan for preparedness necessitated creating a new foreign policy, which came through a drastic shake-up within the Department of State in 1937. The overly cautious William Phillips was shipped off to Rome to replace the bumbling Breckinridge Long, thus causing a vacancy in the undersecretary's slot. The president fought with Hull over this post and won. In this contest, Sumner Welles, sleek and urbane and, like FDR, schooled at Groton, bested R. Walton Moore, a crony of Hull and an eternal optimist who kept telling Roosevelt that the dark storm clouds over Europe really had a silver lining. Roosevelt and Welles thought that Robert Kelley and his East European and Russian Section were obstructionists in American-Soviet relations; consequently, late in the year Kelley was shipped off to a first secretary's post in Turkey. East European Affairs were absorbed into a new European Affairs branch headed by J. Pierrepont Moffat. The Russian Section saved its files and library from being completely dispersed or destroyed only by diligent and surreptitious efforts. Charles Bohlen simply hid some of the library in brown paper wrappers in the attic of the State Department, and the rest was sent over to the protective custody of the Library of Congress where it disappeared in the general collection.[32]

Another part of the president's plan to shift the direction of American foreign policy actually began on August 25, 1936 when Davies received a summons to the White House where, over a lunch in the executive offices, Roosevelt asked him to accept an appointment he

---

[30]Roosevelt, *Roosevelt's Foreign Policy*, p. 135.

[31]Gordon A. Craig and Felix Gilbert, eds., *The Diplomats, 1919–1939* (Princeton: Princeton University Press, 1953), p. 653.

[32]Kennan, *Memoirs*, p. 85.

had refused in 1913 when proffered by President Woodrow Wilson. Although Davies's egocentrism slants his recollection of his diplomatic career, his account of the meeting provides at least a rough reality of Roosevelt's purpose. The president told Davies he desired to send him to Moscow as a part of his effort to preserve the peace, if possible, and to assign him later to Berlin when Ambassador William Dodd retired sometime during the next year. Roosevelt impressed on Davies the importance of the two capitals in the unfolding drama that could lead either to peace or war, and the president was "not overly sanguine that peace could be preserved, nevertheless, he wanted to contribute in every proper way to prevent war in Europe, if that were possible." World peace or world war, FDR confided, depended on Hitler.[33]

Because the president mentioned a transfer to Germany within one year, Davies assumed Roosevelt planned to use him as his agent for peace, a troubleshooter in the hot spots of Europe. Davies thereafter took upon himself the role of roving ambassador, with Moscow as an occasional home base. There was certainly no way that he could have misunderstood his assignment in Moscow to be as broad as he later assumed it to be. He and his wife Marjorie Post Davies dined with the Roosevelts on January 2, 1937, and the president gave his new ambassador to Russia fairly specific instructions.

Roosevelt told Davies that Soviet intransigence on the debts had injured prospects for closer relations. Due to the resultant strain, Davies's position should be one of dignified friendliness, characterized by a definite reserve with a clear intimation that FDR and Secretary Hull were deeply disappointed in the Soviets' failure to live up to what seemed to the Americans a clear obligation. The president instructed the new ambassador not to seek further negotiations; such initiatives should be left up to the Russians who, after all, should realize that it was of greater importance to them to improve relations than it was to the Americans. Roosevelt thought Davies should sit back and await developments, but in the meantime he was "to make every effort to get all the first hand information, from a personal observation where possible, bearing upon the strength of the regime, from a military and economic point of view; and also seek to ascertain what the policy of their government would be in the event of a European war."[34]

There have been various conjectures on why Davies was assigned to Moscow, why the Russian Section was disbanded, and who the culprit was in planning its dissolution. The surmises range from a liberal

---

[33]Joseph E. Davies, *Mission to Moscow* (New York: Simon & Schuster, 1941), pp. xi–xiii.

[34]Ibid., p. 6.

plot, headed by Eleanor Roosevelt, Harry Hopkins, Welles, and others who recruited journalist Drew Pearson to their cause, to simply an internal struggle for position and influence within the Department of State.[35] Surely there is some truth in all the assertions, but they do not speak directly enough to Roosevelt's motivation or, more precisely, do not single out the overriding consideration that Franklin Roosevelt decided it was time to do what he could to confront the disintegration of the world peace structure and was determined to have people sympathetic to his posture.

From the vantage point of 1938, Whitney Shepardson and William Scroggs observed that the events of late 1936 and 1937 had somewhat sobered America, awakening it to existing dangers: "The truth slowly revealed itself that a world revolution was under way, that a world war was possible, and that nations were offered the choice of submitting to the rising tide of force or of resisting it."[36] FDR assisted in the awakening through his warnings, and his rearmament program slowly began to attract public support.

Roosevelt's shake-up of the State Department did not ensure a more active foreign policy. Some of the people who moved into the new positions were not as opposed to isolationism as Roosevelt might have desired, and most problematic for him, for better or worse, he was stuck with Cordell Hull. The secretary was aware of the possibility, and even the probability, of a developing world war and its accompanying threat to American security, but he balked at any move to prepare for it publicly because public opinion terrified him. Even when FDR was willing to take halting steps to create public awareness of the threats, Hull demurred; for example, when the president, in his Constitution Day speech of 1937, decided to extoll the virtues of democracy as opposed to fascism, Hull thought the language too strong. At a cabinet meeting where the subject was discussed, Harold Ickes interjected that such language had not seemed to bother the Nazis when they condemned democracy at the Nuremberg party rally, and he could see no reason why the president's mild admonition could not be made in return. Roosevelt, Ickes thought, seemed determined to disregard Hull's advice when he retorted, "That is right." Ickes reflected on the

---

[35]For details of these interpretations see Kennan, *Memoirs*, pp. 82–86; Moore-Bullitt correspondence, January–July 1937, R. Walton Moore Papers, Franklin D. Roosevelt Library, Hyde Park, New York; Maddux, *Years of Estrangement*, pp. 89–94; and Martin Weil, *A Pretty Good Club: The Founding Fathers of the U.S. Foreign Service* (New York: W. W. Norton, 1978), pp. 88–96.

[36]Whitney H. Shepardson and William O. Scroggs, eds., *The United States in World Affairs: An Account of American Foreign Relations, 1937* (New York: Harper, 1938), p. 6.

secretary of state's attitude, noting that "Hull has become so timid that he tries to walk without casting a shadow."[37]

At the critical juncture when it was necessary to give Roosevelt sound counsel on how to arouse Americans to the needs of security, Hull became a dead weight to the administration. Because of his service in the House and Senate, he was highly sensitive to congressional and public sentiments: "He was, in fact prone to overestimate the isolationist attitude of the nation and to underrate the chances of executive leadership. Quick to see potential objections to any positive program, he was inclined to argue that too bold a course would . . . provoke serious dissension at home which, in turn, would be exploited by the dictators."[38] Hull was aware of the dangers but not at all ready to take action. When the president decided in 1937 and thereafter to try to help the victims of aggression by improving relations with the Russians, the secretary opposed rapid change of America's Russian policy. His motto was: whatever you do, do it slowly.

When Roosevelt forced Hull to accept Welles, the president was attempting to place at the top level of the State Department someone who was more inclined to see the world crisis as he did; other shake-ups in the department were aimed at gaining an edge in carrying out FDR's foreign policy wishes. The problem was that the streamlining of the department left in key positions many individuals who opposed Roosevelt's policy. Kelley may have been sent off to Turkey and his East European Division merged into the Division of European Affairs, but these actions were not going to help Roosevelt's cause. Freshly returned from Australia, Moffat directed the new division and was even more determined than Kelley not to have any dealings with the Soviets, or anyone else for that matter, who might cause America to enter a collective security agreement.

James Clement Dunn of the European Division worked assiduously to prevent the New Dealers from taking over the State Department. He was the force that kept the Europeanists in the department in the premier position to call the shots. In 1937 he was appointed political adviser on European affairs, got Moffat his new assignment, and in general made sure that the secretary was under control at all times as Dunn "flew back and forth like a shuttlecock" between his own office and Hull's.[39] Thus, when Roosevelt decided to promote

---

[37]Ickes, *The Inside Struggle*, p. 211.

[38]William L. Langer and S. Everett Gleason, *The Challenge to Isolation, 1937–1940* (New York: Harper, 1952), p. 17.

[39]Weil, *A Pretty Good Club*, p. 81.

better relations with the Soviets as a means of dealing with the expanding world crisis, he had two formidable opponents who controlled the pen of his chief adviser on foreign policy, Cordell Hull. The drift toward war, in Moffat's estimation, was Britain's fault, with attendant catastrophic results: "In his view, the First World War had spawned Bolshevism; and the second would extend its sway; and yet the British were making it inevitable. . . . Moffat [grew] more and more bitter at the British as appeasement waned."[40] This was not because he held Neville Chamberlain's view that perhaps the Soviets and Germans would do one another in, for Moffat was convinced that a general war would spread Bolshevism.

Certainly the Dunn-Moffat perspective was merely one part of the Department of State's inside conflict on policy, but it was the controlling position. The department's overseas representatives were not nearly so hidebound in their determination to avoid commitment. Norman Davis, for example, was greatly disturbed by the efforts of Congress to restrict the president's freedom of action and wrote to Roosevelt on February 4, enclosing a memorandum expressing his views as to the inadvisability of any rigid neutrality legislation that would hamper the president in exercising his constitutional responsibilities in conducting foreign affairs. Davis agreed with Roosevelt when he said the world was passing through a crisis, during which the president would be faced with numerous delicate and intricate problems that would require him to have maximum freedom of action. Davis believed that, "if he [Roosevelt] is to conduct our foreign relations wisely, and in the best interests of the United States and world peace, it is essential that he retain wide discretionary powers to deal with situations in which he alone is competent to judge the requirements. Congress should not encroach upon the constitutional powers of the President to determine the foreign policy of the country."[41] Thus, to encroach, Davis concluded, was to violate 150 years of American constitutional development.

George Messersmith was another of the Europeanists who supported a more active foreign policy aimed at thwarting the totalitarian powers, and he viewed the Nazi menace as more dangerous than the Soviet one. Therefore, as he cast about for means either to avoid or prepare for war, the president had some support in the State Department for his campaign to create a more forward policy. When Roosevelt decided to move closer to the Russians, Messersmith tried to promote the effort by encouraging Secretary Hull to approach them quickly.

---

[40]Ibid., p. 96.
[41]Davis to FDR, and enclosure of February 4, 1937, PSF, Neutrality, Box 33.

III

In 1936 President Roosevelt had flirted with the idea of bringing the various powers together in a major peace conference, and, writing to Ambassador Dodd on August 5, he asked him to feel out the Germans on this concept. Either Dodd or Davies let the news of the inquiry slip to Ambassador John Cudahy who, after seeing Dodd and Davies at their respective embassies, wrote to the president, hoping the rumor was not true: "I am certain a Wilsonian pronouncement in favor of peace while it would create a great stir would be forgotten in two weeks time. Also any attempt to assemble the leaders of European states for a statement of their objectives and grievances would result in nothing but propaganda and recriminations and would leave things worse than before."[42] Cudahy was leery of a conference with nothing determined in advance concerning a concrete course of action.

President Roosevelt continued to toy with the idea of a peace conference, but in one respect he took Cudahy's advice to heart when the ambassador suggested that "the ultimate issue is between Germany and Russia, not between Communism and Fascism or between forms of government and political philosophies, but between the intense internationalisms of Germany and Russia."[43] He reminded the president of the historical antecedents for a conflict, as progressive warlike Germany looked at backward land-rich Russia. In the final analysis, Cudahy concluded, the day of reckoning would come over conflicting German and Russian territorial objectives, with Germany assuming the offensive. "That is the ultimate issue."[44] Despite cheerful predictions from Assistant Secretary of State Moore, Roosevelt responded that he had to agree with Cudahy and assuredly told the ambassador "do not believe rumors that I contemplate any move of any kind in Europe— certainly under conditions of the moment."[45] It was at this juncture that the president decided to send Davies to Moscow. Roosevelt repeated Cudahy's observation as his own in a letter to Phillips of February 6, 1937: "Every week changes the picture and the basis for it all lies, I think, not in Communism or the fear of Communism but in Germany and fear of what the present German leaders are meeting for or being drawn toward."[46]

---

[42] *FRUS: Diplomatic Papers*, vol. 1, *General, 1937* (Washington, DC: Government Printing Office, 1954), p. 24.
[43] Ibid., p. 25.
[44] Ibid.
[45] Ibid., p. 27.
[46] William Phillips, *Ventures in Diplomacy* (Boston: Beacon Press, 1953), p. 203.

President Roosevelt changed his mind and decided that a world conference would be too much. His idea was more in line with his belief that, if he could talk to the important leaders, he could make progress in straightening out the world's problems. In this vein he wrote Dodd on January 9 that the trouble with any such conference is that "it would bring fifty-five or sixty nations around a table, each nation with from five to ten delegates and each nation, in addition, with no authority to agree to anything without referring the matter home."[47] A world conference, he thought, would be impractical; instead, "if five or six heads of the important governments could meet together for a week with complete inaccessibility to press or cables or radio a definite useful agreement might result or else one or two of them would be murdered by the others! In any case it would be worthwhile from the viewpoint of civilization!"[48] Obviously the president did not have in mind his own demise. Underlying Roosevelt's idea of a peace conference was the gambler's psychology, which often appealed to him. He had a hunch that, if a certain course of action were taken, the big stakes might be won. It was a part of his tendency to pursue long odds in the hope of quick returns.[49]

By April FDR's peace conference plan circulated through the Washington rumor mill and was so persistent that Roosevelt decided to deny it at a cabinet meeting. Ickes reported in his diary on April 3 that the president "took occasion to deny the reports that have appeared in the newspapers during the last few days to the effect that, through Norman Davis, Bill Bullitt, and Joe Davies, he is feeling out the principal European countries on the possibility of a peace conference. He said that he is doing no such thing, and apparently he has no such plan in mind."[50] Roosevelt's denial, however, was meant for the benefit of those cabinet members who tended to be nervous about departures in foreign policy.

Hull remembered that FDR had pondered for several years the general idea of inviting the heads of European nations to hold a conference with him at sea where they would sit around a table and work out a lasting peace. To the secretary, it had never seemed that the president had made any real commitment to this idea. In part, he thought Roosevelt had backed off because of negative reaction, especially from the German and Italian ambassadors to the United States

---

[47]Roosevelt, *Roosevelt Letters*, 3:203.
[48]Ibid.
[49]Roosevelt's gambler instinct was demonstrated in an incident related in Frank Freidel, *Franklin D. Roosevelt*, vol. 1, *The Apprenticeship* (Boston: Little, Brown, 1952), p. 310.
[50]Ickes, *The Inside Struggle*, p. 110.

who had received unfavorable responses from their governments. The concept, in fact, seemed to amuse Mussolini.[51]

"Almost before I knew it," Hull recalled, "I found the President completely embracing this project. The colorful drama to be staged in the White House appealed to him." It did not appeal to the secretary of state, according to his recollection, and he argued its futility with the president. Hull specifically remembered telling Roosevelt that "it seemed to me thoroughly unrealistic, just at the time when we needed to arouse public opinion to the dangers abroad and the necessity to rearm to meet those dangers, to turn away from thoughts of self-defense and undertake to revive a completely collapsed movement. To have pursued a theory so credulous would have played into the hands of the Axis."[52]

This was one of several examples from Hull's *Memoirs* of his 20/20 hindsight, after the fact of war had made the peace conference and the efforts to feel out Germany and Italy seem ludicrous. At the time, however, the situation appeared otherwise. Hull responded to Roosevelt's request for his judgment on the message to Mussolini: "Sumner and I heartily approve."[53] Hull may have opposed the idea, but he did not discount entirely the possibility that Germany and Italy might make new moves in the direction of peace if given the opportunity for economic recovery through improved international trade, a fact illustrated in his "Eight Pillars of Peace" speech at the Buenos Aires Conference[54] and in later comments to Canadian Prime Minister Mackenzie King.[55] These policy recommendations did not agree with the secretary's recollection of his realistic, hardheaded advice to the president in 1937.

During that year Cordell Hull made another bid for peace, which followed virtually the same pattern as his Buenos Aires speech and his appeals to British diplomats like Walter Runciman and King. On July 16 the secretary pleaded for the world to strive for peace, observe the sanctity of treaties, and work for the limitation and reduction of armaments. Hull included an excellent statement of what the United States was prepared to do to help: "We avoid entering into alliances or entangling commitments, but we believe in cooperative effort by peaceful and practicable means in support of the principles hereinbefore stated."[56]

---

[51]Hull, *Memoirs*, 1:546.
[52]Ibid., pp. 546–57.
[53]Roosevelt, *Roosevelt Letters*, 3:213.
[54]Hull, *Memoirs*, 1:498.
[55]*FRUS: General, 1937*, pp. 641ff.
[56]Ibid., p. 700.

Such a general proclamation could receive but one response. Every power renounced the evil ways of all the others. Some answered tongue in cheek, others responded with irony, and a few with honest chagrin. Russia was not overly impressed by the secretary's proposal, although TASS gave lip service to the principles involved and noted triumphantly the promptness of Soviet acceptance of Hull's principles and the delay of Germany, Italy, and Japan.[57] Maxim Litvinov asserted Soviet agreement with everything Hull said. Russia, through Litvinov's disarmament plan and permanent peace conference proposal, had attempted to take appropriate action to make these concepts a reality but had found no one willing to act in concert with the Soviet Union.[58]

Anger and disappointment characterized Hull's reaction to the responses. He pointed to the irony of the German, Japanese, and Italian failure to own up to their positions as international desperadoes, while hypocritically announcing full adherence to his stated principles. He was particularly incensed by those who referred to his principles as vague formulas. The Ten Commandments, he said, might be called vague, but "day after day millions of ministers of God throughout the world are preaching these formulae, and I believe there is untold value in this preaching. Society would lapse into chaos if the Ten Commandments were universally broken, just as international society lapses into chaos when the principles of right conduct among nations are widely disregarded."[59] Although this analogy was perfectly in keeping with Hull's moralistic view of foreign affairs, it was slightly flawed. In the first place, the Ten Commandments were not universally honored; second, where they were recognized as a moral force, statutes were enacted to provide police protection to ensure punishment of violators. Hull thought his eight pillars of peace, his eight commandments, should be universally accepted, but he was unwilling to support a policy to implement his program.

Pursuing the police force analogy, Hull stated that anyone who violated the Ten Commandments, when converted to statutes, went to jail. From the view of the punished or the agency of enforcement, there was nothing vague, he said, in these formulas. To Hull, it was unfortunate there was no police force to ensure punishment to nations violating some of the commonly accepted rules of international conduct. In conclusion, he argued that that was "all the more reason, therefore, for some of us never to relax our efforts to convince the people of the world, even if some of the political leaders sneered, that international

---

[57]"Answer of the Various Powers to Hull's Statement," *Izvestiia*, August 9, 1937.
[58]*FRUS: General, 1937*, pp. 705–06.
[59]Hull, *Memoirs*, 1:536.

morality was as essential as individual morality."[60] This was hardly an adequate substitute for a police force, but it was as far as Hull was willing to go. Thus, when President Roosevelt decided to move beyond moral preaching, he signaled a break with his Department of State, whose Washington policymakers, for the most part, were unwilling to follow him.

Failing to promote a general peace conference did not deter Roosevelt from trying to ensure the peace by holding an international meeting. He changed his focus to an attempt to isolate one of the aggressive powers and settle the Far Eastern crisis via a gathering of concerned nations. Welles, who cooperated in FDR's other efforts to arrange a peace conference in 1937, suggested that one dealing with the Far Eastern situation be proposed to the other interested powers, using the Nine Power Treaty of 1922 as the basis for issuing invitations. The day after the president's "quarantine" speech Welles sent a memorandum to Roosevelt, in which he quoted two paragraphs from the Chicago address that he wanted emphasized. After elaborating on the president's appeal to return to international morality, Welles urged him to "inquire of the other governments of the world whether they will be willing to take part in a world conference." He suggested an agenda to deal with principles of international relations, rules of war, rights and obligations of neutrals, and freedom of access to raw materials. Welles also wanted to make sure that an invitation would clearly identify the limits of his proposal, which envisaged "solely the reaching of a common agreement upon standards of international conduct and does not embrace either political, economic, or financial adjustments." His purpose was to line the world up against Japanese aggression, a point he outlined without subtlety. He assumed that all "non-dictatorial" governments would agree to cooperate and that even Germany and Italy would find it to their advantage, but "under present conditions it would appear improbable that Japan would take part. . . . The mere fact that the nations of the world today could by concerted action agree upon anything of vital importance would in itself be a material step forward."[61]

Roosevelt saw Norman Davis and Welles on October 8 and agreed to explore prospects for the proposal. At this meeting, plans were drawn for the Brussels Conference, and the next day an enabling order went forth from Welles, with instructions from the president to go ahead if the invited participants responded favorably.[62] When the British received

---

[60]Ibid., p. 537.

[61]Memorandum, Welles to FDR, October 6, 1937, PSF, State, Sumner Welles Folder.

[62]Memorandum, Welles to FDR, October 9, 1937, ibid.

the invitation, Anthony Eden announced enthusiastically that "in order to get the full cooperation on an equal basis of the United States government in an international conference, I would travel, not only from Geneva to Brussels, but from Melbourne to Alaska, more particularly in the present state of the international situation."[63] Favorable responses in hand, the Americans called for the conference to meet on November 3, and Davis headed the American delegation, assisted by Moffat and Stanley Hornbeck, who had become a special adviser on Far Eastern affairs to Hull. Moffat commented wryly on the makeup of the delegation:

> Our delegation is well balanced. The three of us approach the problem before us with three separate preoccupations. Mr. Davis starts on the premise that the existence of the British Empire is essential for the national security of the United States and that while we should not follow Great Britain nevertheless we should not allow the Empire to be endangered. Stanley Hornbeck reacts to everything that comes up in specific relation to the Far Eastern situation and the Far Eastern situation alone. My personal preoccupation is to prevent at any costs the involvement of the United States in hostilities anywhere, and to that end to discourage any formation of a common front of the democratic powers.[64]

In other words, Moffat saw his responsibility as primarily to ensure that the purpose of the president and Undersecretary Welles would bear no fruit at all; he succeeded.

Hornbeck thought that the Brussels Conference was a great opportunity to stop Japan before it became so powerful that the United States would not only have to fight it but also would face a fully armed and powerful enemy.[65] He was highly suspicious of the motives of London, Paris, and Moscow, all of which, he acknowledged, wanted Japan stopped but were not solicitous of the price China might have to pay, including their rather cavalier attitude about Chinese territorial sacrifices. Hornbeck put it succinctly and smugly: "The United States is not addicted to the practices of power politics, as are the other three."[66]

A fundamental problem at Brussels was that everyone wanted everyone else to take the lead and assure one another they would all

[63]Quoted in Dallek, *Roosevelt and American Foreign Policy*, p. 150.

[64]Hooker, *Moffat Papers*, pp. 182–83.

[65]Marlin K. Friedrich, "In Search of a Far Eastern Policy: Joseph C. Grew, Stanley Hornbeck, and American-Japanese Relations, 1937–1941" (Ph.D. diss., Washington State University, 1974), p. 79.

[66]Ibid., pp. 79–80.

follow—at a safe distance. Hornbeck thought the United States more trustworthy to come to the anti-Axis powers' aid, via economic and other pressures, than vice versa. Davis wanted cooperative sanctions, and Moffat, suspecting ulterior motives on the part of all the powers, wielded a large monkey wrench trying to make sure that they got nothing more from the United States than consultation. Internal politics hamstrung Roosevelt's initial high hopes for the conference, for after promising Davis he would support some form of sanctions, if pursued by the others, he pulled the rug out from under the head of the delegation, leaving him with his commitments exposed to the world as mere posturing. The Brussels Conference was a pure disaster, as Hornbeck noted at its conclusion: "It cannot with any accuracy or with intellectual honesty be affirmed that this Conference has exhausted the possibilities of bringing about peace between Japan and China by processes of conciliation. . . . From the point of view of avoiding really difficult tasks and commitments to concrete effort, the Conference has been a great success."[67] Commissar Litvinov cursed the missed opportunity to do something important. He had gone to Brussels with high expectations and bitterly assailed the failure.[68]

IV

Brussels merely proved the failure of an international conference as the magic formula to ensure the peace, thus narrowing President Roosevelt's focus to his other available options. However, he was warned that his hope to use the Russians to combat aggression was in danger of collapsing, as newsmen and American "experts" on the USSR predicted the rapid demise of Soviet power resultant from the purges. Vladimir Poliakov, who wrote for the *New York Times* under the pseudonym of Augur, predicted "for practical purposes Russia is out of the council of the great powers of Europe." If this were true, a major force for peace in Roosevelt's plans was incapacitated, and this could not be encouraging. However, there were others who contested the thesis that Russia was finished. *Fortune* magazine, for instance, pointedly contradicted Augur: "Before the Soviet Union can be dismissed from military consideration the following questions must be answered: how large is the Soviet Army in active troops and reserves; how well is it armed;

---

[67]Quoted in Richard Dean Burns, "Stanley K. Hornbeck: The Diplomacy of the Open Door," in Burns and Bennett, *Diplomats in Crisis*, p. 109.

[68]Jane Degras, ed., *Soviet Documents on Foreign Policy*, 3 vols. (London: Oxford University Press, 1953), 3:266.

how well could it be supplied in time of war; and for what purposes will it most probably be used?"[69]

In pursuit of his task to evaluate Soviet strength and stability, Davies discounted the idea of Russia's demise. He did so in such a way as to appear foolish, however. He told Roosevelt that the purges would strengthen the Soviet regime because they obviously were rooting out enemies of the state. In the end it was not his assessment that was wrong; it was his method of reaching his conclusions that held him up to ridicule by his embassy staff and the experienced members of the foreign press corps in Moscow. In fact, Davies was correct when he surmised that the purges would not bring Soviet power crumbling down, but the regime survived despite the purges rather than because of them. No doubt, however, he did influence Roosevelt not to give up on the Russians as potential allies in the struggle against the aggressors.

The effect of the purges, as well as their motives, was a subject of considerable speculation by the Foreign Service officers at the American embassy in Moscow. The big question was what really caused Stalin to initiate them and what effect would they have on Soviet prestige and power. Ambassador Davies stood almost alone in judging the accused as guilty, on his understanding of American jurisprudence. During one of the intermissions, he "pompously asked a British correspondent . . . his opinion of the trials." Alfred Chollerton of the *Daily Telegraph* responded that the Soviet Union moved through convulsions and this was the latest and most violent of them. Davies said he was serious and really wanted an answer. He then received a cynical, if accurate, reply: "Mr. Ambassador, I believe everything but the facts." Charles Bohlen was listening to the conversation and recalled that "Davies never did get the point of Chollerton's joke."[70]

Davies was so transparent in his objectives, so obviously obsequious with those in power, so overbearing on those whom he considered his inferiors, and so terribly naive in his diplomatic role that his embassy staff nearly resigned early in his "mission" to Moscow. According to Bohlen, Davies went to Moscow "sublimely ignorant of even the most elementary realities of the Soviet system and of its ideology. He was determined, possibly with Bullitt's failure in mind, to maintain a Pollyanna attitude. . . . He and his wife treated the staff as hired help and rarely listened to its views."[71] Kennan corroborated Bohlen's opinion:

---

[69]"Background of War: The Bear that Shoots Like a Man," *Fortune* 16 (August 1937): 70.

[70]Bohlen, *Witness to History*, pp. 51–52.

[71]Ibid., pp. 44–45.

> [Davies] drew from the first instant our distrust and dislike, . . .
> from the standpoint of his fitness for the office and of his motivation
> in accepting it. We doubted his seriousness. . . . We saw every
> evidence that his motives in accepting the post were personal and
> political and ulterior to any sense of the solemnity of the task
> itself.[72]

Kennan also identified Davies as a publicity hound striving for rapport
with the media in Moscow and listening more to their counsel than to
his professional staff. During the purge trials, for instance, he used
Kennan as his translator, and then during the intermissions, while
talking to reporters, he sent Kennan off for sandwiches.[73] Bohlen and
Kennan were kind in their evaluations, compared to Elbridge Durbrow
who let it be known that "I never worked with a more mentally dishonest man than Joe Davies."[74]

The Russians found and exploited many of Davies's weaknesses
and none more effectively than his passion for Russian objets d'art.
The Soviets made sure that Davies and his wife got nearly everything
they admired, and they admired so much that they single-handedly
drove up the price of black market rubles for diplomatic personnel in
Moscow. According to Robert Williams, Joseph and Marjorie Davies
were willingly and completely conned by the Soviet government:

> They were eager to buy what the Soviet government was eager to
> sell. They were less able to understand that they were, in part,
> pawns in a deadly game, a game in which Stalin was eager to
> manipulate Western opinion while destroying real and imagined
> enemies at home. And Russian art proved a small price to pay for
> the future dividends of *Mission to Moscow*. [Davies's highly flatter-
> ing portrait of Stalin's Russia was published in 1941.][75]

Ambassador Davies, along with many others whom Roosevelt
sent abroad, was told by the president to make as many observations
as possible and to report them. Davies took this to mean that he had
extra liberties as the personal emissary of the president, and he leaned
heavily on the privileges of that position. He reacted to Roosevelt's
request as though he were the only competent observer that FDR had
in Europe, and he therefore felt impelled to visit every country of any
importance in order to give the president the benefit of his observations.

---

[72]Kennan, *Memoirs*, p. 82.

[73]Ibid., p. 83.

[74]Quoted in Weil, *A Pretty Good Club*, p. 92.

[75]Robert C. Williams, *Russian Art and American Money, 1900–1940* (Cambridge, MA:
Harvard University Press, 1980), p. 253.

In August the ambassador journeyed to the major, and many of the lesser, capitals of Europe and reported his findings. With the exception of Lithuania, which maintained friendly relations with Russia because it feared Poland, the general view of Russia was formally correct, as it was toward Germany, because the European nations feared both powers. He told Roosevelt they were all balanced on a tightrope and were afraid of a future coalition between Germany and the Soviet Union. "Cynically they are inclined to believe that such a development is not impossible. They all belittle the achievements and power of the Soviet regime, but one gets the impression that there is a good deal of 'whistling while passing a graveyard.' "[76]

By the end of 1937 Davies managed to avoid residence in his official capacity for 199 days. Of his absences the Department of State recorded 43 on leave with pay, 37 on leave without pay, while 99 were on official business.[77] The ambassador spent so little time working at his primary assignment that he attracted considerable public and private attention. Davies's appointment had been a payment of a political debt for being one of the "Roosevelt-before-Chicago" men.[78] Such "payoffs" gained an inordinate amount of attention, and his frequent absences drew political heat. In view of press publicity, Roosevelt decided to tighten the reins on Davies. He asked Marvin McIntyre, who knew the ambassador fairly well, to break the news, suggesting that McIntyre write bluntly to Davies:

> Frankly, there has been a good deal of criticism of the great amount
> of time you have spent away from Russia since you went there. . . .
> I am confident that everything is all right for the future but that
> most decidedly you ought to stay in Moscow, or at least in Russia,
> without leaving it for the next three months.[79]

McIntyre's letter was a little softer in tone than the one proposed by the president.[80]

The view from the embassy in Moscow at the time of the purges was consistent in rejecting Davies's naive report to the president, in which he wrote that an extensive conspiracy was evident beyond doubt.[81] The Foreign Service officers in Moscow, however, thought the purges had resulted from a combination of factors. Possibly some of the accused

---

[76]Davies to FDR, August 22, 1937, PSF, Box 15.

[77]Williams, *Russian Art and American Money*, p. 251.

[78]John Gunther, *Roosevelt in Retrospect: A Profile in History* (New York: Harper, 1950), p. 263.

[79]FDR to McIntyre, September 22, 1937, PPF 1381, Joseph E. Davies Folder.

[80]McIntyre to Davies, September 22, 1937, ibid.

[81]Davies to FDR, February 4, 1937, PSF, Box 15.

were guilty as charged, but probably most were suspected of opposing Stalin. Quite obviously the masses were being prepared psychologically to accept an essentially isolationist orientation based on a fear of foreigners, especially Germans.[82] The embassy staff did not conclude that Russia was finished as a power in Europe. They merely wanted to provide an accurate assessment of what was occurring and the possible reasons for it. That the Department of State and President Roosevelt were not totally discouraged by the purges was proved by a change of direction in America's Russian policy.

V

Given the Department of State's previous reluctance to give any sign of even implied collaboration with the Soviets after the debt negotiations broke down, a curious incident occurred during the new period of strife between Russia and Japan. For several years the Soviets had attempted to persuade the United States that some token of potential military collaboration should be shown which would give Japan cause to hesitate before it threatened the vital interests of either power in Asia. The department had steadfastly refused to make anything more than general, vague statements in this connection and especially had objected to the visit of American naval vessels to Soviet ports. This policy was altered suddenly during the new Soviet-Japanese border clashes in Manchuria.

Both from the Soviet and American viewpoint this was a significant departure. At a time when most of the major powers were either being ignored or maligned by the Soviet Union, the Americans knew that a visit of their naval units to Russia would alarm the Japanese. Such a move would imply collaboration between the Russians and the United States in certain defensive military operations in the Far East, if the visit were made to a Soviet Pacific port. Loy Henderson saw the invitation for American naval units as a significant gesture by the Soviets, and that among the factors responsible for this expression of friendliness were:

> (a) A growing feeling that the formulators of Soviet foreign policy underestimated the potential importance for the Soviet Union of the friendship of the United States, and overestimated their ability to build dependable alliances for the Soviet Union in Europe;
> (b) A belief that the United States is planning to take a more active interest in the world's affairs, particularly in the Far East;

---

[82]See various observations on these themes, in *FRUS: Soviet Union*, pp. 362–69, 378–85, 398–404.

(c) A desire to strengthen Soviet prestige, which has sharply
declined of late, by making it appear to the world that there is a
rapprochement between the United States and the Soviet Union.[83]

Of the three, the second point was most nearly correct.

In July all the signs, as the Soviets read them, pointed to an
awakened America. *Pravda* analyzed the new look in U.S. policy, reporting that the visit of Admiral Harry E. Yarnell and a naval squadron
to Vladivostok marked the first entrance of American naval vessels
into Soviet waters since the establishment of relations, and "public
opinion welcomes it." The usual caution about friendly enemies was
missing as the Russians pulled out all the stops: "Our relations are
founded not only on lack of political and economic differences between
two countries. The Soviet people admire US business abilities and
technical progress. The United States, we recently saw, also likes us."[84]
The latter reference was to Soviet aviators who had flown across the
North Pole, aided by American aviation mechanics, and who were
greeted in the United States as "hero pilots." A front-page story was
devoted to the warm welcome given to these Soviet fliers by Roosevelt
in Washington.[85] The Russian newspaper recorded the president's gesture as symbolic of a new era in American-Soviet relations.

Pravda further analyzed for its readers—it was hoped some of
them Japanese—the significance of the U.S. naval visit, which "will
soon show our people that the United States' interests coincide with
theirs apropos of preserving peace in the whole world generally, and
in the Far East in particular. . . . The Soviet Union aims not only at
inviolability of the Soviet borders but to achieve collective security as
a guarantee of universal peace."[86] The article asserted that the flight
of the Russian aviators and their enthusiastic reception in the United
States helped to cement American-Soviet relations, and the arrival of
the U.S. naval force could not help but to make them still stronger.
The impression was that the two visits had been coordinated. Henderson, when he telegraphed Soviet reactions to the Department of
State, noted particularly the emphasis that the press placed on the
influence of the United States and the Soviet Union in preserving the
peace.[87]

President Roosevelt approved the visit as he did several other
initiatives toward the Russians in 1937, although the Chief of Naval

---

[83]Ibid., pp. 388–89.
[84]"Greetings to the American Visitors," *Pravda*, July 29, 1937.
[85]"Reception of the Soviet Fliers by Roosevelt," ibid., July 28, 1937.
[86]"Greetings to the American Visitors," ibid., July 29, 1937.
[87]Henderson to Department of State, July 29, 1937, DSF 711.61/621.

Operations Admiral William D. Leahy tried to disabuse Roosevelt of any hope that such contact might be profitable. On August 23 Leahy forwarded Admiral Yarnell's report of his visit. Yarnell had not been very impressed with Vladivostok, the officials he encountered, what he could see of the naval base, or the Russian ships, and he avowed:

> The visit of this force evidently has meant a great deal to these people and considerable preparations were made for our reception and entertainment. As far as I can make out they are quite friendly to the United States and did everything in their power to show this friendship. . . . However, I can not but believe that while general conditions here are worse than they are in other sections of Russia the general appearance of the people and the attitude of the officials is perhaps typical, and if it is, God save us from communism.
>
> While this visit has been interesting and instructive I do not care to repeat it and would not advise its being made on other than infrequent intervals.[88]

In essence, Yarnell thought it was useful to see how Communists operated but certainly the value of association with them was only to their benefit and not to America's.

A favorable new commercial agreement was concluded between the United States and the USSR less than one week after the references in *Pravda* and *Izvestiia* to the American-Soviet rapprochement.[89] The Russian press emphasized the Japanese reaction to the trade agreement. *Izvestiia* quoted *Asaki* and *Nichi Nichi* when both papers stressed the granting of most-favored-nation status to Russia by the United States, which thereby became the first major power to give the Soviets unlimited privileges in a trade pact.[90] An editorial touted the agreement as merely the latest in a series of events that indicated a strengthening of friendship between the two countries. Russia and America, according to the writer, were naturally drawing together because both were threatened by the aggressive posture of the Fascist nations.[91]

Maxim Litvinov granted an interview to an *Izvestiia* reporter in August 1937, in which he asserted that the policies of the United States and the Soviet Union nearly coincided. As evidence, he cited a speech by Secretary Hull who asserted that the peace was indivisible, that all

---

[88]Leahy to FDR, August 23, 1937, with enclosure, PSF, Navy, William D. Leahy Folder.

[89]*FRUS: Soviet Union*, p. 405.

[90]"Japanese Press on the Trade Agreement Between the USSR and the USA," *Izvestiia*, August 9, 1937.

[91]"Soviet-American Trade Agreement," ibid., August 8, 1937.

countries were affected by any outbreak of war anywhere, and that the United States was, therefore, vitally interested in any rupture of the peace.[92] Also, President Roosevelt's stand on the application of the neutrality law in the Sino-Japanese conflict was reported by the Soviet press as a hopeful sign. Although FDR warned Americans to leave China, the Soviets thought it significant when the president announced that he neither intended to alter the number of American naval forces in Chinese waters or to recall U.S. troops.[93]

While the embassy staff in Moscow tried to fathom apparent contradictions in Soviet foreign policy and only half succeeded in discovering the reasons behind the zigzag course followed by the Kremlin, an analyst for the London *Times* assessed it perfectly. "The foreign policy of Soviet Russia," he wrote, "depends . . . no longer on principles which can be found in Marxist textbooks, but on the same considerations of enlightened self-interest which determine the foreign policies of democratic or Fascist countries." If this seemed out of context with the rigid adherence to the party line commonly understood to exist in Russia, he argued, then the observer did not understand the meaning of flexibility in Russia. A change of policy by the leaders was not forbidden. It was opposition to the new policy, once established, that brought one face to face with a firing squad.[94] The Soviet Union, in line with the dictates of human nature and the historical evolution of states with one eye on self-preservation and the other on self-aggrandizement, conducted its international relations more and more in the classical tradition of Russian foreign policy.

VI

Soviet attempts to establish closer military contacts with the United States in 1937 appealed to President Roosevelt and the East European Division of the Department of State but triggered a struggle for control of American security policy by leading figures in the War and Navy departments. Beginning in November 1936, Russia attempted to persuade the United States to build, or sell plans for construction of, naval vessels, especially a battleship that might be used in a showdown with Japan. In March 1937 Robert Kelley and others in the State Department approved of the sale. The president wanted it as a means of promoting collective security by one of the few ways available to him, and Joseph Green, chief of the Office of Arms and Munitions Control,

[92]"At Narkomindel," ibid.

[93]"Statement by Roosevelt," ibid., September 8, 1937.

[94]"Twenty Years of Bolshevism: Soviet Policy Abroad," *International Conciliation* 335 (December 1937): 814.

tried to carry out Roosevelt's wishes. The U.S. Navy, however, used every means at its disposal to prevent the president's desires from being fulfilled.

Soviet efforts to finalize the battleship sale provided a preview of the problems Roosevelt would confront later in persuading the military to give aid to the victims of Fascist and Japanese aggression. The Navy Department's response forewarned the president that his task in aiding the democracies and Russia, through military equipment purchases, would confront willful obstructionist tactics, including almost treasonous plotting to ensure that the commander in chief did not command in the decision process on what means were best to defend national security. This foreshadowed the World War II struggle for control of the diplomatic process between the departments of State, Navy, and Army, characterized by a bureaucratic infighting that ultimately weakened the policymaking function of the State Department.

Army obstructionism came to the fore when Assistant Secretary of War Louis Johnson wrote FDR an insulting letter on September 1. He said he wondered, before he entered the War Department, why the army continued to allow a garrison to be stationed in China when it served no useful purpose, was likely to be a source of embarrassment, and could provoke circumstances "leading to most serious consequences." Then Johnson discovered, on entering his assignment, that the army agreed with him totally and, as recently as June 1936, had urged the withdrawal of the garrison "for the same reasons that appealed to me, but that the State Dept. insisted upon its retention." He questioned why State embarked upon policies that totally ignored the input of the army, a practice "not assumed by the foreign office of any other nation." According to Johnson, other powers made policy only after close consultation with the military.[95]

The fact that Johnson, when he was national commander of the American Legion in 1933 had virtually ordered Roosevelt not to recognize Russia, became the number two man in the War Department, says something about its composition. He "respectfully" had asked Roosevelt to act on his advice by putting the Department of State in its place, subservient to the War Department. Johnson wrote the note, he said, because the attitude of State, considering the situation in the Far East, was "a matter of the gravest concern." He also wanted the navy put under orders to preserve the isolationist position supported by the army, and he proposed that the president "consider directing the Secretary of State to afford an opportunity to the War Dept. to

---

[95]Johnson to FDR, September 1, 1937, PSF, War Department, Louis Johnson Folder.

express its views upon all matters having a military implication, immediate or remote." Having proposed that Roosevelt alter American tradition by inserting the army as a major consultative force on foreign
policy decision making, and by suggesting that the apple of the president's eye—the navy—be forced to coordinate its decision with the
army, Johnson added, almost as an afterthought, "Of course, I want
to follow your wishes completely."[96]

This correspondence illustrated one of Roosevelt's problems in
developing a policy that looked forward to using the military as a
diplomatic instrument. The War Department was essentially isolationist, desired to concentrate its efforts on a purely defensive orientation, and resisted any coordinated policy with which it did not agree.
Such obstructionism was tolerated by Roosevelt during the early 1930s,
but by the end of the decade it had become more irritating to him as
the nations threatened by Fascist aggression required both his attention
and American military aid. Henry Woodring, the isolationist secretary
of war from Kansas, and his assistant secretary were safe in 1937 only
because Roosevelt did not find it necessary, or politically wise, to do
anything about them, but he did not forget. When they continued to
thwart his plans, he delivered the coup de grace in 1940 when "Woodring resigned, Stimson was appointed Secretary of War and Louis
Johnson had to retire."[97]

Roosevelt's desire to sell a battleship to the Soviets was part of
his renewed effort in 1937 to find some way to deal with them in the
interest of collective guarantees of the peace. The president was reinforced in his evaluation of Russia's usefulness, via reports from Davies,
who wrote to McIntyre, who he was sure would pass his observations
on to the president:

> The enemies of this country are discounting the strength of the
> Red Army, and the strength of this government—that is bad for
> Peace. Apparently the War Party in Japan is probing the situation
> to see just how far they are right in their assumption of the weak-
> ness of the Red Army in the East. Trouble is quite likely to break
> out at any time. No one here can tell what the outcome of this
> situation will be. Events move too rapidly.[98]

This was a theme that Davies repeated often and could not help but
influence FDR's perspective to some degree. It seemed only logical,
with mutual enemies, to aid Russia's preparation to fight them.

---

[96]Ibid.
[97]Berle and Jacobs, *Navigating the Rapids*, p. 442.
[98]Davies to McIntyre, July 10, 1937, PPF 1381, Davies Folder.

In November 1936 Soviet representatives had begun exploring the possibility of purchasing warships from the United States. After discovering, in a conversation with R. Walton Moore, counselor of the State Department, that the legal barriers were surmountable, they set up Carp Corporation to handle the negotiations. As State's arms control specialist, Joseph Green told Morris Wolf of Carp that the process was legal, but Secretary Hull could not approve the deal without the concurrence of Secretary of the Navy Claude Swanson. Green continued:

> I warned [Wolf] . . . that I could speak only on the basis of existing laws and policies and on the basis of the present situation, and that he should take account of the fact that if the U.S.S.R. were to become a belligerent, the exportation of naval vessels . . . would undoubtedly be prohibited under the provisions of Section I of the Neutrality Act.[99]

Wolf said he knew the laws and had devised a scheme to handle any contingency. The ship, or ships, would be constructed unassembled and sent to the Soviet Union where they would be put together like a jigsaw puzzle. Green warned him again that the law could change and prevent such a transaction, but Wolf responded that he was prepared to take the risk as long as it was legal and reminded Green that Carp was prepared to commit several hundred million dollars.[100]

Secretary Swanson immediately replied that he did not have sufficient personnel to handle the Soviet order, whereupon Green suggested that there was nothing illegal if the Carp Corporation dealt with a private contractor.[101] The representatives of the Soviet-backed corporation soon found the navy blocking their way in gaining a contract from a private company[102] However, Soviet plans for naval assistance received support from an unexpected source when Kelley opposed the navy's obstructionism. The East European Division endorsed the sale on grounds that may have shocked some of the personnel at the American embassy in Moscow. He asserted that several questions had been considered: would the assistance conflict with any American interest or policy? Was it in American interests to look with favor and possibly facilitate the Soviet plans, or did considerations of policy prohibit such aid? Kelley said his division approved the assistance because they assumed that the Soviet government would eventually evolve into a purely national entity and strengthening Russian naval forces, under

---

[99]*FRUS: Soviet Union*, pp. 458–59.
[100]Ibid., p. 459.
[101]Ibid., p. 460.
[102]Ibid., p. 461.

these circumstances, would not run counter to American national interests.[103]

On April 3 Roosevelt intervened in the matter personally and called Secretary Swanson to account on the issue in a cabinet meeting. The president sensed the source of the bottleneck and told Admiral Leahy that he approved of the deal because it coincided with U.S. interests.[104] Roosevelt was dissatisfied with the progress, and Welles was assigned the task of exploring the matter. He responded that apparently "the difficulties which the Carp Export and Import Corporation has encountered in connection with this proposed transaction result not from the attitude of any Department of the Government but from the inability of the Corporation to persuade the Bethlehem Shipbuilding Corporation . . . to enter into such a contract."[105]

What actually happened was quite a different story. Admiral Leahy had lied to the president. To FDR's face he had said that he agreed with the decision but expressed little enthusiasm to his subordinates who opposed it. A leak, probably from officers under Leahy's command, gained unfavorable publicity from the press. When the White House sent Green to talk to Leahy, he again agreed with the president that the situation required some action but failed to take seriously any possible move to reprimand his subordinates. His real feelings on the matter were clearly stated in his diary where he "revealed his considerable reservations, referring to the directors of Carp, Morris Wolf and Sam Carp, as international villain types and to the Soviet Union as a 'menace' and expressing skepticism about Ambassador Troyanovsky's comments on the similarity of Soviet-American interests in the Far East."[106] Thus frustrated in his effort to aid the Soviets in mutual security interests by his own Navy Department, FDR moved the battleship sale to the back burner. This did not mean, however, that he abandoned his search for security through collaboration with the Soviet Union.

Several times during 1937 Roosevelt found ways to bring the Russians into his plans to secure the peace. In a memorandum to Morgenthau, he suggested a new approach to the Russian debt question which might bear fruit and which had been used by the French in the 1880s to wean the Russians away from German tutelage. This would involve a banking consortium in the United States, guaranteeing Soviet debts that would tie the Russians to America at least until the obligation

[103]Ibid., p. 466.

[104]Maddux, *Years of Estrangement*, p. 86.

[105]Welles to McIntyre, August 21, 1937, with memorandum from Joseph Green of August 20, 1937, PSF, State Department Folder.

[106]Maddux, *Years of Estrangement*, pp. 86–87.

was paid.[107] Roosevelt was still convinced that the debts had to be settled in order to "sell" cooperation with the Soviets to his constituency, both inside the government and among the general public.

Secretary of the Treasury Morgenthau did little after his memorandum from FDR until May. He thought Bullitt had so antagonized the Soviets that it was not the proper time to raise the debt question, but he kept the president's plan in mind.[108] He met with Herbert Feis, Kelley, and several subordinates from the Treasury Department and asked them to bring him up to date on the status of the Russian debt. He wanted to know if there was anything written down on the arrangements. Kelley told him that it was a gentleman's agreement, and the president had spoken of loans to the Russians. Morgenthau also asked if the time were propitious to reopen the question. Kelley said no. Morgenthau then asked why, to which Kelley responded:

> They, of course, lay great stress on the fact that they want very much to settle with us; like to do it, and all that, but if they did it with us they have to do it with France and Great Britain. That was true when Litvinov came over here and he knew it then as now. Unfortunately, the English recently expended a 10,000,000 pound credit without any insistence on settlement of debts.[109]

Morgenthau continued to pursue the subject, via a meeting with Ambassador Troianovskii, another representative from the Soviet embassy, and one from the treasury. In his diary Morgenthau laid out the subject bluntly. "Now I am going to talk very frankly—the two Governments are not getting any closer together." The Russian ambassador agreed. However, Morgenthau assured him that "I don't start something like this unless I first talk to the President." Then Morgenthau got to the reason for resuming debt discussions: "Take a look at China. Look at the chances I took with China when we made those loans and gave them that assistance. The Chinese tell us we saved them. And they are getting stronger every day." He clearly implied that the United States could do the same for Russia in its time of trial. The Russian averred that the Red Army had something to do with strengthening China. Although Morgenthau admitted he might be exaggerating a bit, the important thing was that a weak China meant trouble for both the United States and the USSR; Troianovskii concurred. The treasury secretary then laid his case in the open: "China growing stronger assures Russia and the United States of peace in the

---

[107]FDR to Morgenthau, January 23, 1937, OF 21.
[108]Morgenthau Papers, Diary, Book 69, May 19, 1937, p. 113.
[109]Ibid., Diary, Book 67, May 11, 1937, p. 242.

Pacific. Right?" The Russian said yes. "So," the secretary concluded, "we have a common interest there."

Troianovskii must have thought he was dreaming as Morgenthau asserted that everywhere he looked "Russia and ourselves have the same common enemies." The ambassador then attempted to expand the perspective beyond China, suggesting that similar conditions prevailed in Europe. If cooperation could cover the trouble spots East and West, the chances of preserving the peace would be enhanced. He did not wish to sound too eager; therefore, he asserted that the Soviet Union was in a strong position in world affairs, but "still we are ready to cooperate."[110] It was small wonder that the Soviet press bore so heavily on a new relationship with America. It was not all bluff and gesture; Morgenthau, one of the president's closest advisers, thrust the idea boldly before the Russians and began with the assurance that he did not act without authorization from Roosevelt on such matters.

Not only did Morgenthau extend the olive branch, but Cordell Hull also talked to Troianovskii, with a somewhat more subdued presentation of the same theme. The secretary of state avowed that there were dangerous conditions in the world which dictated that the peace-loving states like Russia and the United States should not let things get worse by allowing the belligerents to have satisfaction from rifts between them over trivial matters. It was time to correct whatever misunderstandings there were in the broader interest of keeping the peace. The failure to settle debts had led to an unfortunate circumstance, with the result that the two powers had not been able to act together on far more important issues. Hull told Troianovskii that this "was a great handicap to peace at a critical period."[111] Since the Americans had made contact and talked earnestly in the name of the president, the Russians believed their long-standing predictions that the United States would ultimately cooperate in self-interest were about to be realized. The important point was that Roosevelt seized the initiative through someone whom he trusted more to do this for him than his own Department of State, whose secretary entered via the back door.

---

[110]Ibid., Diary, Book 70, May 26, 1937, pp. 110–18.

[111]Memorandum of conversation between Hull and Troianovskii, November 27, 1937, PHILIPPINES-YUGOSLAVIA, Box No. 61, Folder No. 250, 1934–1942, Russia, Cordell Hull Papers, Library of Congress, Washington, DC.

VI

American Security Is Threatened: Russia Gains New Importance

AT THE END OF 1937 President Roosevelt wrote James Hilton, expressing an unusual pessimism about the world crisis. He congratulated
him on his novel *Lost Horizon* and suggested that Hilton had accurately
identified the abysmal condition of the world and predicted that the
United States might be the last hope of civilization.[1] The same theme
was pursued by FDR in a letter to Ambassador William Phillips in
September 1938, prophesying that America might have to become the
treasure-house for European civilization, holding forth as Shangri-La
waiting to "pick up the pieces" and "save what remains of the wreck."[2]
He told Phillips that the United States would stand aside and await
the results of the disaster, a course that belied his actual purpose in
1938, for Roosevelt had no such intention. Instead he launched a campaign to make Americans aware of the dangers to the very survival of
democracy, worked to build U.S. defenses, tried various schemes to
avert the impending war, and attempted to bring the Russians to the
side of the democracies, either in defense of the threatened peace or
as an ally should efforts to avoid war fail. The Soviets' responses to
this initiative fluctuated with their assessments of what the Americans
could or would do to promote Russian security.

Roosevelt's first task was to arouse Americans to the nature of
the threat to democracy and their own vulnerability if they stood alone
against the combination of Axis powers. Here he focused particularly
on the precarious position of the United States if Germany controlled
the Continent. Through his press conferences, FDR emphasized the

---

[1]FDR to Hilton, December 20, 1937, PPF 5066, James Hilton Folder.
[2]Roosevelt, *Roosevelt Letters*, 3:241.

frightening reality of a shrinking world that placed American borders closer to Europe and Asia. He pointed out that an attack on the United States need not be a direct one. Over a period of months, he called attention to the prospect of an assault against American strength through a foreign foe gaining control of the economy of Latin America, or by actual invasion of South America or Mexico in order to secure bases of operation against the United States.

Roosevelt told the assembled members of the Associated Church Press that there should be a loosening of the neutrality law, for in many situations its application would work in favor of aggressors. He also informed them that it was necessary to have some organization that would counteract Fascist propaganda in letters to editors and newspaper stories. Then the president settled down to his main point when someone asked a leading question that provided him with the opportunity to tell of America's vulnerability. He explained that U.S. commitments in the Pacific had to include territory, such as the Philippines, where the American flag flew.[3] To the churchmen he asked what they would recommend if a Fascist power supported revolution in Mexico, but he did not receive the answer he wanted and so informed them that it was obvious that the United States could not tolerate such a situation.[4] By the time Roosevelt finished defining the limits of America's vital interests, he had encompassed the entire Western Hemisphere as well as all U.S. possessions elsewhere, plus the strategic approaches to the United States.[5]

When a reporter expressed the opinion that such a task was impossible, FDR said that it would require licking one enemy first and then concentrating on the other one.[6] He laid the groundwork for his campaign, advocating a two-ocean navy. There was probably no one in the room who did not recall at one time having had a special understanding given him directly by the president of why such a naval buildup was necessary for minimum measures of defense. Roosevelt also had in mind the need to isolate an opponent, if possible, so as not to have a two-front war, which accounted for his later efforts to make sure that Japan was kept on the fence as long as possible in order to confront the more formidable menace of Nazi Germany.

On April 21 the president held a special news conference for the Society of Newspaper Editors. He made virtually the same points, using

---

[3]Press Conferences, 11, No. 452-A, April 20, 1938, pp. 325–29.

[4]Ibid., p. 332.

[5]This strategic necessity had been the subject of great interest to Roosevelt when he was in President Wilson's Navy Department. See Freidel, *The Apprenticeship*, pp. 273–74.

[6]Press Conferences, 11, No. 452-A, April 20, 1938, p. 334.

different illustrations concerning the lifting or lightening of the neutrality law, but he did not mention the threat to the United States through Latin America.[7] The next morning, at his regular press conference, he again attacked the neutrality law, with approximately the same emphasis as with the editors and publishers.[8]

Cordell Hull joined Roosevelt's campaign to alert Americans to external dangers, via a speech to the press on March 17. He told the newsmen that the United States steered the middle course between internationalism and isolationism, neither accepting political commitments with other nations nor withdrawing to American shores. But the United States did not intend to surrender any of its rights as a sovereign nation. To waive rights in the face of actual or threatened violations, Hull told the press, could only serve "to encourage disregard of law and of the basic principles of international order, and thus contribute to the inevitable spread of international anarchy throughout the world."[9]

Izvestiia analyzed, in a positive light, Hull's address to the National Press Club and asserted that the secretary of state had indicated that problems in foreign affairs had become questions of universal order or anarchy based on force. According to *Izvestiia*, this view was dictated by the threat of large-scale armed conflict in both Europe and Asia. Hull's request for speeding up the arms program received attention, as did his urging of drastic revision of the neutrality legislation and the need to "cooperate on the basis of common sense where mutual interests prevail" with other threatened nations, "always retaining, however, freedom of choice and action."[10] The Russians read themselves into the category of threatened nations.

Others in the administration and the Department of State, as well as some congressmen, began to sound the alarm about an endangered America. During the development of the Czech crisis, George Messersmith of State wrote Senator Key Pittman on September 1, 1938: "The international situation is really approaching, if not already in it, the most serious crisis since 1914. I think there is ample evidence that Mr. Hitler had made up his mind to go ahead in Czechoslovakia irrespective of what the Czechs might be willing to concede." England and France were destined to be the ultimate victims of Nazi aggression, Messersmith argued, unless the British made their opposition to Hitler

---

[7]Ibid., No. 452-B, April 21, 1938, pp. 365–69.

[8]Ibid., No. 453, April 22, 1938, pp. 381–83.

[9]U.S. Department of State, *Peace and War: United States Foreign Policy, 1931–1941* (Washington, DC: Government Printing Office, 1943), p. 411.

[10]"The Foreign Policy of the United States—Statement by the Secretary of State," *Izvestiia*, March 20, 1938.

absolutely clear and unequivocal. Unless the Nazis were confronted immediately the peace would simply erode away.[11]

These and other admonitions of the impending danger[12] caused Pittman to begin to ring the alarm bell himself, and he wrote to Assistant Secretary of State R. Walton Moore, complaining of the mood that prevailed in Congress and the public which smothered efforts to defend the nation. He attacked "the extreme and foolish pacifist sentiment in this country based entirely on fear," which, he thought, "may dominate Congress at the next session. Fear combined with ignorance is the most difficult opposition to overcome."[13] At the end of the year Pittman told his Senate colleagues that Americans did not like the governments of Germany or Japan, that they opposed dictatorships of any kind, and that "the people of the United States have the right and power to enforce morality and justice in accordance with peace treaties with us. And they will. Our Government does not have to use military force and will not unless necessary."[14] "Unless necessary" was an important reservation, as in 1936 the senator from Nevada had assured an audience that the United States would not fight under any circumstances to enforce treaties or stop aggressors.

Even Moore, the perpetual optimist at the State Department, joined the ranks of those who had become alarmists in the cause for civilization. He urged caution lest the United States be dragged beyond the limits he thought expedient but decided that at least Washington should begin to speak out. In late August he wrote to his friend William Bullitt: "While I am dead against the idea of the United States becoming involved in war, on the other hand I am satisfied that we should be very frank and emphatic in stating our conception of the value of the democratic principle and the dangerous character of the attack on that principle expressed by the policies of the totalitarian nations."[15] Moore asserted that America would not engage in forceful measures to support its theories but was entitled to state them clearly, and this might lead to beneficial results in that "perhaps the constant reiteration of our attitude will have the same result as the constant dripping of water on a solid surface which is after a while worn away."[16] This erosion theory was akin to the president's own idea on how to meet the resistance from public opinion and Congress to preparedness for

---

[11]Messersmith to Pittman, September 1, 1938, Committee Papers, SEN 75A-F9-1 (105H).

[12]Alfred Bergman to Pittman, September 21, 1938, ibid., SEN 75A-F9-1 (105).

[13]Pittman to Moore, October 15, 1938, ibid., SEN 75A-F9-1 (105H).

[14]Statement in the Senate, December 22, 1938, Pittman Papers, Box 162.

[15]Moore to Bullitt, August 31, 1938, R. Walton Moore Papers.

[16]Ibid.

the attack from the Axis powers, which was considerably different than wearing away the aggressors' will to fight. Roosevelt thought that, once he overcame public and congressional opposition, he could add acid to the water dripping on the Axis powers.

Events abroad and Roosevelt's campaign complimented one another in stimulating the requisite concern. Shifting public sentiments were well expressed, as witnessed by a letter to the *New York Times* from a man in Ohio who wrote:

> Ten years ago a proposal to enlarge the United States Navy would have found me in bitter opposition. Today I am finding grim satisfaction in the proposals of the President for a supremely powerful navy. . . . The philosophy of non-resistant pacificism had displayed all of its wares and today it is not only bankrupt but there are good reasons for believing that the verdict of history will place upon it the blame for many of the shocking international crimes committed in the past decade. Theodore Roosevelt was right. Uncle Sam should 'speak softly and carry a big stick.'[17]

The *Times* also reported the resolution of the National Conference on the Cause and Cure of War, not formerly noted for a belligerent posture, which announced the position taken by eleven women's organizations with a total membership of 7 million. They resolved to support legislative measures that "would promote the active cooperation of the United States with other nations in peaceful means to deal with economic or political problems disturbing to the peace of the world." More significantly, however, the delegates approved "even the use of force" in the event a crisis arose that made it necessary to prevent the spread of aggression.[18] On January 29, 1938, 1,800 youth delegates, meeting in New York, endorsed President Roosevelt's quarantine proposal.[19]

Although Roosevelt constantly denied that he paid much attention to what either the media or opinion surveys said, he insisted on getting "reliable" polls as quickly as they were released, or sometimes before they became public. Also, he occasionally commissioned polls by the Princeton survey people, whose techniques he trusted. In 1938 the polls showed a lack of unanimity of opinion. A poll taken in March, for instance, asked: Should the United States go to war to help any Latin American country attacked by a European or Asian power, or should the United States help defend in any way Latin America under such circumstances? Thirty-three percent answered yes; 67 percent said

---

[17]*New York Times,* January 16, 1938.
[18]"An Admirable Peace Program," ibid., January 24, 1938.
[19]Ibid., January 30, 1938.

no. Significantly, the cross section was polled again eight months after the president had inaugurated his education campaign, after events in Europe had accurately proved his concern for the deterioration of the peace, and the press had helped alert Americans to the circumstances there and in Asia. The results of the second survey revealed an even split in favor of aiding or fighting for Latin America.[20]

More important for the president's awareness campaign were two mid-year polls that illustrated more sharply how successful Roosevelt was in arousing opposition to the Axis powers. *Fortune* magazine illustrated that no phase of the president's work was more popular than his international policy and his rearmament program. Of those who declared an opinion, 80.3 percent personally liked the president, as opposed to 11.7 percent who disliked him, an index that he had sufficient personal prestige to feel secure in his pursuit of an active foreign policy. In addition, 63.6 percent approved of his rearmament policy, while only 13.2 percent disapproved, and 50 percent favored his international policy, compared to 15 percent who did not.[21] A poll conducted by George H. Gallup in July reported that the American public favored Great Britain and France in a potential conflict with Germany and Italy by 65 percent, as opposed to 3 percent for the Axis powers and 32 percent who claimed to support neither side. Survey findings also showed that 46 percent of those questioned were already convinced that, in the event of such a conflict, the United States would definitely enter the war against the Axis.[22] Undoubtedly Roosevelt's decision to lead America to preparedness, coupled with events in Europe and China, frightened or angered Americans sufficiently to win increased support for the president's campaign to prepare the country for the defense of democracy.

Reinforced by the knowledge of a change in the public's mood, Roosevelt seized the opportunity to announce sternly to Hitler that "the supreme desire of the American people is to live in peace. But in the event of a general war they face the fact that no nation can escape some measure of the consequences of such a world catastrophe."[23] To Roosevelt, preparedness was not merely intended to arouse Americans to the possibility of a threat but to prepare the nation militarily to meet the dangers. In his press conferences, FDR accelerated his efforts to educate the media to the need for adequate defense in the face of a

---

[20]Hadley Cantril and Mildred Strunk, *Public Opinion* (Princeton: Princeton University Press, 1951), pp. 780–81.

[21]"The *Fortune* Quarterly Survey," *Fortune* 18 (July 1938): 37.

[22]*New York Times*, July 27, 1938.

[23]*Press Releases*, October 1, 1938, p. 219.

monstrous conspiracy to destroy democracy, a plot that would ultimately isolate and then wear down the United States. He told the press
that, without a larger navy—a defense commitment that created a
collective security system in the Western Hemisphere—and a program
to provide assistance to the threatened friends and fellow democracies,
the United States would be the last isolated victim of the totalitarian
powers.

Roosevelt's campaign began to win support almost at once. He
told his press conference of January 4, 1938 that, despite a desire to
reduce government expenditures, this might not be possible because
of future events resultant from world conditions over which America
had no control.[24] By the end of the month, he began to provide information of a more specific nature on defense appropriations but did not
elaborate. He also hazily itemized defense spending by mentioning $2
million for this, $6 million for that, $8 million for something else, and
so forth without adding up the figures for the press. One reporter asked
him to estimate what it would total for 1939, and the president cannily
answered: "I don't know—oh, in 1939—15, 16, 17, 22, 28—about
$29,200,000."[25] Gradually over the next four months the costs escalated,
with the press being brought along relative to the serious need to defend
America. Finally Roosevelt presented the Congress with a request for
expanding the navy, via H.R. 9218, which passed the House Naval
Affairs Committee by a vote of 20 to 3 on March 7, and the Senate
completed action on it May 13, at which time the Naval Expansion
Bill asked for $1,156,000,000.[26]

Harold Callender, writing in the *New York Times*, read Roosevelt's
program clearly; the navy bill was foreign policy in the making. America
might not be allied with any European power, but the intent and effect
were clear. As the U.S. fleet expanded, the Fascists were thwarted
because the Americans made it possible for the Europeans, especially
the British, to focus on defense of other areas against the aggressors.[27]

II

For several reasons, Russia gained a more preeminent position in President Roosevelt's moves to counter the aggressors in 1938. Obviously
the Soviets were among the possible victims of the Axis powers, which
set them aside from other dictatorships; reports from various sources

---

[24]Press Conferences, 11, No. 421, January 4, 1938, p. 11.
[25]Ibid., No. 429, January 28, 1938, pp. 126–28.
[26]*Christian Science Monitor*, March 9, 1938; *New York Times*, May 14, 1938.
[27]Harold Callender, "Europe Weighs U.S. Navy Plan," *New York Times*, May 14,
1938.

to the president clarified the nature of the threat to the Soviet Union; and the Russians were apparently willing to work with the democracies either to avoid the war or to aid in defeat of the prospective enemies.

That Russia was a potential victim of aggression was reaffirmed by Admiral William Leahy when he responded to a request from the president concerning the nature of the world crisis and which nations might be involved in any future conflict. On January 6, 1938, Leahy sent a report from Admiral Harry Yarnell, who maintained that Russia would play a significant role in any Far Eastern conflict, the purges notwithstanding. The Russians, he thought, would quantitatively and qualitatively put up a better fight than the Chinese because of superior equipment. He also believed that Soviet air power far surpassed that of Japan. The situation in Manchuria was serious, and Japan would drive the British out of China and probably the Americans as well. Yarnell was convinced, "with regard to Russia, . . . she will come into the war in the spring."[28]

Another briefing communiqué from Admiral Leahy of January 27 again emphasized the Russo-Japanese antagonism. Captain Riley F. McConnell, chief of staff, commander in chief, Asiatic Fleet, conjectured that Japan was preparing either to attack Russia from Manchuria or to repel an attack by the Soviets. He quoted knowledgeable sources who thought that "the chances are about one in three that Japan will be at war with Russia by the Summer of 1938. Japan's war machine will have had its test and they consider it equal to the task."[29]

In a March 9 memorandum from Sumner Welles, which capsulized a conversation between Hitler and British Ambassador to Germany Sir Nevile Henderson, Roosevelt was reminded of Hitler's anti-Soviet posture. The führer excitedly denounced the Bolsheviks and said that any arms reduction talks by the British with anyone would have to begin with Russia. He implied that his own arms program was not aimed at the British but at the Soviet Union.[30]

Joseph Davies warned that the European democracies were not concerned enough about winning the Russians over to their side. The isolation of Russia was a more serious threat to the democracies of Europe than to the Soviet Union. He thought there was considerable miscalculation of Russian strength and wishful thinking as to its inability to survive politically and economically, thereby leading the democracies either to ignore the Russians or to believe that Germany would turn eastward to pursue the faltering Soviets. Davies contended that the Soviets would prove them wrong:

---

[28]Schewe, *Roosevelt and Foreign Affairs*, 8:31.
[29]Ibid., p. 336.
[30]Ibid., 9:80–83.

The men running this show are strong, able, and, I believe, an idealistic group. They think that they are serving a great purpose when they weed out, by these horrible killings, any 'treachery' which they find. They believe that all great movements for the proletariat have been destroyed by false sentimentalism and weakness and they do not propose to be weak.[31]

Threats from the Japanese and Hitler against the Soviet Union reinforced Roosevelt's hope that a friendly disposition toward the Soviets would aid his campaign to align the Russians with the forces of good, thus establishing a formidable array against the enemies of civilization. It was in this vein that he continued to promote the sale of naval vessels to the Russians, but 1938 saw no improvement in this plan. In 1937 Admiral Leahy and Welles had assured the president that Bethlehem Steel, and not any agency of the government, had thwarted progress on the project. On February 23, 1938, Roosevelt found out differently from Assistant Secretary of the Navy Charles E. Edison, who wrote that Ambassador Troianovskii would seek to meet with the president for a showdown on the matter "as to who is blocking the transaction and why." The Russians were perplexed when the Department of State replied: "Swell—go ahead you have our blessing." They knew that months earlier Roosevelt had ordered the proceedings to be handled expeditiously in the presence of Troianovskii. The Navy Department told the Russians that they approved if it was alright with the State Department, but still nothing happened and the shipbuilders acted as though it had not been cleared.[32]

Edison reported the "low down" on the situation to the president, absolving the Bethlehem people, who understandably wanted a clear authorization so that some congressional investigators would not come down on them later and charge them with selling military secrets. In such a situation all they could say was that they were told to go ahead; they wanted it in writing. Reluctantly, Edison admitted that his investigation of the bottleneck led to the top of his own department: "With the Secretary definitely opposed and most of the Bureau Chiefs opposed or lukewarm, it will take some pretty definite expression from the Commander-in-Chief to those concerned as to policy in this regard." Without such a clear and forceful assertion, he visualized "endless discussions as to how many angels can dance on the point of a needle." Roosevelt may have thought his orders were explicit when he discussed the issue with the secretary of the navy and the bureau chiefs, but it did not "take." Matters stood, Edison concluded, as they had one month

---

[31]Davies to FDR, April 4, 1938, PPF 1381, Davies Folder

[32]Memorandum, Edison to FDR, February 23, 1938, PSF, Navy File, Charles E. Edison Folder.

earlier—"Quo Vadis."[33] This substantiated other warnings Roosevelt received that cooperation with the Russians would have to come through some direct action on his part, or through gaining a debt settlement so that he could move more openly without fear of congressional reaction.

President Roosevelt desired to act in good faith on the Soviet attempt to obtain a battleship from the United States in order to improve the balance of power in the Far East and to assure the Russians that they could count on cooperation from at least one of the democracies in the face of mutual problems with the aggressors. Hull and Assistant Secretary Edison wrote him, asking if objections should be raised to the private contractors going ahead with the project; Roosevelt said no. They then asked: "Shall we go further than merely to state that there is no objection and give some affirmative indication to interested shipbuilders, manufacturers, and naval architects that this government considers the proposed transaction of positive advantage to this country?" FDR answered, "Yes. Give all help."

Concerning final procedures, Roosevelt wrote in the margin of the memorandum: "Handle by a specially notarized office under the Asst. Secty."[34] The president had faith in Edison's loyalty to him and the project and wanted to make sure that it would not be handled by some underling, either without authority or sufficient motivation to see it through. As it turned out, there was no way the project could be brought to fruition without Roosevelt simply commanding the navy brass to stop impeding his orders and taking punitive action when they failed to do so. FDR could issue the orders but could not bring himself to punish the resistors. Therefore, if he were to make progress with his plans to convince the Russians to cooperate, he had to find other ways.

Davies reinforced Roosevelt's conviction that the USSR was a potential victim of the Axis powers and amenable to collaborative efforts.[35] Although Davies was generally naive in his assessments of the Soviet Union and Foreign Service officers were continually amazed that he could view the Russians on the side of the forces of good, he was sometimes more realistic in his evaluation of where the Russians stood in the world crisis than were his more suspicious colleagues in the diplomatic corps. Where career Foreign Service officers looked for duplicity in nearly everything the Soviets did, Davies was able to assume that they were at least human and motivated by self-preservation in many of their actions. In his simplistic analysis, he was forced to his conclusions because there had to be an opposite to the Nazi forces of

[33]Ibid.

[34]Hull and Edison to FDR, June 8, 1938, OF 220, State Department Folder.

[35]Davies to FDR, April 4, 1938, PPF 1381, Davies Folder.

evil. If the Russians aligned with the Germans, the democratic cause was lost; therefore, one had to assume they wore white hats, or at least grey, despite one's revulsion at some of their tactics and ploys. To Davies, the Nazi objectives were to split the forces of good, isolate the Russians from their potential allies, and pick off the democracies piecemeal.[36]

Roosevelt agreed with this viewpoint and was concerned that the British and French, especially the former, were letting Hitler seize more than he should at the expense of others. The president worried over the prospect of the whole continent of Europe falling to Hitler without so much as a peep from those closest to the menace of Nazi control. He did not believe that Hitler would continue against united opposition, but, if allowed to chip away one country at a time while playing the democracies off against one another with Russia as the bait, there would be a long and bloody struggle before the balance could be redressed.

When Bullitt told Harold Ickes that he was convinced British and French policy intended "to permit other nations to have their will of Russia,"[37] there is little doubt that the secretary of the interior passed it on to Roosevelt. Bullitt also said Germany would seize the Ukraine, while Japan took advantage to grab Siberia, but neither of them would be able to digest what they ate and in the end would break under the strain. By "leaving Russia to her fate," the British and French would divert "the threat of Germany from their own lands."[38] Ambassador Joseph Kennedy also believed that English and French policy was aimed at isolating Russia in order to permit Germany to deal with the Communist menace.[39] No two men outside British and French governing circles were in a better position to know the intent of the groups in control of these nations.

Roosevelt was not enamored of this prospect for ensuring the preservation of the peace, at least in part because he was certain that by this juncture Hitler had no intention of stopping his route to conquest until he controlled the world. Therefore, the Moscow post loomed more important than ever, and in July the president cast about for a suitable replacement for Ambassador Davies who had been promised a transfer to Berlin but drew Brussels instead. Roosevelt first offered the position to Sidney J. Weinberg, but he turned it down.[40] The president then decided to leave the post vacant until he found the right

---

[36]Ibid.
[37]Ickes, *The Inside Struggle*, p. 519.
[38]Ibid.
[39]Langer and Gleason, *The Challenge to Isolation*, pp. 122–23.
[40]FDR to Weinberg, July 5, 1938, OF 220-A, Russia Miscellaneous.

replacement. The attempt to persuade Weinberg was in itself significant, as he was a prominent New York banker who had worked with
Davies on a new proposal to develop an acceptable arrangement with
the Soviets to pay their debts to the United States, a project in which
Roosevelt showed great interest.[41] As Davies was leaving Moscow, the
Russians tried to settle the debt question and get on with rapprochement, which they were sure Roosevelt both wanted and needed and
which they certainly found attractive to their own security interests.

Davies made his official farewell visits to the Foreign Office on
June 5. First he called on Mikhail Kalinin who told him that world
conditions had caused the difficult problems facing diplomats in Moscow, and Russians had to isolate themselves from external enemies,
notably Germany and Japan. He praised Roosevelt's Chicago speech
and hoped this indicated the possibility that the United States would
become more active in the protection of world peace. The U.S. ambassador then proceeded to Molotov's apartment where he received a
surprise. Stalin walked into the room and sat down for a two- and one-
quarter hour frank discussion, the first Davies had had with the Soviet
dictator during his tenure in Russia.

Stalin made his purpose in talking to Davies quite clear. He
stressed that the European situation was growing worse, in part due
to the reactionary Chamberlain government, which was determined to
make Germany strong and place France in a dependent position tied
to British policy, "with the purpose of ultimately making Germany
strong as against Russia." Stalin said he did not believe Chamberlain
truly represented the British people and that he would probably fail
because the Fascist dictators would drive too hard a bargain. Stalin
asked whether Davies was conversant with the negotiations on the
construction of a battleship in the United States for the USSR and
wondered what was causing delays. Davies responded that "quite frankly,
it was difficult for me also to understand . . . but that I thought the
matter had recently given indications of going forward more rapidly."
Stalin then guardedly voiced a suspicion about American intent to carry
through on the deal. Stalin could not really believe that, if Roosevelt
wanted the ship built, his underlings would not jump to the task. The
Russians never understood the inner workings of the American political
process. If anyone in the USSR consciously or unconsciously thwarted
Stalin's orders, they went to Siberia or the firing squad. With his own
absolute power in such matters undoubtedly in mind, Stalin remarked:
"If the President of the United States wanted it done he felt sure that

---

[41]Davies, *Mission to Moscow*, pp. 372, 374, 543.

the Army and Navy technicians could not stop it, and that it could be lawfully done."[42]

In his memoirs Maxim Litvinov commented on Stalin's proclivity to act like a shrewd merchant, and this session with Davies bore out the commissar's description. Stalin talked of the problems hindering cooperation between the Russians and the Americans when, after all, they both wanted the same thing: to block the success of the aggressors. He saved his major item for last. The debt seemed to prevent closer collaboration, but he was aware of a banking group in America that worked closely with President Roosevelt and that would advance Russia money or credits to pay it off. Davies seized the opportunity to lay out exactly what a settlement of the debt question could mean and what its past history encompassed. The bitter recriminations had been unfortunate, he admitted, because relations had been resumed to provide exactly the sort of pressure on the aggressors Stalin had mentioned. Haggling over the size of the debt followed, with Stalin suggesting that perhaps the Americans might settle for payment of the Kerensky debt. Davies argued that there was no use in even approaching his government with such a proposal. Stalin retreated somewhat, and the matter was left for further discussion by the appropriate authorities.[43]

Davies forwarded the summary of his conversation to Hull on June 9, which in turn went to the president. However, the day before the ambassador had sent a memorandum directly to Roosevelt, outlining the proposal as he understood it, along with suggestions on how to clarify the amount of the debt, interest rates, and method of payment, especially focusing on whether the Export-Import Bank should be involved. Davies thought there would be similar problems to those which had created a stalemate earlier if the issue were handled exclusively through the Export-Import Bank; whereas, if private bankers controlled the arrangements, either alone or through the bank, with the Soviets agreeing to legal limits of its operation, the matter could be settled.[44]

Troianovskii illustrated how important the meeting was when he immediately sought an interview with Secretary Hull who recorded that the Russian ambassador came in bubbling with excitement that Stalin had gone to see Davies when he was at the Foreign Office and had spent so much time discussing crucial matters with him. Troianovskii averred that this meant a real turning point in U.S.-Soviet relations. At last the debt question and other minor matters, which

---

[42]Schewe, *Roosevelt and Foreign Affairs*, 10:231–38.
[43]Ibid., pp. 241–46.
[44]PSF, Russia, Davies Folder; Schewe, *Roosevelt and Foreign Affairs*, 10:247–48.

had kept them from real cooperation, would be settled. Troianovskii covered Hull with unguents, claiming that the sentiments expressed in two of the secretary's recent speeches had helped to bring this about. The Russian spoke with great enthusiasm about the prospects for rapprochement between the two nations and the beneficial results that would accrue to them and the world from such a unified course of action. Hull responded as Davies had to Stalin. Joint pressure on behalf of the peace had been the objective of the United States from the outset of recognition:

> I emphasized to him in this connection the fact that this was precisely what we had in mind when we decided to recognize the Soviet Republic some years ago, but regarding which we had been woefully disappointed. I added that he could imagine the gratification, therefore, of myself, the President and others to see this new step by Stalin. . . . I again emphasized the immense satisfaction it gives us to see this step by the Soviet Government, which should mean so much to our countries and to the stability, peace and order of the world.[45]

Hull was apparently startled but elated by the Soviets' change of heart and eagerly sought, in another memorandum, to cement the gain by urging the pursuit of rapprochement.[46] The whole affair was a tragicomedy. Hull apparently believed that persistent "correct" relations with the Russians were about to pay off and that despite misgivings the selection of Davies had returned some benefits by the ambassador's decision to remain friendly with Litvinov and other Russian leaders. When Davies returned to America, Hull congratulated him on his work in Moscow. In a conversation of June 24, the secretary emphasized the importance of the USSR, "not only with reference to the Japanese-Chinese situation but also in connection with possible European peace." Davies recalled that Hull said "in his quiet way . . . very generous and kind things as to the success of my mission to Moscow, which these proposals which I brought back had demonstrated." The groundwork that this change of attitude in Moscow created, Hull believed, "was a very important thing for the future in these hazardous days of international threat from the 'aggressor bandits' in the world."[47]

A far more significant ingredient lay behind the Soviets' "change of heart." In 1937 Roosevelt had decided to examine the prospects for

---

[45]Memorandum of conversation between Hull and Troianovskii, June 7, 1938, PHILIPPINES-YUGOSLAVIA, Box No. 61, Folder No. 250, 1934–1942, Russia, Hull Papers.
[46]Memorandum of June 18, 1938, ibid.
[47]Davies, *Mission to Moscow*, p. 371.

closer military collaboration with the Soviets if war erupted in Asia. He pursued this directly through Davies, and he specifically did not want the embassy personnel or the State Department to know about it.[48] The ambassador referenced this matter in his report of the meeting with Stalin. Hull knew about the initiative and supported it, although perhaps not entirely approving its secret nature. In his report Davies also recorded Stalin's assurance that the Soviet Union was confident of its ability to defend itself. Davies then continued:

> Early in this discussion, I broached the particular matter which President Roosevelt had discussed with me orally during my visit last January. To my surprise, in view of previous information [Davies had discussed the issue with Litvinov but got no encouragement] it was favorably received. I was committed not to disclose these discussions to anyone except the President and the Secretary of State.[49]

Davies made sure he would maintain the contact as confidential by using either Soviet interpreters or Colonel Philip R. Faymonville, the American military attaché in Moscow, whom the Soviets trusted but the embassy personnel did not. Davies reported to Roosevelt concerning his plan:

> With reference to the establishment of a secret liaison for the inter-change of military and naval information with the Soviet Government, upon which I reported to you personally, the matter was left open pending the appointment of my successor at Moscow.
>
> Messers Stalin and Molotov, as I stated to you, were both most cordial and friendly in their desire to effect such an arrangement but were deeply concerned (and I can understand their reasons therefor) lest through leaks, the information might be obtained by their enemies. They were desirous that all such information should be kept between the heads of the Governments and only the immediate chiefs thereof.
>
> They expressed confidence in the judgment, capacity and fairness of our Military Attache, Lieutenant Colonel Philip R. Faymonville. The personality there under such an arrangement is a matter of vital consequence to them.[50]

---

[48]Maddux, *Years of Estrangement*, p. 96; Davies to FDR, January 18, 1939, OF 3601; Schewe, *Roosevelt and Foreign Affairs*, 13:125.

[49]Schewe, *Roosevelt and Foreign Affairs*, 10:237.

[50]Davies to FDR, January 18, 1939, OF 3601; Schewe, *Roosevelt and Foreign Affairs*, 13:125.

When the Russians asked for a loan of $200 million to cover their debt to the United States, the Americans dropped the matter because the request proved to be another illustration of the Soviets' belief that, if FDR wished to settle the debt in this fashion, he could do so despite the Johnson Act, which prohibited loans to governments in default on previous obligations. When Roosevelt, due to his inability to override the obstructionism of his naval officers, also failed to pursue the military liaison issue, via the construction of a battleship for the USSR, Russian and American leaders became even less trustful and further isolated from one another. The "ifs" involved here are significant. If the Russians could have worked with the Americans on a realistic military contingency plan in the Far East, they might have felt more comfortable in taking a stronger stand in Europe. Then they would have been almost positive of U.S. involvement, even if an attack came from Germany in the west, for the Soviets were sure that the Japanese would take advantage of such a conflict to enter the war, thus automatically involving the Americans at least in Asia and probably in the general war, as it could not be isolated into two separate conflicts. On the other side of the issue, if the Russians had gone ahead with the debt settlement, Roosevelt would have been relieved of the burden of remaining aloof from the Soviets for internal political purposes and might have felt freer to follow up on the military liaison idea.

Within the State Department, Assistant Secretary Messersmith also recommended a move toward reconciliation with the Soviets for all of the reasons that motivated Roosevelt, Hull, Davies, and the Russians. He sent the secretary of state a memorandum that was a follow-through of a January 2 conversation with Hull, who had expressed concern over what was happening in Russia and the degree to which the United States was in the dark. Messersmith also had noted the difficulty that American diplomats had in establishing continual contact with the decision makers in the USSR, a situation that he thought compounded the problem of knowing what went on and of exercising influence on Soviet policy.

Messersmith made several suggestions instead to alter this situation and proposed urgent action on them. He reminded Hull that the Russians knew America was arming to defend itself in the face of increasing disorder in the world and that they were going to be extremely important in the developing crisis. Their Foreign Office did not make policy so contact there was useless. Stalin and his immediate associates were the only ones who could shape Soviet foreign policy; therefore, an American official, with authority to act, should speak to Stalin. Messersmith lamented Russia's ignorance of events in the outside world and the lack of intelligence from American diplomats on what happened in Russia:

I venture to suggest that someone should go for us to Russia, quietly and unostentatiously, who would under very specific instructions from the President and the Secretary get in touch with Stalin and his immediate associates. . . . I do not venture here to take up what we might say but I do wish to go on record as believing that we should seriously consider a step in this direction now as a part of that initiative and formulation of clear definite policy which I think we should not delay.[51]

Messersmith was wrong in his assertion that the American embassy did not know what was going on in the Kremlin. He might more accurately have said the staff suspected the motives and intent of Soviet policy and disdained closer ties for this reason. He was certainly correct, however, in his affirmation that the United States wielded little influence because Americans did not have continual access to the top. Roosevelt recognized this and tried to do something about it. Why nothing happened was at least partly FDR's fault; his suspicion of the State Department delayed a coordinated approach at a time when Hull and Messersmith thought it important. Roosevelt's caution was perhaps warranted, for he knew there were leaks coming from somewhere, especially in regard to policy initiative and the appointment of new ambassadors.[52] His suspicions rested in part on advice he received from friends and others close to him who were committed New Dealers and did not trust the conservatives, who they were sure infested the State Department. Eleanor Roosevelt warned her husband of the conservative and resistant nature of the average career Foreign Service officer, and Felix Frankfurter reminded him that these were the people opposed to his Russian policy. Secretary of the Interior Ickes harped on it in private discussions with the president, as did Henry Morgenthau, Jr.

Roosevelt hoped that a new and appropriate appointment to Moscow might continue the contacts established on Davies's last day there, but the selection was not easy. After Weinberg turned down the president, several petitioners sought the position, some of whom were given serious consideration. Soliciting the job, Jerome Davis of the Yale Divinity School, who previously had prepared a memorandum on recognition for the president, wrote to Mrs. Roosevelt who then asked her husband to read the part about Davis's expertise and willingness to go to Russia.[53] William Gibbs McAdoo wanted the president to consider Jean Paul Getty for the post, and FDR asked Secretary Hull to speak to him about this.[54] A number of other letters in OF 220-B promote

[51]*FRUS: Soviet Union*, pp. 504–05.
[52]Schewe, *Roosevelt and Foreign Affairs*, 8:44, is just one of numerous complaints Roosevelt registered on this to Welles.
[53]Memorandum, Eleanor Roosevelt to FDR, September 14, 1938, OF 220-B.
[54]Memorandum, FDR to Hull, June 4, 1938, ibid.

some candidates, solicit the position for the writer, and in various ways try to influence the president by political pressure, cajolery, or by their credentials for the job. There were at least one dozen letters promoting the candidacy of Charles H. Stuart of the international consulting engineering firm of Stuart, James, and Cooke, which had done business with the Soviet Union since the early 1920s. Roosevelt sent a memorandum to Hull, suggesting that they should fill the position quickly. He passed on several names for the secretary's consideration, among them Pierrepont Noyes, Ira Nelson Morris, and Stuart. The president also asked Hull if he wished to submit any names, reminding him that the three men mentioned all had enough private means to take the job.[55] Through his reference to private means, Roosevelt made it clear that he was not going to select a career person for the Moscow embassy.

Roosevelt's eagerness to find a replacement was related in part to Davies's breakthrough, but it also was spurred by reports the president had received concerning the Soviet-Japanese rivalry in the Far East. FDR's daily digest from the State Department announced on July 22 that, "although the Japanese Ambassador made renewed protest in regard to the presence of Soviet troops in territory claimed to be part of Manchuria, he indicated at the same time that if the troops were withdrawn his Government would be willing to set up a joint commission to delineate the frontier at the point of question."[56] This was a concession the Japanese would not have made one year earlier. It indicated that Soviet statements concerning the strength of their position in relation to Japan were more than just talk. A summary of events of August 5 corroborated the importance of Soviet power in the Far East and emphasized its strategic value. On the basis of reported conversations between Moscow and Tokyo, the State Department concluded: "The Soviet Government had made and is standing on proposals, the acceptance of which by Japan would involve a diplomatic victory for the Soviet Government and a diplomatic defeat for the Japanese."[57] An apparent collaboration between the United States and the Soviet Union might accomplish FDR's objective of keeping the Japanese on the fence while the forces of democracy dealt with the larger menace in Europe. This could only appear to Roosevelt as a fulfillment of part of his expectations in resuming relations with Russia. The Soviet Union was acting as a deterrent to expanding Japanese ambitions in Asia.

---

[55]FDR to Hull, May 14, 1938, PSF, No. II, Departmental Files, Box 33, State Department File, Cordell Hull Folder.

[56]Memorandum, State Department to FDR, July 22, 1938, OF 20, State Department Folder.

[57]Memorandum of August 5, 1938, ibid.

III

What was happening in Europe garnered a great deal of attention and concern from the president, who tried hard to make the Axis powers believe that the United States might engage in war to defend the democracies. However, he also wanted to make sure that an American response to war would not be taken for granted. This was a delicate line intended to make the Germans and Japanese believe that they could provoke the United States to war and therefore not to play fast and loose with American interests while at the same time to convince the democracies they had to defend their own rights if they wished America to stand with them. President Roosevelt did not want the British and French to be too certain of U.S. aid lest they act recklessly. The American plan emerged clearly in a State Department briefing to the president in preparation for a major foreign policy address he would deliver at Queens University in Ontario, Canada. Adolf A. Berle noted for the president's attention:

> The German Army is now partly mobilized and maneuvering in Bavaria within striking distance of the Czech frontier. We have to allow for the possibility that things may be on the way to a blow-up. . . . The theory of the speech is an endeavor to create a certain amount of doubt abroad as to what our intentions may be. This, it is thought, may have a moderating effect.[58]

One reason Roosevelt placed more hope on some sort of American-Soviet cooperation was his loss of confidence in the British and French to defend the peace. Chamberlain's duplicity alarmed the president and sent him scurrying for information and alternatives that might block the Nazis. Ambassadors Kennedy and Bullitt both cabled FDR in late August, relating communications between Chamberlain and the French and between Chamberlain and the American ambassador in London. On August 31 Bullitt reported a conversation with Georges Bonnet of the preceding evening, in which the French premier announced that the British had instructed their ambassador in Berlin to inform the German government that, if German troops crossed the Czech frontier and France chose to go to war against Germany, "England would go to war on the side of France."[59] On the same date, Kennedy reported that Chamberlain opposed the group in the British cabinet,

---

[58]Berle to FDR, August 15, 1938, PSF, No. II, Departmental Files, State Department File, Adolf A. Berle Folder.

[59]Bullitt to Hull, August 31, 1938, PSF, France; Schewe, *Roosevelt and Foreign Affairs*, 11:118.

who wished to declare war if Hitler marched into Czechoslovakia, and
would not go to war unless forced to, no matter what the French did.
Berle attached a note to the memorandum, informing FDR of Kennedy's report and stressing the discrepancy between the Bullitt and
Kennedy cables. Berle surmised that either Chamberlain was lying or
trying to bluff the Germans.[60]

Roosevelt was furious and expressed his suspicions of Chamberlain's motives to Morgenthau on September 1. He thought that either
Chamberlain was not telling the truth or that the press had distorted
the prime minister's position. However, he also thought it possible that
Chamberlain told one story to the Germans and the French and another
to the Americans. "It is a nice kettle of fish," Roosevelt remarked.[61]
As he continued to talk, FDR became more irate. He told Morgenthau
that the British prime minister was slippery, he could not be trusted
under any circumstances, and he was playing the usual British game—
peace at any price. Roosevelt thought that when the drama was played
out Chamberlain would attempt to place the blame on the United
States for either fighting or not fighting; therefore, if Britain went to
war it was because they had support from the Americans, or if they
did not fight it would be because the Americans would not support
them. The president fumed that Chamberlain "was interested in peace
at any price if he could get away with it and save his face."[62]

Roosevelt believed that the only thing he could do was to appeal
to the involved parties to sit back and consider the consequences of
their action. On September 26 he urged continued negotiations on the
Czech crisis and asserted that the fate of civilization hung in the balance. He sent this message directly to the German chancellor, the
president of Czechoslovakia, and through the Department of State to
the British and French prime ministers.[63] The president followed his
initiative the next day with a message appealing to Hitler and an identic
one to Mussolini.[64] The dictators treated Roosevelt's appeal with
contempt.

The German and Italian leaders may not have taken Roosevelt's
request seriously, but the Soviets did. *Izvestiia* reported Bernard Baruch's declaration to the press that, in the face of possible aggression
by Germany, Japan, and Italy, the United States had to extend its
armaments program. He mentioned FDR's favorite illustration of the

---

[60]Berle to FDR, August 31, 1938, PSF, State Department File, Berle Folder; Schewe, *Roosevelt and Foreign Affairs*, 11:121.

[61]Morgenthau Papers, Diary, Book 138, September 1, 1938, p. 20.

[62]Ibid., p. 34.

[63]*Press Releases*, October 1, 1938, pp. 219–20.

[64]Ibid., p. 224; *Peace and War*, p. 427.

threat of aggressors through Latin America, which the Russians thought indicative of American awareness of the Nazi threat. Baruch urged America to respond to Axis aggression by spending several billions of dollars immediately for defense plus establishing closer relations with South America. According to *Izvestiia*, America was serious in its intent to confront aggression through energetic steps to fulfill orders for new weapons for U.S. arsenals by the summer of 1939.[65]

All sorts of conjectures reached the Department of State and Roosevelt about Soviet policy, in the face of the discussions at Munich. The consensus was that the Russians were left out of the talks and were feeling threatened as a result, and certainly they did not trust the British to arrive at any agreement that would be satisfactory to them. Early in the year Litvinov had expressed his concern over Nazi plans for Eastern and Central Europe and had tried to get the British committed to "a grand alliance," which he deemed a necessity after the *Anschluss* because he foresaw a march on Czechoslovakia as Hitler's next move.[66]

In September Colonel Faymonville sent a G-2 report from Moscow, in which he suggested that the Russians were prepared, under the provisions of the Soviet-Czechoslovak Treaty of Alliance, to act if the Germans attacked the Czechs. The Soviets were inclined to live up to the terms of the treaty, most particularly if France did, but would wish to act in any case. However, Soviet military leaders were "openly critical of British policy and appear to believe that the Runciman mission is endeavoring to bring about a state of affairs under which the Sudeten provinces will be detached from the territory of the Czechoslovak Republic." What the Romanians and the Poles decided to do would determine how the Russians would try to meet commitments of land forces. They might send air support and assume naval operations against the Germans, but "a general European War such as would be precipitated by a German attack on Czechoslovakia would find the Soviet Government in a mood to conserve its own military forces to the greatest possible extent."[67]

Whether or not the Russians would have acted if Britain and France had upheld their commitments to the Czechs remains a subject of heated debate. In fact, they might have done so in order not to be left out of any territorial settlement that would emerge if the Allied

---

[65]"Washington Worried by Fascist Aggression: Grandiose Program of New Armaments in the USA," *Izvestiia*, October 18, 1938.

[66]*FRUS: Diplomatic Papers*, vol. 1, *General, 1938* (Washington, DC: Government Printing Office, 1954), p. 447.

[67]G-2 Report 3800, September 15, 1938, 6-1, 2657-D 1/5, EE 104, War Department Records, DSF, National Archives, Federal Records Center, Suitland, Maryland.

forces were victorious. It was logical for the Russians to want to participate because they feared British intentions under the Chamberlain
leadership, which they thought aimed at isolating the Russians, a task
that would prove more difficult if the Soviets carried out their commitments to an alliance. The failure of British and French policymakers
left them with other concerns, as a report from Faymonville at the end
of the year indicated. The military attaché had been asked on August 30
to assess what the Soviets thought Japan would do in light of the current
crisis. He responded that the Russian leaders were aware that Japan
was completely in control of the military, which was determined to
"extend and retain its conquests in China and to strengthen Japan for
an eventual attack against the Soviet Union." The assault might come
for any of several reasons, including Japan being urged by its German
or Italian allies "to create a diversion against the Soviet Union in the
Far East while an attack on the western boundaries of the Soviet Union
is launched." Given this assumption by the Soviet leadership, there
was absolutely no way they would commit to Czechoslovakia alone,
no matter how badly they might wish to do so.[68] Whatever happened
in Europe was now in the hands of the British and French leaders, as
the Americans and Russians watched and waited with a sense of fore-
boding and not a little contempt for the Anglo-French leadership.

IV

Deterioration of Soviet security plans, and the drastic slide toward war
on Russia's eastern and western borders, helped to dictate its approach
to the Americans in 1938. Russian security measures, subject as they
were to constant shifts and alterations in line with the changing world
situation, noticeably showed nothing but friendly gestures toward the
United States. As the Soviets prepared for the possibility of withdrawal
and isolation, they identified potential enemies by singling them out
for attack by closing their embassies and other such hostile moves.
Molotov charged, in a speech of January 19, that certain foreign consuls
engaged in illegitimate espionage and sabotage activities, thus those of
Poland, Germany, Japan, Italy, Iran, and Turkey were restricted; the
United States was a noteworthy exception.[69]

Russia wished to promote an alliance between the supporters of
the peace. Troianovskii gave public notice of this intent in a speech at
the University of North Carolina, announcing that the threat to world
peace was a real and present danger and "the only way out of this

---

[68]G-2 Report 3850, November 21, 1938, 6-1 2657-D 1/7, EE 107, ibid.
[69]Degras, *Soviet Documents*, 3:151.

danger . . . is for Great Britain, the United States, and the Soviet Union to form an alliance." The problem, he said, was "no nation wants to lead the way; they think they may precipitate a war and so they want to pass the buck."[70]

Russian spokesmen bent over backward to convince America that cooperation in defense of the peace was in its best interests. Ambassador Troianovskii told the City Club in New York that his country was being placed on record as backing democratic nations, desiring continuance of their democratic forms of government, and urging "the democracies—including Russia, which he said was a government of Socialist-democracy and not communism—to present a united front against fascist peace breakers."[71] Obviously Troianovskii had been assigned the task of working on public and private opinion in the United States, as he delivered speech after speech pointing up the threat to security posed by the Nazi and Japanese aggressors.

Russian news writers continued to tout Cordell Hull as a realist promoter of an alliance for peace. When Hull came to the defense of a sane policy, *Izvestiia* gave him full credit as it quoted the secretary of state: "Cooperation is common sense. We must take into consideration the strength of other peace-loving nations and aim our strength to supplement theirs, as does every other country, or else the aggressors will be aided."[72] In June *Pravda* reported a major address by Hull to the American Bar Association in Tennessee, in which he joined Roosevelt's criticism of isolationism. To the Russians, the speech was important because it reflected the official U.S. position. They thought American officials were "taking into account the lessons of the first World War" and had become convinced "that the United States has no hope of not being involved in [another war] no matter where." What *Pravda* found most promising was a new mood among the American public which was shifting to support a policy aimed at "joint cooperation and opposition to aggression."[73]

Pravda thought it was significant that Congress was about to review the whole problem of American foreign policy, including the neutrality law. In line with this more aggressive policy, "The State Department intends in the near future to conduct a campaign, by mobilization of public opinion, in favor of the foreign policy of the government."[74] The Russians became even more excited about America's new and forceful stance when Roosevelt attacked "the Fascist

[70]*New York Times*, February 9, 1938.
[71]Ibid., February 27, 1938.
[72]"The Foreign Policy of the United States," *Izvestiia*, February 14, 1938.
[73]"On International Themes—The Speech by Hull," *Pravda*, June 5, 1938.
[74]"The Foreign Policy of the USA," ibid., June 22, 1938.

barbarians" in a speech to the National Education Association on
June 30. Although several countries might attempt to turn back the
progress of civilization, Roosevelt said, the United States would act to
preserve it.[75]

Litvinov tried to tell the democracies that facts had to be faced;
they had no choice but to join the Russians in opposing the aggressors.
The Soviet Union had two choices because it had armed and announced
a firm policy of resistance as soon as designs on its territory had become
obvious, whereas Western states, in failing to prepare, were bereft of
alternatives. Russia could cooperate with the democracies in the preservation of the peace, or it could make deals with other powers and
let the rest of the states fight it out. As Litvinov warned the democracies,
"Whatever deals the capitalist States may enter into among themselves . . . the aggressors will always seek new prey in those territories
whose masters have shown their flabbiness and their inability to defend
their positions."[76] It remained unstated that in doing this the aggressors
would have to secure themselves from attack by the Soviets; yet, the
threat of such a possibility was implicit. The time had come for the
Western states to decide whether they feared the threat of communism
by infiltration more than they feared the threat of fascism by force.[77]

Litvinov's speech proved to be a calculated warning that the time
had really come, in Roosevelt's words, "to fish or cut bait." After
Munich, when the Soviets considered themselves to be the object of
British disaffection, the warning became even more explicit when Litvinov told French Ambassador Robert Coulondre that Russia would
withdraw behind its frontiers, watching Germany grow fat on the rest
of Europe. When the Continent was subdued, whom would Hitler turn
on—militarily prepared Russia or weak foundering England? The
answer, Litvinov thought, was England, and then it would have to beg
for Soviet favors. In effect, he told Coulondre that the Western democracies had helped make Russia a power with which to be reckoned.[78]
Litvinov also tried to disabuse them of the idea that America might
save them by an intervention that would make a deal with the Soviets
unnecessary. The United States, he said, was too isolationist for anyone
to rely on its cooperation unless "in Europe itself there is . . . formed
before hand a firmly welded group opposing aggression with an appre-
ciable chance of success."[79]

---

[75]"Roosevelt Against Fascist Barbarians," *Izvestiia*, July 2, 1938.
[76]Degras, *Soviet Documents*, 3:293.
[77]Ibid., p. 292.
[78]Robert Coulondre, *De Staline à Hitler* (Paris: Hachette, 1950), p. 171.
[79]Degras, *Soviet Documents*, 3:290.

Litvinov clearly stated his fear concerning the course of events to Davies, which the ambassador then forwarded to the secretary of state. Davies wrote that Litvinov was sure that a Fascist peace was being imposed on Europe, except for England and Russia. The latter could not count on outside aid and had to continue its own self-sufficiency. He concluded that only a new government in England could save the day.[80]

In view of growing Soviet pessimism, Roosevelt and Hull came to believe that cooperation with the Russians was necessary to prevent them from joining the enemy camp. Certainly the president and Hull thought that at a future date, when the crisis grew more severe, Russia and America might need one another. A dispatch from Moscow stressed that Munich had isolated the Soviets, and, in lieu of European allies, they sought closer ties with the United States, as the writers of the communiqué believed was indicated in an *Izvestiia* article called "The Two Giants" and one from *Krasnaia-Zvesda* entitled "Soviet-American Relations."[81]

The embassy personnel thought the United States had the Soviets in a position to take advantage of their eagerness in order "to bring about a profitable settlement of outstanding matters of which the solution has been delayed owing to difficulties either actual or assumed which the Soviet Government has adduced in the course of past negotiations." This reference was primarily to debts and propaganda, which reflected the basic concern of the embassy and its disinclination to take seriously the prospect of real cooperation with the Soviets in the interests of security; the embassy staff had not been apprised of the attempt to deal with this question earlier in the year. It was their understanding that Secretary Hull considered cooperation as constituting "genuine friendship." They therefore notified him that it should be stressed that no statement could be found in the articles, which they had forwarded to the State Department from the Soviet press, that they thought indicated a real desire for friendship, as Hull understood it, on the part of the Kremlin. The personnel concluded that "it may be assumed that the Kremlin does not envisage cordial relations with the capitalist governments on any permanent basis but rather as a temporary expedient dictated by the more immediate objectives of Soviet policy."[82]

One of the articles referred to in the embassy dispatch illustrated indeed a most "friendly" disposition toward the United States. The Soviets made no effort to hide their conviction that their concept of

---

[80]*FRUS: Soviet Union*, p. 544.
[81]Ibid., p. 593.
[82]Ibid., pp. 593–94.

friendship was based on mutual self-interest and expediency. Alex Sandrov, writing in *Izvestiia*, identified the Soviet perception of mutual needs and benefits:

> The Munich policy . . . has placed new problems before even the most powerful capitalist state which took no part in the Munich agreement, namely the United States of America. The leaders of American policy . . . have long been aware of the real significance of events in question [in Europe and Asia] and are able to evaluate and characterize with calmness and strength the state of affairs which has arisen.[83]

Sandrov visualized a group of realists in charge of American policy; therefore, it was easy to imagine that, even before the crisis of September 1938, Roosevelt, Hull, Ickes, Welles, and others who opposed the "lying campaign of the isolationists" had indicated clearly that they knew peace was indivisible and that the safety of the United States depended on the security of other states. This meant there would have to be a break in the isolationist tradition, for the United States in no way could remain indifferent in the face of outright violations of their interests, especially from Japan, and American statesmen "often proclaimed the necessity of collective action in repelling aggression."[84] That no action followed strong statements, such as the "quarantine" speech, Sandrov attributed to the struggle to overcome isolationism and to the attitude of Great Britain.

By the time Sandrov's article appeared, the Soviets had gone into virtual isolation. They had abandoned hope of getting any effective assistance from France, and it seemed obvious to them that Great Britain was trying desperately to salvage peace at Russia's expense. Russia then turned in a last effort toward rapprochement with the United States, the one nation it believed it had the most in common and the least possibility of imminent conflict. Sandrov pointed out, in fact, that the two nations had similar vital interests that were being threatened by aggressors in both Europe and the Far East, and he thought the time had come when the United States had to choose a course for the future:

> Both countries can yet meet [on the road to the active defense of peace] and that would have the most salutary influence on the international situation. At this time we should remember the words

---

[83]Alex Sandrov, "The Two Giants," *Izvestiia*, November 16, 1938.
[84]Ibid.

of Litvinov in his speech at the banquet in New York on November 24, 1933, 'who can doubt but that the united voices of the two giants will compel themselves to be taken into consideration, and that their joint efforts will weight the scales to the benefit of peace.'[85]

The two giants, however, were separated by a wide gulf. Many Americans, including some who made foreign policy, imagined that in part U.S. isolation from Russia was ideological. The Soviets were told repeatedly that a fear of public opinion made the Americans skittish, and this they found hard to comprehend. They believed that, if the Roosevelt administration really desired, it could seize the leadership of public opinion and turn it in the direction of collective action. When apparently FDR's preparedness campaign was occurring, via speeches of Ickes and others who sounded the alarm against Germany, the Russians assumed that a "new cooperative policy" would follow, especially when they were encouraged to believe that President Roosevelt and Secretary Hull both wanted this. *Izvestiia* stressed this new Roosevelt foreign policy that sought accommodation with the foes of aggression.[86]

What the Russians did not know was that the United States had no policy but merely an attitude. It felt endangered and at first recoiled. When the threat did not dissolve, President Roosevelt rushed forward to do verbal battle without being sure of the locus of the battlefield or the exact nature of the weapons. Both giants considered themselves to be isolated, but, by the end of 1938, there was perhaps more justification for this feeling in Russia than in the United States. In later years Soviet historians looked back on the events of 1938, searching for some foundation for American policy and concluded, like the American revisionists, that the government could not have been so incredibly blind to U.S. interests. They therefore believed that there was some Machiavellian master plot aimed at embroiling Russia in a destructive war with Germany. Only after the failure of this policy did the United States attempt rapprochement with Russia to defeat the Nazis.[87] The Russians could not believe that the Americans were still feeling their way in the treacherous seas of diplomacy, with more attention focused on the rocky shoals of congressional isolationist obstruction than on

---

[85]Ibid.

[86]"New Facts in the Strategy of the USA," *Izvestiia*, December 4, 1938.

[87]This thesis is fully developed in the Soviet historical journal. See U. V. Arootunian, "The Role of American Diplomacy in the Organization of the Munich Conference," *Voprosi Istorii*, no. 2 (February 1958): 76–95.

the storm centers about to erupt in Europe and Asia. President Roosevelt knew the explosion was imminent and life threatening but could not make up his mind about which lifeboat could provide the best security in the forthcoming tempest as he scurried from one to another testing their timbers.

VII

The End of Innocence

FRANKLIN ROOSEVELT began his annual address to Congress on January 4, 1939 much as he had the preceding three years, but there was a note of increased determination and urgency to his message:

> We have learned that God-fearing democracies of the world which observe the sanctity of treaties and good faith in their dealings with other nations cannot safely be indifferent to international lawlessness anywhere. They cannot forever let pass, without effective protest, acts of aggression against sister nations—acts which automatically undermine all of us.[1]

The threatened governments would have agreed, except perhaps for a mild protest from the Soviets over the term "God-fearing." There was, however, a wide variance of opinions on what constituted "effective protest." Neville Chamberlain wanted it to mean American willingness to follow England's lead, although he did not expect for a moment that such a thing would happen. French officials would have been satisfied with a declaration that America had to defend vital interests that required maintenance of the European status quo. They were slightly more hopeful of this than the English, at least in part because, without U.S. support, their prospects for confronting a Nazi onslaught were slim to none. The Russians counted with less realism than the Paris government on the Americans providing them with more than a declaration. Soviet leaders believed that an alliance was still possible with the United States incorporating the principle of collective security for the Far East, if not elsewhere. Roosevelt's approach to Russia in 1938 led the Soviets

---

[1]Samuel I. Rosenman, ed., *The Public Papers and Addresses of Franklin D. Roosevelt*, vol. 8, *War and Neutrality, 1939* (New York: Macmillan, 1941), p. 3.

to believe once again that, when he spoke of effective protests, he was too realistic not to deal finally with them with more than words in the name of collective security.

At first, *Izvestiia* responded cautiously to Roosevelt's message.[2] However, after the American press had vociferously proclaimed FDR's message as an indication of a great departure in foreign relations, the Russians quoted American newspapers liberally. *Izvestiia* noted that the U.S. press considered Roosevelt's address a "definite warning to the fascist aggressors," and that it might include economic sanctions.[3] British and French reactions were also liberally quoted. The London *Times* applauded the broad support in America for the president's message, while the French press similarly foresaw Roosevelt acting directly against the aggressors. Presumably Roosevelt signaled a new firmness intended to provide "strong support for the opponents of Munich."[4] On January 8 the Russians quoted the *New York Daily Worker*, which assessed Roosevelt's speech as a sharp challenge to international and internal reactionaries. The American Communist paper claimed that the president's opponents were disturbed by his anti-Fascist attack because public opinion supported him and made his position even more secure.[5]

In general, the Soviet press accurately reported the American reaction to Roosevelt's speech. Letters and telegrams to the White House predominantly applauded FDR's firmness in the face of the aggressors. As a spokesman for the American League for Peace and Democracy, Edwin S. Smith of the National Labor Relations Board wrote:

> [It] . . . was the high-water mark of your thinking and expression in regard to the ultimate issues which confront the country. Your emphasis on the fact that frustration of aggression abroad and preservation of democracy at home are component parts of an indivisible program seemed to me of the utmost importance. I hope you will find many occasions to drive this idea home.[6]

Smith asked the president to address the membership of his organization with a message that would reach millions of people who belonged to "the most realistic peace group in America," one that stood for the principle that the time had come to take "a firm stand against the

---

[2]"Message of Roosevelt to Congress," *Izvestiia*, January 5, 1939.
[3]"Reactions to the Message of Roosevelt," ibid., January 6, 1939.
[4]Ibid.
[5]"Reactions to Address by Roosevelt," ibid., January 8, 1939.
[6]Smith to FDR, January 5, 1939, PPF 3541, American League for Peace and Democracy Folder.

aggressors." He contended that his organization would back Roosevelt in refusing to sell arms to aggressors while supplying the victims.[7]

President Roosevelt was taken by the idea and asked a secretary to request the Department of State to submit a draft of a message (roughly along the lines of Smith's suggestion), which FDR could send to the Congress of the American League for Peace and Democracy. The department, however, thought that the president had said all there was to say in his address to Congress. Sumner Welles responded that it might be pressing Roosevelt's luck to ask for specific measures against aggressors while the administration was still trying to get support for adequate defense.[8] Welles thought that the post-"quarantine" speech position was still in effect and that the United States had an attitude and was still searching for a program.

Those who wrote to the president, opposing preparedness and interference, frequently became irrational about it. Most who supported him did so almost with a note of resignation. The editors of *The United States in World Affairs* evaluated reactions to Roosevelt's attack on the aggressors and judged that his suggestions received a cordial reception, despite the fact that "in this latest message Mr. Roosevelt definitely aligned the country on the side of one group of nations with an intimation that they might count on something more than moral support."[9]

Roosevelt proved this conjecture concerning his intent when he met with the Senate Military Affairs Committee on January 31. He reminded them that during the Napoleonic Wars the United States had tried to avoid the conflict by strangling itself with restrictive legislation, but it had not worked; instead, it ultimately led America to war with Great Britain. The president made a candid admission to the senators that the United States was again jeopardized by aggressors. He brought it close to home by using his illustration of the designs Europeans had on Latin America back in the early nineteenth century, designs that were once again being contemplated by antidemocratic forces in the world, and, if Latin America were threatened, the United States would be involved. Roosevelt told the members of the committee that he had a reason for giving them a history lesson:

> Mind you, this must be confidential because I know the rule of
> every President is that if you tell more than two Senators it gets

---

[7]Ibid.

[8]Memorandum, FDR to State Department, January 5, 1939 and response, Welles to FDR, PPF 3541.

[9]Whitney H. Shepardson and William O. Scroggs, eds., *The United States in World Affairs: An Account of American Foreign Relations, 1939* (New York: Harper, 1940), pp. 6–7.

out. Try to keep it as confidential as you can. . . . I don't think
we want to frighten the American people. That is one thing we
don't want to do . . . at this or any time. We want them to gradually
realize what is a potential danger.

Well about three years ago, we got the pretty definite information that there was in the making a policy of world domination
between Germany, Italy and Japan. That was when the first anti-
Comintern Pact was signed. . . . There exists today, without any
question whatsoever—if I were asked to prove it I could not prove
it, of course—what amounts to an offensive and defensive alliance.[10]

President Roosevelt said there were two ways one could approach
the danger. Americans might hope someone would assassinate the leaders or that they would fall from internal upheaval, which is what the
European victims of Napoleon's aggression waited for to their own ill
fortune. The other alternative was to defend oneself by helping the
potential victims of aggression. If the senators entertained the notion
that Hitler could be diverted by appeasement, Roosevelt tried to turn
the idea aside. Hitler was not merely crazy but thought of himself as
a reincarnation of Julius Caesar and Jesus Christ, and the world was
at his mercy because of his power, unless his victims did something
about him. The Americas were threatened because, after the domination of Europe, the Western Hemisphere was a logical and inevitable
next step for the aggressors. FDR reminded the senators that Hitler
had said as much in his speech of January 30. To the president, the
scenario would be clear:

Hitler would dominate Europe and would say to . . . the Argen-
tines, 'Awfully sorry, but we won't buy your wheat, meat or corn
unless you sign this paper.' And the paper that the Argentine is
asked to sign says, 'Number one, we will take your corn and pay
for it in our goods and we will pay for your cattle in our goods
and we will pay for your wheat in our goods. Then, next, you have
got to turn over all your military defenses and training to our
officers. Oh, yes, you can keep the flag.'[11]

One by one Roosevelt ticked off the Latin American republics—
Brazil, Venezuela, Colombia—to which these pressures would be
applied. He pointed out the distance by bomber from Colombia to the
Panama Canal. Germany's 1,500 bombers could strike from there to
other vital targets, while the United States had about 80 planes with

---

[10]Conference with the Senate Military Affairs Committee in the White House, January 31, 1939, PPF 1; Schewe, *Roosevelt and Foreign Affairs*, 13:197–223.
    [11]Ibid.

equivalent range. "Those are things you ought to regard. How far is it from Yucatan to New Orleans or Houston? How far from Tampico to St. Louis or Kansas City? How far?" He advised the committee not to think that this was chimerical. After all, how many of them would have said six years earlier that Hitler would be where he was in Europe and in a position to dominate the Continent. Thus the lesson of security, its relationship to Roosevelt's expanded defense budget, and the sale of aircraft was brought even closer to home.[12]

President Roosevelt's assertion proved correct that, if he told more than two senators anything, it was not a secret. But from the president's perspective, leaks concerning his blunt talks with the Military Affairs Committee created positive results. After the information he had fed to the senators became public knowledge, a Gallup survey asked: "If Germany and Italy go to war against England and France, do you think we should do everything possible to help England and France win, except go to war ourselves?" Sixty-nine percent thought all aid should be provided, compared to 31 percent against.[13]

On April 20 Roosevelt held his yearly session with the American Society of Newspaper Editors, warning them that the situation was serious; the best odds were even that war would come and that the aggressors would win. He said he had been held over the coals and called an alarmist because he had spoken the truth. "I do not think it fair," he continued, "to give this country . . . the impression that everything is all quiet in Europe when it isn't." This was Roosevelt's master performance with the media directors. He knew that time was running short in confronting a growing totalitarian aggression, and he decided to be as frank as political expediency would allow. He used his illustration of a European continent in the control of Hitler by giving the editors a geography lesson, which he claimed most Americans needed. Then he gave them a history lesson, using more graphic illustrations of what would have happened to the United States if Napoleon had won his wars in Europe. Gradually the president worked his way toward the dire threat to Latin America of a Nazi-controlled Europe and the economic pressure that could be put on all the Latin nations whose livelihood depended on selling to Europe. When Roosevelt got to Mexico, he pointed out how many German planes there were compared to those in the New World, their range, accessibility to Mexican bases, and the threat they would bring to New Orleans and Kansas. He said the odds in favor of war and an Axis victory did not even count Japan

---

[12]Ibid.

[13]Henry Morgenthau, Jr., to FDR, February 22, 1939, OF 200; Schewe, *Roosevelt and Foreign Affairs*, 13:355.

in the equation and reminded the editors of the growing Japanese interest in Latin America, particularly in Mexico.

Roosevelt parried questions that tried to lead him to say that the United States would inevitably be involved if there should be a war in which America helped the European opponents of the dictators. His telling argument was that it would make no difference because Hitler would place a Chinese wall around the United States, whether the country aided the victims of aggression or not. If he did not scare the editors, he forced them to face certain realities that he had come to confront. Whatever the United States could do to keep the war from the Western Hemisphere and to prevent the collapse of the foes of the Axis was mandatory, or America would be the ultimate isolated victim.[14]

In the midst of his campaign to arouse the editors, Roosevelt continued to educate the working press who attended his regular press conferences. After his return from the fleet maneuvers in early April, he told the press he would be back in Warm Springs, Georgia, in the spring "if we don't have a war." The use of the collective pronoun in the statement received considerable editorial attention, and he advised the reporters that they should read a story appearing in the *Washington Post.* The editorial asserted that none knew better than the president that "his office makes his most casual public observations subject to interpretation as a matter of national policy."[15] It also set the stage for the president's calculated development of a foreign policy initiative and then observed: "To those who would protect themselves by closing their eyes the President addressed his warning." Explicitly, Roosevelt wanted the public to know that a war in Europe would vitally affect the United States because it would endanger American security. "By 'we' he undoubtedly meant western civilization," the editorial stated. In this, there was special significance because, in addition to stimulating national thinking, the message emphasized that until a world war actually started it was not inevitable:

> In using the collective 'we' the President told Hitler and Mus-
> solini, far more impressively than he told Warm Springs, that the
> tremendous force of the United States must be a factor in their
> current thinking. He told the Axis powers . . . that a war forced
> by them would from the outset involve the destinies of a nation
> which, as they fully realize, is potentially far stronger than Ger-
> many and Italy united.

[14]Press Conferences, 13, No. 540-A, American Society of Newspaper Editors, in the State Dining Room of the White House, April 20, 1939, pp. 284–324.
[15]Ibid., No. 538, April 11, 1939, pp. 267–68.

To make that plain at this crucial time is to help in preventing war.[16]

By calling the reporters' attention to the *Post* editorial, FDR affirmed its conclusions. *Current History* called the editorial "historic" because of the emphasis the president had given it as an expression of his own policy, plus the effect that his endorsement could have on events in Europe.[17] Certainly Roosevelt wanted the aggressors to believe that they would face America in any further attack. He sent a request to Hitler that, in the interest of peace, Germany would guarantee not to attack the thirty-one nations named in the message. "In making this statement," he said, "we as Americans speak not through selfishness or fear or weakness. If we speak now it is with the voice of strength and with friendship for mankind. It is still clear to me that international problems can be solved at the council table."[18]

The chargé of the German embassy in Washington reported that the message to Hitler was the result of the failure of the Anglo-French alliance policy. In other words, it was born of desperation;[19] it was hardly likely to convince Hitler that there was any need to pay much attention to Roosevelt's appeal. Hitler's response was a planned embarrassment to the president. Joachim von Ribbentrop, the Reich's foreign minister, sent a circular note to the German embassies in most of the thirty-one nations mentioned in Roosevelt's message, asking for an official notice from their governments as to whether they felt threatened by Germany. Hitler was sure they would say no, but, in order not to have his ploy backfire, the note specifically excluded Britain, France, "and their satellites," Poland, and Russia.[20]

II

As Roosevelt worked to create an awareness of the danger to American security and the need to do something about it, he tried to clear away the impediments to his program to defend the country and aid the victims of aggression. Existing neutrality legislation posed one of his major blocks to an outgoing plan to aid the democracies and their friends. The administration's ability to make drastic alterations, or to eliminate the law altogether, proved a test of executive authority in

---

[16]Ibid., p. 268.

[17]"A Newspaper Editorial Which May Be Historic," *Current History* 50 (May 1939): 47–48.

[18]Rosenman, *War and Neutrality, 1939*, p. 203.

[19]Public Record Office, *Documents on German Foreign Policy, 1918–1945*, series D, vol. 6: *The Last Months of Peace, March–August 1939* (London: Her Majesty's Stationery Office, 1956), p. 245.

[20]Ibid., pp. 264–65.

the control of foreign affairs, which was carefully watched from abroad and especially from the Soviet Union. When the president told a press conference that the war referendum concept was a serious threat to American security and that the neutrality laws had injured the cause of world peace,[21] his remarks appeared in *Izvestiia* two days later.[22]

A *Pravda* correspondent interviewed Senator Elbert D. Thomas of Utah, trying to find out the chances for a more forceful policy anchored on legislation that the senator was sponsoring. Thomas said that his bill, which was supported by the administration, would give the president the right to name aggressors when they began a war that violated a treaty with the United States. This would enable Roosevelt to be legally authorized to sell weapons and supplies to the victims and forbid sales to aggressors. Thomas also declared isolation at an end because of the awareness of public opinion in the United States and the changes in the world situation. The interviewer wanted to know if America would be able to join other nations in opposing aggressors, and Thomas responded that it was necessary to work out a program to eliminate war, renew confidence in international law, and seek friendship with other states. Although the United States had to remain on the sidelines, nothing should prevent the public from expressing its attitude toward any immoral international act. "And in practice?" the Russian journalist asked. Thomas thought public opinion was more unified than ever and would support the sale of planes and ammunition to democratic countries. He concluded that collective security in the Western Hemisphere would be a reality.[23] The Russian approved the new public awareness but not collective security centered only in the New World.

Numerous witnesses before the Senate Foreign Relations Committee supported attempts to crack the neutrality law. They testified that the law was injurious not only to American security but also to the general peace of the world. Henry L. Stimson told Key Pittman that he sincerely hoped the senator would "be able to accomplish something in the Congress which will at least strike the shackles off the foreign policy of the American government should war break out."[24] In April a document prepared for the president on the procedure to be followed in the event of a European war recommended that "the first priority before anything effective could be done was to amend

---

[21] Press Conferences, 13, No. 528, March 7, 1939, pp. 173ff.

[22] "Statement by Roosevelt," *Izvestiia*, March 9, 1939.

[23] "The Foreign Policy of the USA—Conversation with Senator Thomas," *Pravda*, March 22, 1939.

[24] Stimson to Pittman, April 25, 1939, Committee Papers, SEN 76S-F9 (141), Neutrality Hearings Folder.

drastically the neutrality law in favor of aiding the democracies."[25] In the same vein, William Bullitt recommended on May 19 that, if the Germans moved against Great Britain and France, American supplies should be made available immediately. He thought that "Ribbentrop and others who desire war are arguing that the Neutrality Act will not be changed, that supplies to France and England from the United States will be cut off, and that Germany, therefore, may risk war with impunity."[26]

During his press conference of July 4, FDR fretted over the delay in changing the neutrality legislation.[27] *Izvestiia* reprinted the president's attack, emphasizing his comments that revision could help to prevent war. The Russians thought it significant that even Republican newspapers were vilifying the isolationists and favoring reexamination of the neutrality law in order to grant Roosevelt more leeway in foreign policy.[28] The Soviets thought that America's usefulness in the developing war hinged on whether the president could assume leadership at home. This would determine whether the United States would be a force in the delay or outcome of war, a matter that came into sharp focus on July 18 at a meeting between Roosevelt's people and the Senate Foreign Relations Committee. The press had been saying for some time that there was an important struggle going on between the executive and legislative branches for control of foreign policy and that Congress was acting as a deterrent to an active program by the White House to avoid war. If the president could break the congressional stranglehold, he could more forcefully oppose the aggressors. The Russians were told repeatedly by Ambassador Davies that Roosevelt was a man of action who could be counted on to view events realistically in Europe and the Far East. If Roosevelt won the contest, the Russians believed America might really tie itself to a European defense commitment. When the showdown came with the Foreign Relations Committee, FDR addressed the assembled group with the dramatic charge, "Our decision may well affect not only the people of our own country, but also the people of the world. . . . I've fired my last shot. I think I ought to have another round in my belt."[29]

Senator William Borah accused the president of overdramatizing the situation and assured the assemblage that there would be no war

---

[25]Undated, unsigned memorandum for the president, "In the Event of a European War," PSF, Neutrality, Box 33,

[26]Memorandum, Bullitt to FDR, May 19, 1939, PSF, Neutrality, Box 33.

[27]Press Conferences, 14, No. 560, July 4, 1939, pp. 3ff.

[28]"The Struggle Over the Neutrality Law—Statement by Roosevelt," *Izvestiia*, July 6, 1939.

[29]Langer and Gleason, *Challenge to Isolation*, p. 143.

in Europe in the near future. He opposed any alteration of the existing neutrality legislation, at least at the time. Roosevelt asked Hull to tell Borah the dire warnings coming from the American embassies. The secretary of state solemnly recounted the bad news: "If Senator Borah could only see some of the cables coming to the State Department about the extremely dangerous outlook in the international situation, I feel satisfied he would modify his views."[30] Borah disagreed; he did not believe his views would be altered at all. A few days later Roosevelt recounted this exchange to the press:

> Senator Borah did intimate rather clearly and definitely that his information, his private information from Europe, was better than the information received by the United States Government. . . . The Secretary of State asked him if he intended that as a suggestion that the State Department information was not as good as his own private information. He finally said that he had meant to infer that.[31]

Vice-President John Nance Garner, according to one version of the meeting, interceded and took a straw vote to see if revision of the neutrality law could receive enough support to get through the current session of Congress. When he tallied the results, he turned to the president and said: "Well Captain, we may as well face the facts. You haven't got the votes, and that's all there is to it."[32] On July 21 Roosevelt announced at his press conference that he had done his best, but the senators had turned him down. He denied emphatically the story about Garner's poll. Richard Harkness asked Roosevelt if the vice-president had said, "Captain, we may as well be candid; you haven't got the votes." If the Langer and Gleason account is accurate, this let Roosevelt off the hook. He could say in all innocence that Garner did not say that, but Roosevelt further stated, in order to place the blame squarely on the Republican isolationists,

> When it became perfectly clear from a statement by the Republican Leader that the Republicans would vote en masse for postponement until January, and then Senator Barkley said there would probably be sufficient Democrats to go along with them to prevent a vote being taken if Congress stayed in session, nobody had to say anything more. That was obvious.[33]

---

[30]Hull, *Memoirs*, 1:650.
[31]Press Conferences, 14, No. 564, July 21, 1939, p. 34.
[32]Langer and Gleason, *Challenge to Isolation*, p. 144.
[33]Press Conferences, 14, No. 564, July 21, 1939, p. 34.

Roosevelt asserted several times that the burden was off his shoulders. Senator Charles L. McNary of Oregon spoke for the committee and assumed responsibility for any miscues that might result from the refusal to act. "In other words," the president said, "they accepted the responsibility of saying to the Executive Branch of the Government, 'There is nothing further you can do to avert war.' "[34]

In this fashion, Roosevelt squarely laid the blame for not further aiding the democracies on the Republicans and isolationists in Congress. A correspondent sent the president a copy of a letter he had written to Borah which accurately analyzed Roosevelt's intent and scored the senator for not supporting FDR's effort: "I do not believe in getting involved in a war but I do believe that a 'poker game' is highly desireable at this time, and I think this is what the President had in mind all along."[35] No doubt with mixed emotions Roosevelt was called away from the game just when it became necessary to play for the highest stakes with the last of his chips.

Izvestiia noted that the struggle was over and Roosevelt had lost. Hull and FDR had staked their case on the argument that the danger of war in Europe was imminent and had tried to alter the neutrality law in the hope of influencing the outcome of events. The Russian newspaper reported that the president and the secretary of state announced that they still believed that failure to review the neutrality law had weakened the U.S. position in international affairs.[36] The Russians soon gave evidence that they agreed.

III

Before the Russians gave up on American support for preserving the peace or confronting the aggressors, they tried one more time to establish a firm coalition against the Axis powers. As this effort developed, the Soviets carefully evaluated Roosevelt's progress in turning aside the isolationist obstructions to American involvement in the external world and attempted to gain concrete commitments from Great Britain and France. In case this plan failed, Stalin also began preparations for an alternative course that would mend the breach with Germany and put pressure on the Japanese to leave Russia alone and concentrate their efforts on other objectives. Stalin's ploy did not go unnoticed by American observers and gave Roosevelt added impetus in his endeavor

---

[34]Ibid., p. 36.

[35]Letter of July 19, 1939, OF 1561, Neutrality.

[36]"Meeting of Roosevelt and Hull with Representatives from the Senate," *Izvestiia*, July 21, 1939.

to become an active force in world affairs. Russian plans for the future were of as much concern to the Americans as vice versa.

At the beginning of 1939, from the Soviets' perspective, collaborative efforts with the United States in defense of the peace seemed promising. New signs of American determination to aid the victims of aggression, although directed toward France, gave hope of something developing between Russia and the United States as a result of the Franco-Soviet alliance. *Izvestiia* reported Roosevelt's meeting with the Senate Military Affairs Committee, in which the president attempted to clear the way for the sale of warplanes to the French. During the last week of January, a U.S. military plane carrying a Frenchman crashed with secret equipment aboard. The Hearst press charged that a covert military alliance existed between the United States and France. At a press conference the president explained that the Frenchman's presence was the result of a legitimate sale of aircraft authorized by Washington.[37] The Russian press eagerly repeated reports from American newspapers about Roosevelt reputedly saying at the meeting with the Senate Military Affairs Committee that America's first line of defense was in Europe and that the United States would provide all possible aid to Great Britain and France to strengthen the democratic countries against the Rome-Berlin-Tokyo Axis.[38]

The campaign of the reactionaries, *Izvestiia* noted, had grown in intensity in the United States, trying to counteract Roosevelt's efforts to arouse public awareness of the threat to peace. Despite this, support was growing for an outgoing American policy to meet the aggressors:

> The number of supporters of Roosevelt's foreign policy is increasing even among Republicans. Thus, for example . . . Mark Sullivan . . . and others formerly critics of Roosevelt, now completely approve of his foreign policy. The Washington *Post* and the . . . Washington *Star* censure the attacks of Hoover on Roosevelt. . . . The correspondent for the *New York Times*, Krock, points out that Roosevelt, regardless of the neutrality law, intends to order aid to England and France against Germany and Italy.[39]

Kremlin leaders wanted all potential friends and enemies alerted to their willingness to fight or make friends. On January 19 chargé d'affaires in Moscow Alexander C. Kirk sent the Department of State part of an editorial that had appeared in *Journal de Moscou*, printed by the Russian government for the edification of the embassy staffs, with

[37]Press Conferences, 14, No. 522, January 31, 1939, pp. 102ff.
[38]"Statement by Roosevelt to Senate Committee," *Izvestiia*, February 2, 1939.
[39]"The Foreign Policy of the USA," ibid., February 8, 1939.

the notation that it did not appear in any of the Russian language papers:

> The uproar which has been raised in the European press around what is called the 'Ukrainian problem' is very significant. It may be noted that in regard to this question certain French and English newspapers are making more noise than even the fascist aggressors themselves. It is not difficult to guess the reason . . . they are suggesting to Hitler to leave Western Europe in peace and to go in search of his prey [to the East].[40]

There was a two-fold message the Russians wished to pass on: first, to the French and British, and whoever might be aligned with them, that the Soviets knew their game and did not believe it would work; and, second, to Germany, asking if they would be so stupid as to attack an armed and prepared Russia determined to resist them when the gate lay open to unquestionably weak France and Britain. There was an implicit invitation to both sides to talk things over.

Kirk suggested to the State Department that the editorial obviously aimed at foreign consumption. The reasons for it, he thought, could be either "to conceal the real concern of the Soviet Government over the possibility of Nazi aggression in the Ukraine," or it might even be "based on reassuring statements which [Litvinov] may have received from Berlin . . . as to Hitler's immediate intent in regard to the Ukrainian question." The chargé concluded that, no matter what the circumstances, the Soviet Union was feeling the pulse of both sides to ascertain the signs of the most life. He believed that at the current stage of development, "whatever its attitude or aims may be, any positive move by the Kremlin in foreign affairs will, it is believed, depend on the development of events abroad."[41] Certainly Kirk's prediction was accurate, and events abroad boded ill for Soviet attempts to promote collective security. America, however, still remained the unknown quantity. Roosevelt, the Russians knew, was fighting for recognition of the threat to American security[42] and rushing to build an effective defense mechanism,[43] but the prospects for success were much in doubt.

It became more and more obvious to American analysts in the State Department that the Russians could go either way in deciding with whom they should side. Kirk wrote Hull on February 22, reporting rumors afloat in Moscow that Litvinov might be removed as commissar

---

[40]*FRUS: Soviet Union*, p. 731.
[41]Ibid., p. 732.
[42]"Roosevelt Worried by Conditions in Europe," *Izvestiia*, February 20, 1939.
[43]"Questions of Defense in the USA," ibid., February 23, 1939.

of Foreign Affairs and assigned to replace Troianovskii as ambassador
to the United States. If such a change occurred, it would seem likely
that collective security, which had been championed by Litvinov, had
been abandoned in favor of a policy of rapprochement with Nazi Germany, to which Litvinov had been strongly opposed.[44]

Shortly after this communication Roosevelt and Hull decided
finally to appoint a replacement for Joseph Davies in Moscow. Laurence
A. Steinhardt's assignment to Russia was announced on March 5 and
was welcomed in the USSR, where the Soviets felt slighted by the
lengthy delay in appointing an ambassador.[45] Steinhardt, however, was
not required to report to his new post until August. If the United States
hoped to influence the Kremlin to divert a Soviet-German rapprochement, the delay was disastrous.

On March 3, 1939, the Soviets tried to establish an unusual
contact with the Americans. Although the purpose was unclear, it no
doubt had to do with Litvinov's final desperate effort to promote collective security. The Soviet ambassador to France requested a "casual"
meeting with William Bullitt, who was aware that there was no such
kind of meeting between a Soviet diplomat and himself. He knew he
was persona non grata in Moscow, and no Russian in his right mind
would contact him socially. Bullitt immediately telegraphed the secretary of state, inquiring if there were any new developments in
American-Soviet relations that he should know about before meeting
the Russian, or if there were any implications in Chamberlain's visit
to the Soviet embassy in London the previous day. Hull responded that
there had been no change in relations with Moscow other than Steinhardt's appointment as ambassador, which had not yet been announced.
He also assured Bullitt that State had no "exact" information as to
Chamberlain's visit.[46] In fact, his visit was in response to Soviet efforts
to move the British to active collaboration, and the Russians no doubt
wished to ensure some degree of U.S. cooperation. The Department
of State knew more than Hull indicated to Bullitt, but the secretary,
with his usual caution, declined to act; the United States was still
playing the role of observer despite Roosevelt's efforts to meet the world
crisis.

Hull received some alarming information concerning possible
changes in Soviet policy which related to the failure of Russian efforts
to move closer to Britain, France, and the United States. Kirk wrote
on March 14, warning of a prospective Soviet-German rapprochement.

---

[44]*FRUS: Soviet Union*, p. 737.
[45]*New York Times*, March 5, 1939.
[46]Bullitt to Hull, March 3, and response of March 4, 1939, DSF 711.61/670.

He reported that members of the German embassy were quite pleased with the tone of Stalin's reference, in a speech of March 10, to international affairs and "have even offered the opinion that there was a possibility that if these remarks were presented in the proper manner and by the proper officials in Berlin to Hitler an amelioration in the political situation between the Soviet Union and Germany might be developed."[47] Another dispatch from Kirk on March 16 advised the State Department that the Russians indicated they thought they had the situation in the Far East well in hand, and the decisive victories of Russian troops the preceding July and August during the Chang-kufeng incident on the Manchurian border illustrated to the Soviets that Japan's aggression could be controlled. Marshal Voroshilov boasted that "the Red Army was prepared at any time to repeat in intensified form this lesson."[48]

On April 6, ten days before Kirk predicted that the Soviets might attempt to mend fences with Germany, he wrote to Hull that the position of quasi-isolation, to which Russia had been relegated during Munich, and the eclipse of the policy of collective security had placed the Russians in a position that made them wait on the initiative of others, except in the case of improving relations with their immediate neighbors. "In the ensuing months," Kirk wrote, "England and France were singled out for special condemnation as wreckers of the policy of collective security," thus signaling a change in orientation:

> [T]he violent campaign which the Soviet press had been carrying on against Germany slackened and symptoms have even been detected of a possible inclination on the part of the Soviet Government to reduce the element of friction in its relations with Germany. Stalin himself in his latest declaration places the blame on others for poisoning Soviet-German relations.[49]

Kirk warned Hull that it was the change in attitude toward Germany that should receive close attention. The Soviet Union, he thought, was primarily interested in self-defense and second in what it could get for itself. Based on these considerations, Stalin's policy would roughly follow a general pattern, which the chargé outlined for Hull. Stalin would await developments abroad and then gauge whether they proved threatening to the USSR. In the meantime, he would avoid any commitments that might restrict his freedom of action or ensnare Russia in a conflict that did not represent its immediate interests:

---

[47]*FRUS: Soviet Union*, pp. 744–45.
[48]Ibid., pp. 745–46.
[49]Ibid., p. 751.

> Even in the presence of commitments he will pursue a realistic
> policy in varying, according to the shifting demands of those inter-
> ests, the manifestation of attitudes toward foreign countries. . . .
> Finally, in the face of a menace that seems imminent, he will
> endeavor to extend the system of collective action and to align
> himself therewith in order to lessen the danger to Russian frontiers
> on all sides.

In the final analysis, Kirk concluded, if war came and in any
way threatened Russian security, Stalin would fight. It would be a
defensive operation, if at all possible, thus reducing to a minimum the
strain on the nation's resources. Stalin would look forward to the advantages that the USSR might derive from internal upheavals in other
countries in the process of fighting a war. Kirk observed shrewdly that
the Communist state in Russia had undergone a transformation into
Stalin's personal fiefdom, where the Soviet dictator had concentrated
all power in his own hands. This did not alter Soviet antagonism to
the capitalist states; Stalin, in mobilizing the forces of the Soviet Union
to the service of his dictatorship, should not be expected to ignore that
hostility, "both as a defensive and offensive weapon for the safety and
profit of his regime."[50] In other words, he could be expected to use the
slogans of communism to represent the national aspirations of Russia
and his own personal ambitions. This was a prediction too soon forgotten.

As the *Christian Century* pointed out in mid-April, the big question
for world security was: "What will Russia do?" Whatever it was it
proved a question to be settled before either Chamberlain or the Axis
powers were ready for a final showdown:

> Neither side dares make more than marginal moves until it is
> known what Stalin is going to do. . . . If he decides to stay neutral,
> on the theory that he has no more to lose by seeing Hitler turn
> westward than Chamberlain formerly thought he had to lose by
> seeing the Fuhrer march eastward, then the axis powers are likely
> to conclude that the hour for their great gamble has arrived. But
> until the decision is made we expect to see that outbreak of a
> general war postponed.[51]

What Russia should do provided the subject of considerable discussion in the Kremlin, where Litvinov argued against a commitment
to Hitler. The commissar still believed that an alliance could be arranged
with Britain as the key, for, if the British were drawn into war, the

---

[50]Ibid., pp. 752–53.
[51]"What Will Russia Do?" *Christian Century* 56 (April 19, 1939): 505.

Americans would follow, which would be Germany's undoing. Litvinov discounted the French as having much effect one way or the other except that, as an ally placed on Germany's border, the British, French, Russian, and American combination would mean "Hitler will either get scared and stop, in which case he will have to face economic crisis," or, confronting a hostile world, he would fanatically plunge into war and be crushed because "Germany cannot fight on two fronts." As Litvinov argued, "With the inexhaustible industrial might of the United States our victory is ensured."[52] Stalin countered that, if Russia came out as the initiators of a world front against fascism, it would end by standing alone; no one would fight to defend communism. Litvinov thought his days were numbered unless Stalin believed he could still be useful as a smoke screen while the German negotiations went on, or as an ace in the hole in case the German plan evaporated.[53]

Even if the scenario was not played exactly as recorded in Litvinov's notes, something approximating it occurred. Certainly, as these events took place, there was no room left for British and French maneuvers; they either had to commit to a program that would persuade Stalin that theirs was the winning side, or face all of the armed powers in a formidable array against them. The only role remaining for the United States was to declare with them or see the democracies in terrible straits and American security resting on the tenuous staying power of overmatched British and French military forces. In playing for time, Roosevelt found little solace in the news he received from Moscow.

In some measure the Soviet decision to cast Russia's lot with Hitler rested on events in America. When the Russian press reported the last phase of the struggle for a more active American foreign policy, the interest was more than casual in the outcome. On March 10 *Izvestiia* quoted a letter from Stimson to the *New York Times*, which asked that the United States stand with other powers against aggressive Fascists who threatened the security of the United States. The Russians emphasized Stimson's request for America to support "clearly" the Western powers in opposing the aggressors, in which case they would not dare carry the war any further.[54] "Clearly" was the key word. The Russians had reached the point where they believed that positive agreements had to be made with the Axis powers or the West, and there were groups that favored each side in the struggle. Since both were viewed as enemies of the Soviet system, Kremlin policy would be dictated purely by Stalin's calculation of who would win. If Congress refused

---

[52]Litvinov, *Notes for a Journal*, pp. 291–92.
[53]Ibid., pp. 292–94.
[54]"Statement by Stimson," *Izvestiia*, March 10, 1939.

to load Roosevelt's guns by removing restrictions on aid to the democracies and the British and French refused to take negotiations with the Russians seriously, they felt no qualms in dealing with Hitler.

Immediately after Munich the Russians began to search out prospects for rapprochement with the Germans, who put out similar feelers to the Russians at the same time.[55] Stalin made his move via a speech he delivered to the Eighteenth Party Congress on March 10, which Kirk relayed to the State Department the following day. Kirk reported Stalin's discussion of the political aspects of the international situation. The Soviet premier contended that the policy of capitulation adopted by the democracies was based on the fear of destroying the Fascist wall that stood between Russia and the West. The democracies did not turn against the Fascist powers, even though they were far stronger economically and numerically, because they hoped in vain that the Fascists would concentrate their energies toward the East. The United States, Kirk said, was connected by mention of the instigations of the North American press, which spread "false stories" about Russian military weakness and other such comments in the hope of convincing the Germans that Russia would be an easy mark.[56]

Kirk made no comment on the most important implication of the speech, wherein Stalin cautiously offered the olive branch to Germany:

> We stand for peaceful, close, and good neighborly relations with all neighboring countries which have a common frontier with the Soviet Union. We stand and will stand on that position insofar as these countries will maintain such relations with the Soviet Union and insofar as they do not attempt to infringe directly or indirectly [on] the interests, integrity, and inviolability of the frontiers of the Soviet state.[57]

Considering the Soviets' proclivity for Aesopian language, this was an unusually direct invitation to the Nazis to come to the conference table ready to deal. If, however, the invitation was not clear enough, Stalin made it even more explicit:

> The tasks of our Party in the realm of foreign policy are: (1) to continue in the future as well as to carry on the policy of peace and of strengthening of business-like ties with all countries; (2) to observe caution and not permit our country to be drawn into

---

[55]A. Rossi, *The Russo-German Alliance, August 1939–June 1941* (Boston: Beacon, 1951), p. 5.

[56]*FRUS: Soviet Union*, pp. 739–40.

[57]Ibid., p. 741.

conflict by the provocateurs of war, who are accustomed to using others as cats' paws.[58]

Because the Soviets were engaged in direct negotiations with the British and French, this could only be a warning to them and an invitation to the Germans. Stalin obviously was not interested in pulling anyone's chestnuts from the fire who did not want, themselves, to assume the risk of getting burned. The Russians would as soon go with the other side, which already had its hands in the fire, grabbing for all the chestnuts.

That Stalin aimed at rapprochement with Germany is a matter of record. Molotov said so on August 23 after the Nazi-Soviet Pact was concluded. In the presence of Ribbentrop and Stalin, Molotov "raised his glass to Stalin, remarking that it had been Stalin who—through his speech of March of this year, which had been well understood in Germany—had brought about the reversal in political relations."[59]

The first overt move toward rapprochement came from the Russians on April 17, 1939, when Soviet Ambassador Alexei Merekalov visited Baron Ernst von Weizsäcker, the secretary of the German Foreign Ministry. Previously Merekalov had avoided any official contact after the presentation of his credentials on June 5, 1938. The two men sparred for awhile before the state secretary gave the Russian the opening he wanted. Weizsäcker said he had noticed that the Soviet press of late had been letting up on Germany, to which Merekalov responded: "Russian policy had always moved in a straight line. Ideological differences of opinion . . . did not have to prove a stumbling block with regard to Germany. . . . There exists for Russia no reason why she should not live with us on a normal footing. And from normal, the relations might become better and better."[60]

IV

While Russia negotiated with Great Britain and France, the outcome of which might decide the issues of war or peace, the United States remained, by choice, a bystander in the proceedings. Ambassador Davies wrote to the secretary of state on April 18, suggesting that he might be able to go to Moscow, if Hull and the president so desired, and exert his influence to see that the discussions going on there resulted

---

[58]Ibid.

[59]U.S. Department of State, Raymond J. Sontag and James S. Beddie, eds., *Nazi-Soviet Relations, 1939–1941: Documents from the Archives of the German Foreign Office* (Washington, DC: Government Printing Office, 1948), p. 76.

[60]Ibid., pp. 1–2.

in a firm agreement between Britain, France, and Russia. Davies argued that American intervention would be sufficient to settle the matter, partly because of the personal prestige of Roosevelt, Hull, and Davies. To Hull, it was preferable "not to run any risk"; he was afraid, "from a domestic point of view such a visit, however carefully prepared, might be misconstrued."[61]

President Roosevelt's reticence stemmed from a different concern than Hull's. Although he encouraged the Russians to reach an agreement with the British and warned Stalin that Hitler was treacherous and would turn on him, he had little hope that the British would take a forward position.[62] Under Chamberlain's prime ministership, FDR simply did not believe the British could lead a coalition against Hitler. He wrote Professor Roger B. Merriman of Harvard's Department of History, expressing his anger at the Chamberlain government's tendencies to ignore reality and pass the buck. The president said he wished British leaders would stop their " 'we who are about to die salute thee' attitude." Lord Lothian called at the White House to say he had been wrong in his belief that England could negotiate with Hitler as a rational leader. He suggested that only America could pick up Britain's fallen mantle and defend democracy. Roosevelt "got mad clear through" and told Lothian that the British leaders had to conquer their defeatism before they could expect firm support from "their American cousins."[63] This pessimism was not likely to promote much faith in the fruition of an Anglo-Soviet alliance.

Roosevelt had heard the rumor that Litvinov might be replaced as foreign commissar and sent to the United States as ambassador. When instead the number two man in the Russian embassy in Washington, Konstantin Umanskii, drew the assignment, the Americans were upset, and FDR was even more worried about the American-Soviet relationship. Bullitt once called the new ambassador a "filthy little squirt"[64]; Roosevelt was not much more impressed with him. The president reluctantly accepted Umanskii's credentials but warned, "Double the guard!"[65] They were justified in their concern, as Umanskii was a party flunky who rose to preeminence in the diplomatic bureaucracy as a sycophantic follower of Litvinov. Where the Soviet leadership was concerned, his assignment illustrated a lessening of importance for

---

[61]*FRUS: Soviet Union*, p. 757.

[62]Maddux, *Years of Estrangement*, p. 99.

[63]FDR to Merriman, February 15, 1939, PSF, Great Britain; Schewe, *Roosevelt and Foreign Affairs*, 13:324.

[64]Bullitt, *For the President*, p. 148.

[65]FDR to Hull, April 27, 1939, OF 220.

the American post. Unlike Troianovskii, he was more an agent of the government bureaucracy than a diplomat.

Umanskii's appointment was not the only disturbing sign from the Kremlin. Kirk had warned the State Department to begin worrying if Litvinov should be removed as foreign minister, and on May 3 the announcement came of the commissar's "resignation." While the Americans accurately read the danger signs in Litvinov's departure, the British were taken aback and fumbled for a rational explanation. Sir William Seeds, British ambassador in Moscow, reported Molotov's succession and conjectured that the new appointment might only mean the disappearance of Litvinov and the strengthening of the Foreign Affairs Commissariat in making Soviet policy decisions. Rumor had it that Vice Commissar Vladimir Potemkin had maneuvered to dump Litvinov and Molotov was only an interim appointment. It did not seem that Potemkin, who was in Turkey at the time, was directly involved in the coup, but he might emerge as commissar of Foreign Affairs when the smoke settled. The change might signal a shift away from Litvinov's foreign policy of collective security in favor of a return to isolationism. Ambassador Seeds said it was too early to tell about any changes, but that the conversations with the Russians in Moscow were going very well.[66]

At the Foreign Office in London, Muller was less sanguine when he added a minute to the dispatch. He thought a return to isolation did not bode well for British efforts to woo the Soviets to the side of the democracies. Laurence Collier, one of the Soviet experts, agreed that a trend toward isolationism was probable and in practice would work to Germany's advantage. In his opinion Britain should move to counteract this disastrous course: "Even now, perhaps, we have a chance of avoiding this by being more forthcoming on the vital question of *reciprocal* guarantees against aggression."[67] No one seemed to take seriously Collier's suggestion that it was time to be "forthcoming" with the Soviets and to exchange mutual guarantees against attack.

Sir Percy Loraine, the British ambassador in Italy, gave the first inkling of a Nazi-Soviet arrangement. He reported that his French colleague propounded "the astonishing theory that Stalin has sacked [Litvinov] in order to make an arrangement with Germany which would of course enable the latter to attack Poland and retake the Corridor with relative impunity." Loraine found this difficult to swallow, and this skepticism was corroborated by his counselor of embassy

---

[66]Foreign Office File, FO 371/23685, Political, Northern, Soviet Union, FILES 233, pp. 2253 to END–235, 1939, N 2282/233/38, May 4, 1939, Public Record Office, London.
[67]Ibid.

who was told by his Soviet counterpart that Molotov's ascendancy would not be accompanied by any change in policy. Sir Alexander Cadogan said he had no information on the actual cause of Litvinov's resignation, although there had been reason to believe for some time that the commissar's position was not secure. He thought one possibility was that Stalin was "disgruntled at [the] failure of His Majesty's Government and [the] French government to respond adequately to Soviet overtures and is moving towards [a] policy of isolation." Cadogan added another theory that he thought less likely: Stalin wanted to dump Litvinov's policy of trying to conclude general pacts and henceforth would favor specific ad hoc commitments. He did not think that Stalin wanted to deal with Germany, but the Soviet dictator might believe isolation and complete neutrality would be best if the British and French would not guarantee Soviet territory against German attack.[68]

Most British Foreign Office analysts refused to credit any rumors that foretold a pact between Hitler and Stalin. It did not make sense to them, at least until the discussions with Great Britain and France had run their course. Sir Eric Phipps, ambassador to France, wrote the Foreign Office from Paris that Stalin was bluffing, trying to induce the British and French to accept the Soviet proposals for mutual guarantees and encirclement of Germany. To him, Stalin was trying to force them into a firm alliance by making them think that Litvinov's dismissal had some dire consequences if they did not agree with the Soviet plans. Certainly the dismissal would please Germany because Litvinov was a Jew, Phipps conjectured, but it hardly seemed likely that Stalin was going to move before the Soviet encirclement plan had been rejected. This was a proposal from the Russians to surround the Germans with Allied powers, forcing them to back down. Such a plan brought Chamberlain to the Russian embassy where he met with Soviet Ambassador Ivan Maisky.[69] Collier added a comment to the dispatch which should have alerted the Foreign Office; he reminded his colleagues that the Russians already knew "that [the Soviet plan] was not to be accepted in essentials."[70]

Phipps's anti-Soviet posture and disregard of Russia's role as possibly decisive in the developing European crisis dearly cost both the British and French. Before Litvinov's dismissal the commissar made one last effort to work out a deal with them to commit themselves to

---

[68]Loraine to Cadogan, May 4, 1939, and response of May 6, 1939, FO 371/23685, Political, Northern, Soviet Union, FILES 233, pp. 2253 to END–235, N 2263/233/38.

[69]Ivan Maisky, *Memoirs of a Soviet Diplomat: The War, 1939–43* (New York: Charles Scribner's Sons, 1968), p. 4.

[70]Dispatch from Phipps, May 5, 1939, FO 371/23685, Political, Northern, Soviet Union, FILES 233, pp. 2253 to END–235, 1939, N 2293/233/38.

an alliance. The proposal was made through Paris, and the French government asked Phipps to contact London for an opinion; however, he failed to forward the proposal, as he saw no urgency in the matter. Bullitt then asked Sir Robert Vansittart why Britain had not responded and was told that His Majesty's government had not received any such plan. Bullitt hurried to Paris to persuade Édouard Daladier to contact London personally through the French ambassador there. Britain rejected the overture and made its own suggestions to the Soviets, whereupon "Russia lost faith in the possibility of England and France's joining in opposition to Germany."[71]

The Soviets pursued their rapprochement with the Nazis all the more forcefully and made sure the Germans got the point of Litvinov's dismissal. The Soviet counselor of embassy in Berlin, Giorgii Astakhov, called on the Foreign Office and "tried without asking direct questions to learn whether [Litvinov's dismissal] would cause a change in . . . [the German] position toward the Soviet Union."[72] The German chargé in Moscow, Werner von Tippelskirch, already had written the Foreign Office, assuring Ribbentrop that the appointment of Molotov to succeed Litvinov was especially significant because Litvinov was not only the chief advocate of rapprochement with Great Britain but also actually had been engaged, at the time of his removal, in conducting conversations aimed at cementing his policy by an alliance. "The decision," according to Tippelskirch, "apparently is connected with the fact that differences of opinion arose in the Kremlin on Litvinov's negotiations." The Nazis took the sacking of Litvinov the way the Russians hoped they would. After the Nazi-Soviet Pact was signed, Hitler told his generals on August 22 that reaching an understanding with Russia rested on the Soviet commissar's departure; "the replacing of Litvinov was decisive."[73]

A writer for the *Christian Century* agreed with Collier, proclaiming that the replacement of Litvinov meant that England and France had refused to meet Russia's terms in their discussions and that Stalin was announcing he had no interest in schemes based on limited liability. According to *Christian Century*, "An inclusive, general guarantee, probably applying to the Far East as well as to Europe may be the only kind of agreement which Stalin will consider, and Litvinov's retirement may be punishment for failure to insist on such an alliance."[74]

---

[71]Bullitt, *For the President*, pp. 340–41. Orville Bullitt reached this conclusion, based on a combination of his brother's papers and information he gathered from Charles Calan Tansill, *Back Door to War* (Chicago: Henry Regnery, 1951), pp. 528–29.

[72]Sontag and Beddie, *Nazi-Soviet Relations*, p. 3.

[73]Rossi, *Russo-German Alliance*, p. 16.

[74]"Litvinov Gives Up Office," *Christian Century* 16 (May 17, 1939): 628.

George Soloveytchik provided the best analysis among American journalists, surmising that Litvinov's fall was the result of a blend of several considerations. He thought that the Russians wished to force the British and French to hurry their decisions. This stemmed from a determination to show the world Russia's legitimate objectives had to be met or it would retreat into isolation. Most ominous, he concluded, was a "wink to Germany that the way to a possible understanding has been cleared of one of its main obstacles." Soloveytchik believed it made little difference to Stalin which way the wind blew as long as it came up strongly in his favor. A Russia allied with Germany or benevolently neutral toward Germans, however, could bode no good for Great Britain and France.[75]

In June the Soviet press set forth the terms for an alliance with England and France. Molotov, *Pravda* stated, presented them with the minimum conditions necessary to establish a "united peace front." The USSR could not ensure the security of the nations connected with England, such as Poland, without reciprocity, which implied the need of recognizing which countries were "tied" to Russia.[76] *Pravda* quoted a significant question from a French newspaper: "Do we or do we not want a union with the USSR?" If this were desirable, then it stood to reason that England and France had to protect Russia against any attack through the Baltic states. The rejection of an alliance would mean that the Baltic area would have to be sacrificed to the Germans, and "the Soviet Union does not want this and neither do we."[77] In plain language the French paper asked whether France and Britain desired Russian assistance sufficiently to acknowledge Soviet spheres of influence in East Europe because that was clearly the price that had to be paid for Russia to stand against the Nazis and to help keep Poland independent.

Great Britain either chose not to get the point or did not feel free to pursue the course suggested, and the French were tied to a British response. Nazi negotiators felt no such restrictions; they made specific arrangements concerning the fate of Poland and the Baltic states, plus offering pacification of Russia's relations with Japan insofar as they could do this. Russia's arrangements with Germany did not come until long after the terms for rapprochement were offered by it to England and France. The requisite quid pro quos were presented to the British

---

[75]George Soloveytchik, "Litvinov and After," *Contemporary Review* 155 (June 1939): 673.

[76]"Questions of Foreign Policy," *Pravda*, June 7, 1939.

[77]Ibid.

negotiators in April and again in May.[78] The hint of June was indeed the last chance; by that date the Germans welcomed the opportunity to normalize relations with the USSR.[79] On July 3 the Germans showed the Russians the handwriting on the wall concerning the fate of Poland, and on August 10 they suggested an arrangement with the Soviets which would divide Poland, the "upstart" nation.[80] Four days later Molotov told German Ambassador Friedrich-Werner von Schulenburg that what happened regarding Poland depended on Germany; he demanded that the Germans cease supporting Japanese aggression. Soviet efforts to link Poland and Japan to their cooperation with the Nazis was all too clear as the German ambassador wrote Weizsäcker:

> A member of the American Embassy here, which for the most part is very well informed, stated to one of our aides that we could at any moment upset the British-French negotiations, if we abandoned our support of Japan, sent our military mission back to China and delivered arms to the Chinese. . . . Something of this sort would, perhaps, have to take place if we are to make any progress.[81]

It did not prove necessary for the Germans to go so far as to abandon the Japanese. The Russians were satisfied instead with the exertion of German influence to pacify Russo-Japanese relations,[82] the division of East Europe into spheres of influence, and the fourth partition of Poland.[83] Japan did not like the prospect of rapprochement with the Soviet Union, but, without Germany and Poland to exert pressure from the other end, the Japanese did not feel secure in attacking a militarily prepared Russia while still involved in China. The nonaggression pact with Russia would be delayed another two years, but the Kremlin leaders had effectively eliminated the threat from Japan. The rapid development of moves and countermoves between Germany and the USSR pushed the Soviets to reach and pass the point of no return, while the democracies were still arguing over what they could afford to offer.

---

[78]Winston Churchill argued in May that the time had come when delay would be fatal to Western security; England immediately had to make an alliance and recognize some of Russia's security demands. See Winston S. Churchill, *The Second World War*, vol. 1, *The Gathering Storm* (Boston: Houghton Mifflin, 1948), p. 365.

[79]Sontag and Beddie, *Nazi-Soviet Relations*, pp. 26–27.

[80]Ibid., pp. 29, 45.

[81]Ibid., p. 47.

[82]Ibid., pp. 52–53, 70–73.

[83]Ibid., pp. 61–63, 66–67, 72–73, 86–87, 90–91.

President Roosevelt knew that important decisions were about to be made in the Soviet Union. On July 29 he left on a fishing trip, accompanied by Colonel Faymonville who had recently returned from his assignment as military attaché in Moscow. As the *New York Times* reported, "It was said at the White House that the President desires to have a general talk on Russian affairs with Colonel Faymonville, because of the latter's knowledge of the country, but that there was no special significance in the holding of the discussion."[84] The White House press corps knew better. By habit, FDR only took people on his fishing trips whom he liked as companions or with whom he desired uninterrupted talks for specific purposes. The president hardly knew Faymonville except by reputation as a knowledgeable observer of the Kremlin's policymakers. Roosevelt may have been willing to accept the colonel's advice precisely because the attaché's superiors in the army and opponents in the State Department were the people who tried to thwart efforts for closer collaboration with the Russians.

When the Nazi-Soviet Pact was announced on August 21, the president seemed to be expecting it, or at least it did not evoke any startled comments from him. His press conference of August 25 took place before he could be thoroughly briefed on what had transpired between the Russians and the Germans. Roosevelt brushed aside questions alluding to the agreement that he said he hoped would not lead to war.[85] Cordell Hull recorded that events in Europe "moved toward disaster with doubled acceleration following the announcement of the Soviet-German pact."[86] Shattered by the prospect of war, Hull marked the Soviets as contributors to the uneasy circumstances.

Jay Pierrepont Moffat also recalled the reaction in the State Department to the Russo-German Pact. August 21 had begun with an apparent easing of the European crisis, but then several telegrams began to come in indicating a different tenor, which by late afternoon cast a pall over the department:

> At about half-past five the bombshell came through of the German-Soviet Nonaggression Pact and the impending voyage of Ribbentrop to Moscow. . . . It looks to me as though Germany had promised Russia no objection to the latter taking over Estonia and Latvia and, in effect, agreeing to some form of new partition of Poland. Sumner Welles, Adolph Berle, and I discussed its effect

---

[84]*New York Times*, July 28, 1939.
[85]Press Conferences, 14, No. 573, August 25, 1939, pp. 120–23.
[86]Hull, *Memoirs*, 1:660.

back and forth, but we differed on the way it might affect the events of the next few days.[87]

Eleven days later the effect became frighteningly clear.

V

Bullitt called on September 1 to tell the president of the Nazi blitzkrieg on Poland, to which Roosevelt replied: "Then it's happened!"[88] On this calm note he accepted the apparently inevitable outbreak of the Second World War. He told the press that precautions had to be taken against agitation in America "aimed against our system of government, propaganda in favor of communism or dictatorships." A reporter asked him what he had said after communism, and Roosevelt responded: "Dictatorships. Systems of government that are contrary to ours."[89] In this fashion, the president obliquely connected the Soviet Union to the outbreak of war but would say no more about Russia's role in the whirlwind of events occurring in Europe.

Roosevelt walked a tightrope where Russia was concerned. His intelligence sources told him the Russians might have acted in coldly realistic self-defense, having failed to reach any accommodation with the Western powers. Even Soviet participation in the dismemberment of Poland brought no startled response from the president.[90] The Russians deliberately delayed making a move toward Poland until the Germans had done the dirty work and Warsaw had fallen, which made them appear less villainous to the world. The Nazis knew this was the effect Russia sought. On September 14 Ambassador von Schulenburg informed the Foreign Office from Moscow that Molotov had told him that the Red Army was ready to move on Poland but "For the political motivation of Soviet action (the collapse of Poland and the protection of Russian 'minorities') it was of the greatest importance not to take action until the governmental center of Poland, the city of Warsaw, had fallen."[91]

President Roosevelt showed anger and animosity toward the USSR when Stalin decided to bring Finland, or a portion thereof, into the ring of Russian defenses. The first overt Soviet move against Finland brought an immediate response from FDR who wrote Steinhardt, instructing him to approach President Mikhail Kalinin and tell him

---

[87]Hooker, *Moffat Papers*, p. 250.

[88]Gunther, *Roosevelt in Retrospect*, p. 303.

[89]Press Conferences, 14, No. 576, September 5, 1939, p. 140.

[90]Ibid., No. 580, September 19, 1939, p. 177.

[91]Sontag and Beddie, *Nazi-Soviet Relations*, pp. 92–93.

the president of the United States wanted to remind the Soviet government of the long and deep friendship between America and Finland. Roosevelt said he felt free to contact Kalinin "because of our joint efforts a number of years ago which resulted in the resumption of friendly relationships between Soviet Russia and the United States." He reminded Kalinin of the many Americans of Finnish extraction who would naturally be concerned over the fate of their homeland. He hoped Russia would not strain its relations with the United States by making demands on the Finns "which are incompatible with the independence, integrity, and vital interests of that Republic." Roosevelt told Steinhardt to close by expressing the president's desire that this would be taken in the nature of friendly advice.[92]

Concern for the security of Finland was not the only reason for FDR's appeal; he feared the internal domestic reaction in America. Those who worried about the Communist bogeyman at home would raise the cry against treacherous activity from the enemies of humanity. Roosevelt knew this would happen and would inevitably lead to some noise from Democratic conservatives and Republicans who, in general, intended to discredit the president and injure his chance of running in 1940. The Poles, who did not receive as sympathetic a hearing from public opinion as did the Finns, due to the ease with which Polish defenses disintegrated and because of the part Poland played in the dismemberment of Czechoslovakia, would join with the other minorities absorbed by Russia to take the opportunity for vengeance. Also, well-meaning Americans, who just liked to pull for the underdog, would exert pressure on the administration to break relations with Russia at a time when the United States could ill afford to do so.

Although Roosevelt was angry at the Russian demands on Poland and Finland, he tried to offer restrained advice because the last thing he wanted to do was to drive the Kremlin irretrievably into an active alliance against Britain and France. Russia's benevolent neutrality toward Germany was bad enough; he did not wish to complicate matters further by risking an embroglio with the Soviets. In a letter to his friend Lord Tweedsmuir on October 5, FDR summed up his dilemma: "I am literally walking on eggs, and, having delivered my message to the Congress,[93] and having good prospects of the bill going through, I am at the moment saying nothing, seeing nothing and hearing nothing."[94]

---

[92]FDR to Steinhardt, October 11, 1939, PSF, Box 15.

[93]This probably referred to the president's request for the repeal of the embargo provision of the Neutrality Law of September 21, 1939. See Rosenman, *War and Neutrality, 1939*, p. 512.

[94]Roosevelt, *Roosevelt Letters*, 3:279.

Franklin Roosevelt publicly held his peace on Russia but could not resist privately venting his feelings about Stalin's treachery. He accurately judged the American reaction to Stalin's attack on Finland, at least partly because he felt the same outrage. Finland was the epitomization of everything that the Americans admired—independent, a republic based on free elections, frugal, businesslike, upstanding, and moral. Devotion to one's obligations was a trait Americans admired in others because they admired it in themselves. All the good things in life were called to mind by the recollection that, in a time of default and recrimination from other countries, Finland had gone to work and paid back its World War obligations without complaint or trying to "worm out." There was a natural inclination, which FDR felt and knew other Americans would express, to favor the "little guy." On November 30, 1939, the day Russia attacked Finland, Roosevelt wrote to Ambassador Joseph Grew, informing him of the assault: "The whole of the United States is not only horrified but thoroughly angry. People are asking why one should have anything to do with the present Soviet leaders because their idea of civilization and human happiness is so totally different from ours." He thought the Russians had failed to act as civilized twentieth-century human beings.[95]

Roosevelt had to make a public statement on the matter, and he made it more restrained than his private comments when he announced on December 1:

> Despite efforts made to solve the dispute by peaceful methods to which no reasonable objections could be offered, one power has chosen to resort to force of arms. . . . All peace-loving peoples in those nations that are still hoping for the continuance of relations throughout the world on the basis of law and order will unanimously condemn this new resort to military force as the arbiter of international differences.[96]

The president made certain that there were no opportunities to question him on his statement.

On the same day that Roosevelt made his announcement to the press, he wrote Lincoln MacVeagh, ambassador to Greece, venting his own moral indictment: "Just back from Warm Springs in the midst of this dreadful rape of Finland. . . . I wonder what the next Russian plan is?"[97] In a December 13 letter to Francis B. Sayre, high commissioner of the Philippines, he expressed his perplexity and concern over Russia's

---

[95] Ibid., p. 290.

[96] Press Conferences, 14, No. 602, December 1, 1939, pp. 332–33.

[97] FDR to MacVeagh, December 1, 1939, PPF 1192, Lincoln MacVeagh Folder.

action: "No human being can tell what the Russians are going to do next, and I think the Japanese actions will depend much on what Russia decides to do both in Europe and the Far East—especially in Europe."[98] Roosevelt may not have understood Russian motives, but by guess or analysis his comment concerning Japan was one of his shrewder observations on foreign affairs.

Most of the press conference of December 5 centered around efforts by the newsmen to persuade Roosevelt to say something about the severance of relations with Russia, so loudly demanded in Congress and the press, but he adroitly dodged the issue by again asserting that the Soviet attack was dreadful.[99] Dreadful might have been the word Roosevelt used to the press; frightening was the way he evaluated the attack to William Allen White. Writing to White he outlined the new lineup of forces in Europe, and he frankly appealed to the Kansas editor for help. The president thought it necessary to do some quick awakening of the American people to the facts of international life.

Roosevelt analyzed for White what had happened between Russia and Germany. There were several schools of thought on the cause and effect of the pact, including one in which Germany took the Russian bear by the tail to keep England out of the war and then became much alarmed when the bear quickly devoured part of Poland, the Baltic states, and attacked Finland while posing a threat to other countries such as Norway, Sweden, Romania, and Bulgaria. Another, and equally creditable, view claimed there was a fairly definite agreement between Russia and Germany for the division of Europe. Their desire for control extended to all of Europe's colonies, and it was this prospect that frightened Roosevelt the most:

> If the latter is true, and Germany and Russia win the war or force a peace favorable to them, the situation of your civilization and mine is indeed in peril. . . . We greatly underestimate the serious implications to our own future. . . . It is really essential to us to think in broader terms and, in effect, to warn the American people that they, too, should think of possible ultimate results in Europe and the Far East.
>
> Therefore . . . my problem is to get the American people to think of conceivable consequences without scaring the American people into thinking that they are going to be dragged into this war.[100]

---

[98]Roosevelt, *Roosevelt Letters*, 3:291.
[99]Press Conferences, 14, No. 605, December 5, 1939, pp. 343–45.
[100]Roosevelt, *Roosevelt Letters*, 3:293–94.

It was at this point that Roosevelt decided that whatever he could do to prevent the Russo-German cooperation from developing further he had to do or civilization as he knew it was finished.

President Roosevelt did not want to overreact to Russian provocations, at least not to the extent of severing relations. He did, however, wish to impress on the Soviets that they could go too far and thus endanger continued diplomatic relations. They were creating problems for American citizens in Russia, printing insulting articles about U.S. policy and otherwise provoking an American response. This moved the president to write Hull and Welles:

> I am inclined to think that the day may come soon when it will be advisable to bring the situation to the direct attention of Oumansky. He can well be told that the failure of his government to answer my telegram regarding bombardment of citizens and the failure of his Government to let our Ambassador communicate with the City of Flint[101] tend to show such a complete disregard of the ordinary politeness and amenities between civilized governments that the President honestly wonders whether the Soviet Government considers it worth while to continue diplomatic relations. We need go no further than this but it would put a certain burden on the Soviet Government itself.[102]

Russian leaders had passed beyond the stage where they thought they need be concerned about American public opinion. By virtue of their agreement with Germany, for all practical purposes they already had absorbed Estonia and Lithuania, [103] and the Germans had made it clear to Finland that it could expect no help from them against their Soviet ally.[104] The German Foreign Ministry instructed its representative in Finland on October 9 to tell the Finnish government that probably the Russians would not demand much territory. The Finns replied the following day that they would concede some islands in the Gulf of Finland, but, if Russia wished more than that, it would have to fight.[105] This moved the German minister in Helsinki, Wipert Blücher, to suggest that his government intercede with Russia to assist Finland in confining Soviet claims within stated limits.[106] It was too late. The

---

[101]The *City of Flint* was an American vessel stopped by the German pocket battleship *Deutschland*, which was charged with carrying contraband and was manned with a German prize crew that took it to Murmansk where the Russians refused to permit the American crew to talk to embassy officials and vice versa.

[102]Roosevelt, *Roosevelt Letters*, 3:296–97.

[103]Sontag and Beddie, *Nazi-Soviet Relations*, p. 112.

[104]Ibid., p. 121.

[105]Ibid., p. 123.

[106]Ibid.

division of Eastern Europe had been made sometime before, and the country was out of Germany's sphere of influence. Finland would just have to fight.

Stalin had been the master plotter behind the entire maneuver, from the first feeler after Munich to the thrust at Finland. He had never been comfortable in the company of the Western democracies for they did not, for the most part, speak the same language of statecraft that he did. Hitler was another matter. Stalin understood Hitler and vice versa. The Nazi führer genuinely believed he could trust Stalin once the bargain was struck; he thought Stalin understood the alternatives. He told his military chiefs that "Stalin and I are the only people who have considered the future."[107] There was a problem, however; Stalin could not live forever and if he died some radical might seize control. Hitler told Admiral Erich Raeder that Russia would behave as long as Stalin lived, or was not overthrown, and "as long as we ourselves do not have any serious crises."[108] In this, Hitler assessed Stalin about as accurately as was possible. In another respect he judged the Russians more shrewdly than many Westerners. He did not assume that the Soviet Union had entirely surrendered its belief in communism, as did the more gullible Ribbentrop, but he did tell Mussolini that Russia was "undergoing a far-reaching evolution, and the path which Stalin has taken appears to lead toward a kind of Slav-Muscovite nationalism and to be a move away from Bolshevism."[109]

Stalin swore to Ribbentrop that the Soviet government took the pact seriously and would not betray its partner.[110] In the final negotiations, Stalin played a little of the game he thought the British had been playing with him at Munich. He told Ribbentrop he was right in his contention that England was weak and wanted to let others fight for its presumptuous claim to world domination. If England controlled the world in spite of this weakness, Stalin continued, then it was due to the stupidity of those who let themselves be bluffed.[111] It was in this frame of mind that Stalin intensified the harassment of French, British, and American diplomats and citizens in Russia.

On November 14, 1939, Ambassador Steinhardt had written to Hull, recounting British and French responses to Soviet harassments. Despite provocation, the two governments would not break relations with Russia for the simple reason that such a response would be cutting off their noses to spite their faces; Britain, he said, had found this to

[107]Rossi, *Russo-German Alliance*, p. 75.
[108]Ibid., p. 76.
[109]Ibid., pp. 76–77.
[110]Sontag and Beddie, *Nazi-Soviet Relations*, p. 76.
[111]Ibid., p. 74.

be true in 1927 when it severed ties with Moscow. They had discovered that it was impossible to obtain reliable information about Soviet activities without a diplomatic establishment in the Russian capital. One of the British embassy officials told Steinhardt: "Both British and French Governments would maintain their diplomatic establishments in Moscow intact under all circumstances short of an outright declaration of war."[112] Whatever Roosevelt and Hull thought about Stalin's crude power plays, they knew they could not afford to sever relations.

Despite his refusal to be stampeded into breaking relations with the Soviets and his concern over doing anything that would further push the Russians in the direction of the enemies of the peace, Roosevelt viewed the Soviet leadership in a new light. In part, this was because he so desperately needed assistance in blocking the path of the aggressors. The Soviets' defection from the democracies had left the president with fewer alternatives in his search for an effective anti-Fascist coalition. In this vein, FDR lost his fascination for the Russians and saw them as the new ogre in Europe, not because they were worse than the Germans but because he had expected better of them. There was also possibly a twinge of bitterness because the Soviets had turned out to be practitioners of the art of realpolitik, which FDR found distasteful in international relations despite his own tendency to lean occasionally toward such a policy. He found that the Russians were not merely Americans with different names after all. There was a hint of this reaction in his message to Kalinin, in which he referred to the experience they had gone through together when the United States had recognized the Soviet Union in 1933. A failure to respond to this appeal for the recollection of comradeship left a sour taste, a feeling of betrayal, a reflection that the Russians had departed from the path of virtue; they had brought about the end of innocence.

---

[112]*FRUS: Soviet Union*, pp. 793–94.

Epilogue

Waiting for Armageddon

DURING THE 1930s, Franklin Roosevelt placed as much focus on the American-Soviet relationship as on his dealings with any power outside the Western Hemisphere. His realism told him that there was ample cause to seek support from a major power in preserving the peace; Russia was an available force, mutually threatened, and similarly searching for supporters who opposed war. Why he failed to cooperate as fully with the Soviets as he desired can be partially explained by his fear of the isolationist climate, opposition within the Department of State, the timidity of Secretary Cordell Hull, and the failure of the British and French to establish a collective security front with Russia, which would have allowed Roosevelt to deal with an established bloc against the disturbers of the peace.

Failure of the larger objectives of Roosevelt's Russian policy was not solely the fault of the Americans, for Soviet reluctance to give him room to commit to broader cooperation bore a share of the blame. The Russians were told repeatedly that any further rapprochement depended on a debt settlement, and Stalin and his Kremlin colleagues did not believe it, to the frustration of their own growing security needs. Communist ideology dictated to some degree the Russians' expectations of American responses to their requests for cooperation against the Japanese and Germans. Capitalist greed would make the Americans forget the debt and seek broader trade with the Soviets, which in turn would give them a means of demanding other kinds of U.S. commitments in order to gain the trade advantage. Also, the Russians constantly touted the inevitability of an imperialist war that would ensnare the Americans in Asia, if not elsewhere. These "inevitable" forces would deliver the Americans to a cooperative arrangement without any overt act from the USSR.

Finally, Soviet leaders were at least partly trapped by a misreading of Roosevelt's control of the foreign policy process and their perception of American "realism" as it was advertised by the liberal press in America and attacked by the conservatives. If the president was an "internationalist," as many of his advisers contended, then eventually his words promising to move against disturbers of the peace would have to be followed by concrete acts. Thus, the Russians, like Roosevelt, moved erratically, expecting that historical forces would serve them if they occasionally prodded the United States with a stick and dangled a carrot in front of the skittish Americans. Every pronouncement by Roosevelt or Hull that the aggressors had to be stopped raised the Soviets' expectations for promised U.S. assistance.

There were several occasions during this decade when Soviet and American leaders believed that their opposite numbers had finally decided it was time to get together in some active program to thwart their enemies. These moments arrived after the fashion of a courtship ritual, wherein the wooers, fearful of losing one another, sent out signals calling for reconciliation but did not want to be the first to rush forward. Usually these attempts coincided with judgments by Stalin and Roosevelt that they were in danger of becoming isolated victims of the aggressive powers. No cooperation followed because the Russians and Americans found excuses to stand aside and await some show of "sincerity" by the Kremlin or Washington which would permit them to collaborate on their own terms.

Ironically, Roosevelt's best hope for fruitful collaboration with Russia was Maxim Litvinov, the very person William Bullitt and Hull chose to blame for the failure of closer cooperation. For his part, in the face of the Nazi and Japanese threats, Litvinov knew that Stalin would grow impatient if the commissar could not bring off the collective security scheme with the democracies. He also knew that the United States was the key to the success of this operation. Litvinov believed that recognition by the United States was both essential and possible; it was essential in order to give Japan something to worry about, thereby relieving the pressure from the East, and possible because the United States, under new leadership, might be able to see the benefit that could be derived from reducing the effect of Japanese power in the Far East. Recognition seemed to verify his assumption of American realism; therefore, quite logically, Litvinov assumed that the Americans might be expected to participate thereafter in some aspect of the struggle for collective security.

If the collective security plan was not entirely Litvinov's in conception, it became his in practice. Stalin stayed out of the center of the diplomatic limelight during this phase of Russian foreign policy, but Litvinov always knew where the center of power was and from 1937 on what failure would mean.[1] Stalin allowed him the better part of a decade to persuade the democracies to make agreements concerning commercial and defensive measures. Litvinov's dominance as foreign commissar depended on the success of rapprochement with Great Britain, France, and the United States. Failure of this policy was sure to see his decline and even his possible elimination. When Litvinov was dismissed on May 3, 1939, the democratic states should have paid more attention than they did to what this meant.

The Kremlin warned repeatedly that a failure of collective security would lead to more drastic measures on its part to ensure Russia's safety. The vacillation and halfhearted policy of Great Britain and France in their approach to the depredations of the aggressors, as the Soviets pointed out themselves, put Russia in the driver's seat where it could sell its wares to the highest bidder. France made its bids in its arrangements with the USSR of 1935 and after. These were useless, however, without complementary agreements with Great Britain in Europe or between the United States and Russia in Asia, for Germany had to be threatened effectively from one direction or the other, and Russia could not help France to block German advances with an unchecked Japan roving its Siberian frontiers. The failure to make realistic bids to the Soviets must be laid at the feet of Great Britain and the United States, for France had little choice but to follow their lead.

Primarily Great Britain must bear the brunt of the responsibility for the failure of European security measures. This was not because Neville Chamberlain carefully laid out a plan to turn Germany loose on repugnant Bolsheviks (this was more of a hope than a policy); rather, the British policymakers, particularly Chamberlain, seriously misread the changing power factors in both Europe and Asia and especially miscalculated Hitler's determination to control continental Europe, which no British government could tolerate. Chamberlain and several Foreign Office experts badly misunderstood the degree of importance Russia bore on the outcome of their maneuvers and certainly underestimated the Soviets' power and flexibility to arrange affairs to fit almost any combination of forces working to the Soviet Union's advantage. To no avail they were warned by some of the Soviet experts in the Foreign Office against isolating the Russians. If Chamberlain failed

---

[1]Henry L. Roberts, in his carefully reasoned article on the Soviet foreign minister in *The Diplomats*, noted that Litvinov, in his private remarks from 1937 onward, gave a number of hints of a possible German-Soviet rapprochement. These were at least in part directed toward making the Western powers aware of the results that would flow from a failure of collective security. See Craig and Gilbert, eds., *The Diplomats*, pp. 344–77.

to wear down the totalitarians in internecine warfare, a simple calculation of alternatives should have indicated that Russia would very
likely play turnabout. Great Britain, unprepared as it was for conflict,
was in a poor position to set the armed powers against each other
without some sort of commitment to one of them, and Russia was the
only power determinedly against an extension of the war at that time.
The British prime minister also failed to perceive how important it was
for him not to alienate Roosevelt, but how thoroughly he managed to
do just that.

The president misunderstood the alternatives too. He thought it
useless to commit the United States against the Axis because he was
sure that, if he was too forthcoming, he would deliver the country into
the hands of the isolationists in the next election. Roosevelt had a right
to worry whether an outgoing policy would accomplish anything except
political defeat at home, yet he seemed unable to act straightforward
in circumstances even more crucial to security than those that moved
him repeatedly to criticize his predecessors for their lack of leadership.
Many of his advisers on preparedness argued that a bold stance would
deter the aggressors, and, when he ventured to announce that the
Americans could not stand idly by and see the world go up in flames,
FDR wrote to friends, telling them that he had given the dictators
pause to think and perhaps had averted war. His mistake, however,
was in not distinguishing between bold statements—announcements
that America would defend itself—and declarations that it would fight
against any further aggression.

In the final analysis, it was not President Roosevelt's failure to
enter into effective agreements with the Russians for securing the peace
in the 1930s that gave cause for criticizing the conduct of American
foreign affairs, for such an alliance would have been good only so long
as the Russians found it of special aid in the preservation of their own
security. Criticism is justified because the Roosevelt administration
followed a policy of drift in foreign affairs until the United States found
itself in the position of being forced to choose between the lesser of
two evils among the totalitarian states if democracy were to survive at
all. American aid might not have helped. Great Britain and France
might not have responded to a more direct leadership policy from the
United States, but the results of the attempt could scarcely have been
more injurious than the policy of inaction that evolved and emboldened
the dictators.

President Roosevelt should have remembered his own wise advice
when he wrote his congratulations to David Lawrence for an editorial
that the journalist had written entitled "Minding Our Own Business."
FDR had commended Lawrence's central thesis "that a superficial

policy of minding our own business may often times result in the neglect of our business altogether."[2] The neglect of American concerns in foreign affairs in the 1930s, reflected in Roosevelt's refusal to face some hard facts in American-Soviet relations, focuses attention on his administration's lack of a foreign policy in general. Both the president's and Hull's statements often made it seem that there was a policy, and this made the Russians believe that the threads of the American position would be woven together into a finished fabric. This belief continued into 1939 when the Kremlin leaders decided that the United States would not actively participate in international politics except in a very limited defensive capacity. Germany and Japan became convinced that the Americans meant it when they said they would not fight unless attacked, and the Russians finally believed it also.

President Roosevelt was not alone in bearing responsibility for the failure to develop a foreign policy. He was correct in directing attention to a whole host of congressmen, editors, and publishers who refused to see a connection between a secure America and a peaceful world. Members of his administration also bear blame for this, however. It was extremely unfortunate that, at a time when sound advice might have helped the president to meet the danger, the higher officials of the Department of State refused to consider an effective program to meet the onrushing crisis. This could be attributed to the novices whom the Roosevelt administration introduced to the intricacies of diplomatic maneuvering, but mainly it was due to a lack of understanding of the broad political questions that faced the government in the conduct of its international relations.

American policy, if it can be called such, was based on the belief that European and Asian problems could be solved by the restoration of economic security and by pulpit pounding. When Hull preached his sermons on economic justice and fair play and sternly lectured the dissentient powers on their immorality, he won points for both his high-mindedness and moralism but was seldom congratulated on his realism. When moralism failed, Hull and other American officials turned to muttered incantations and the old Wilsonian habit of watchful waiting as a substitute for action.

By the end of 1939 President Roosevelt awoke to some of the deficiencies of the moralistic approach, but, since he was not sure what could be done about it, he simply prepared America to defend itself against the onslaught that was certain to come. He tried to help with arms shipments to the victims of aggression but otherwise let events rush to meet him. As Roosevelt waited, Stalin abandoned Litvinov's

---

[2]FDR to Lawrence, May 16, 1939, PPF 5990.

policy of rapprochement with the West and rekindled in the Russian heart old dreams of empire. While the *Drang nach Osten* had not yet run its course, almost by accident the Soviets' drive to the West already had begun as Stalin secured from his Nazi enemies of yesterday an entering wedge in East Europe to a new Soviet empire. Russia ended 1939 committed to a European policy secured by an alliance with Hitler, while Roosevelt ended the year worried about how he might separate the armed powers from one another. Americans and Russians had sown mutual seeds of suspicion, which remained buried as they struggled with the more immediate question of security.

Roosevelt certainly tried to bring the Russians into his plans to preserve the peace or win a possible war. Recognition proved his intent to frighten or bluff the Japanese and to give Hitler reason to pause in his designs for aggression; the consideration to allow American naval units to visit Soviet ports carried the same purpose. Various efforts to reach a debt settlement and to cooperate on aid to China through both the State and Treasury departments also illustrated FDR's willingness to include the Russians in his plans to stop aggression. And the proposal to sell a battleship to the Soviet Union further proved Roosevelt's intention to treat it as an ally. Each of these efforts, however, fell short of accomplishment because mutual self-interest and overconfidence led to almost arrogant assumptions that Kremlin and Washington leaders could have their own way without real concessions.

Although Roosevelt saw only a limited role for American-Soviet relations, it was an important one. He hoped to align 165 million Russians with the Americans as a public opinion force on the side of peace. He believed that, if he made it apparent that relations were intimate, this would not only impress the dissentient powers but also would free the Soviets from concern about an imagined threat from America so that they could feel safe in confronting their real enemies—Germany and Japan. Through this apparent American-Soviet rapprochement, it might be possible to bluff the aggressors into holding back in the face of a possible U.S.-Soviet bloc in cooperation with the other threatened nations. Perhaps Roosevelt's approach was naive when he thought Japan and Germany would worry about "possible" alliances against them, but at least his intent was based on recognizing the true threats to the status quo. Part of the problem with the president's policy was that it aimed at preserving a status quo against forces determined to alter it, which therefore required more than bluffs and gestures to prevent changes in the world balance of power.

As Roosevelt came to realize the nature of the challenge he faced, he knew America was threatened and that the Soviets were his only hope among the arming powers of standing with the democracies against the dictators. In this sense, Stalin was important to him as a possible counterforce to the enemies, even though the president knew him to be a dictator as well. So long as Stalin seemed to wish to avoid a large-scale international conflict, despite his faults, this put him on the side of the angels. People like Joseph Davies reminded FDR that his choices were limited and that, although Stalin was ruthless, he was the only available choice to beat back the forces aiming for war and revision of the world order. Roosevelt therefore tried to make the Russians an important part of his foreign policy program. He may have hoped that the British and French would decide to stand up to the potential aggressors, but he thought that Russia was his ace in the hole if this did not occur, and more and more he feared that the British were not going to meet the challenge.

Both the Americans and Russians wanted peace and to use each other in its preservation, but they desired it for different reasons. Failure to recognize one another's objectives was to cause bitterness, recrimination, and suspicion, which were only buried in the larger necessity to defeat a common foe too terrible to countenance. In 1939 this was not yet clear, however, and the year ended with Roosevelt seeking some means of fitting the Soviet Union back into his plans to thwart the Axis powers and fearing he might fail. With the coming of the Second World War, the next crisis was upon the president, and he met it with the same bon vivant attitude that he met most crises in his life. To be sure he worried about it, but it did not give him ulcers. In fact, he was still able to express his optimism in the late spring of 1940 in a letter to Ambassador Joseph Kennedy: "These are bad days for all of us who remember always that when real world forces come into conflict, the final result is never as dark as we mortals guess it in the very difficult days."[3] Perhaps Franklin Roosevelt's optimism was necessary because the alternative was to sink in despair. He knew Russia was as important to his plans to win the war as it had been to preserve the peace, but circumstances once again forced him to play the waiting game.

---

[3]Roosevelt, *The Roosevelt Letters*, 3:312.

Bibliography

Archives and Manuscript Collections

Library of Congress, Washington, DC
    Cordell Hull Papers
    Key Pittman Papers
National Archives, Washington, DC
    Committee Papers: U.S. Senate Committee on Foreign Relations
    U.S. Department of State Files (DSF), Record Group 59
National Archives and Federal Records Center, Suitland, Maryland
    U.S. Department of State Files
Public Record Office, London
    Foreign Office Files (FO)
Franklin D. Roosevelt Library, Hyde Park, New York
    R. Walton Moore Papers
    Henry Morgenthau, Jr., Papers
    Franklin D. Roosevelt Papers
        Official File (OF)
        President's Personal File (PPF)
        President's Secretary's File (PSF)
        Press Conferences

Government Publications

Public Record Office. *Documents on German Foreign Policy, 1918–1945.* Series D., Vol. 6, *The Last Months of Peace, March–August 1939.* London: Her Majesty's Stationery Office, 1956.

U.S. Department of State. *Foreign Relations of the United States, Diplomatic Papers.* Vol. 4, *The Far East, 1937.* Washington, DC: Government Printing Office, 1954.

———. ———. Vol. 2, *British Commonwealth, Europe, Near East, Africa, 1933.* Washington, DC: Government Printing Office, 1949.

———. ———. Vol. 1, *General, British Commonwealth, 1934.* Washington, DC: Government Printing Office, 1951.

———. ———. Vol. 1, *General, 1937.* Washington, DC: Government Printing Office, 1954.

———. ———. Vol. 1, *General, 1938.* Washington, DC: Government Printing Office, 1954.

———. ———. *The Soviet Union, 1933–1939.* Washington, DC: Government Printing Office, 1952.

———. *Nazi-Soviet Relations, 1939–1941: Documents from the Archives of the German Foreign Office.* Edited by Raymond J. Sontag and James S. Beddie. Washington, DC: Government Printing Office, 1948.

———. *Peace and War: United States Foreign Policy, 1931–1941.* Washington, DC: Government Printing Office, 1943.

———. *Press Releases.* Washington, DC: Government Printing Office, 1933–1939.

Published Documents

Bullitt, Orville H., ed. *For the President: Personal and Secret.* Boston: Houghton Mifflin, 1972.

Degras, Jane, ed. *Soviet Documents on Foreign Policy.* Vol. 3. London: Oxford University Press, 1953.

Nixon, Edgar B., ed. *Franklin D. Roosevelt and Foreign Affairs.* Vols. 2, 3. Cambridge: Belnap Press of Harvard University Press, 1969.

Roosevelt, Elliott, ed. *The Roosevelt Letters.* Vol. 3. London: George G. Harrap, 1952.

Roosevelt, Franklin D. *Roosevelt's Foreign Policy: Franklin D. Roosevelt's Unedited Speeches and Messages.* New York: Harper, 1942.

Rosenman, Samuel I., ed. *The Public Papers and Addresses of Franklin D. Roosevelt.* Vol. 4, *The Court Disapproves, 1935.* New York: Random House, 1938.

———. Vol. 5, *The People Approve, 1936.* New York: Random House, 1938.

———. Vol. 6, *The Constitution Prevails, 1937.* New York: Macmillan, 1941.

———. Vol. 8, *War and Neutrality, 1939.* New York: Macmillan, 1941.

Rossi, A. *The Russo-German Alliance, August 1939–June 1941.* Boston: Beacon Press, 1951.

Schewe, Donald B., ed. *Franklin D. Roosevelt and Foreign Affairs.* Vols. 9, 10, 11, 13. New York: Clearwater, 1979.

Interviews

Feis, Herbert. National Archives, Washington, DC. Spring 1958.

Perkins, Frances. University of Illinois, Urbana, Illinois. Spring 1958.

Roosevelt, Eleanor. Hyde Park, New York. Summer 1959.

Books

Adams, Frederick C. *Economic Diplomacy: The Export-Import Bank and American Foreign Policy, 1934–1939.* Columbia: University of Missouri Press, 1976.

Bennett, Edward M. *Recognition of Russia: An American Foreign Policy Dilemma.* Waltham, MA: Blaisdell, 1970.

Berle, Beatrice Bishop, and Jacobs, Travis Beal, eds. *Navigating the Rapids, 1918–1971: From the Papers of Adolph A. Berle.* New York: Harcourt, 1973.

Bishop, Donald G. *The Roosevelt-Litvinov Agreements: The American View.* Syracuse: Syracuse University Press, 1965.

Bohlen, Charles E. *Witness to History, 1929–1969.* New York: W. W. Norton, 1973.

Browder, Robert Paul. *The Origins of Soviet-American Diplomacy.* Princeton: Princeton University Press, 1953.

Burns, James MacGregor. *Roosevelt: The Lion and the Fox.* New York: Harcourt, 1956.

Burns, Richard Dean, and Bennett, Edward M., eds. *Diplomats in Crisis: U.S.-Chinese-Japanese Relations, 1919–1941.* Santa Barbara: ABC-Clio, 1974.

Cantril, Hadley, and Strunk, Mildred. *Public Opinion.* Princeton: Princeton University Press, 1951.

Churchill, Winston S. *The Second World War.* Vol. 1, *The Gathering Storm.* Boston: Houghton Mifflin, 1948.

Coulondre, Robert. *De Staline à Hitler.* Paris: Hachette, 1950.

Craig, Gordon A., and Gilbert, Felix, eds. *The Diplomats, 1919–1939.* Princeton: Princeton University Press, 1953.

Dallek, Robert. *Franklin D. Roosevelt and American Foreign Policy, 1932–1945.* New York: Oxford University Press, 1979.

Davies, Joseph E. *Mission to Moscow*. New York: Simon & Schuster, 1941.

DeSantis, Hugh. *The Diplomacy of Silence: The American Foreign Service, the Soviet Union, and the Cold War, 1933–1947*. Chicago: University of Chicago Press, 1980.

Dodd, William E., Jr., and Dodd, Martha, eds. *Ambassador Dodd's Diary, 1933–1938*. New York: Harcourt, 1941.

Edwards, Tryon et al. *The New Dictionary of Thoughts*. New York: Standard Books, 1949.

Feis, Herbert. *Characters in Crisis*. Boston: Little, Brown, 1966.

Filene, Peter. *Americans and the Soviet Experiment, 1917–1933*. Cambridge: Harvard University Press, 1967.

Fischer, Louis. *Men and Politics*. New York: Duell, Sloan & Pierce, 1941.

Freidel, Frank. *Franklin D. Roosevelt*. Vol. 1, *The Apprenticeship*. Boston: Little, Brown, 1952.

Grew, Joseph C. *Ten Years in Japan*. New York: Simon & Schuster, 1944.

Gunther, John. *Roosevelt in Retrospect: A Profile in History*. New York: Harper, 1950.

Hoff-Wilson, Joan. *Ideology and Economics: U.S. Relations with the Soviet Union, 1918–1933*. Columbia: University of Missouri Press, 1974.

Hooker, Nancy Harvison, ed. *The Moffat Papers: Selections from the Diplomatic Journals of Jay Pierrepont Moffat, 1919–1943*. Cambridge: Harvard University Press, 1956.

Hull, Cordell. *The Memoirs of Cordell Hull*. Vol. 1. New York: Macmillan, 1948.

Ickes, Harold L. *The Secret Diary of Harold L. Ickes*. Vol. 1, *The First Thousand Days, 1933–1936*. New York: Simon & Schuster, 1953.

———. Vol. 2, *The Inside Struggle, 1936–1939*. New York: Simon & Schuster, 1954.

Kennan, George F. *Memoirs: 1925–1950*. Boston: Little, Brown, 1967.

Langer, William L., and Gleason, S. Everett. *The Challenge to Isolation, 1937–1940*. New York: Harper, 1952.

Libbey, James K. *Alexander Gumberg and Soviet-American Relations, 1917–1933*. Lexington: University Press of Kentucky, 1977.

Lindley, Ernest K. *The Roosevelt Revolution*. New York: Viking, 1933.

Litvinov, Maxim. *Notes for a Journal*. New York: William Morrow, 1955.

Maddux, Thomas R. *Years of Estrangement: American Relations with the Soviet Union, 1933–1941*. Tallahassee: University Press of Florida, 1980.

Maisky, Ivan. *Memoirs of a Soviet Diplomat: The War, 1939–43*. New York: Charles Scribner's Sons, 1968.

Moore, Harriett L. *Soviet Far Eastern Policy, 1931–1945*. Princeton: Princeton University Press, 1945.

Payne, Howard C.; Callahan, Raymond; and Bennett, Edward M. *As the Storm Clouds Gathered: European Perceptions of American Foreign Policy in the 1930s*. Durham, NC: Moore, 1979.

Phillips, William. *Ventures in Diplomacy*. Boston: Beacon Press, 1953.

Range, Willard. *Franklin D. Roosevelt's World Order*. Athens: University of Georgia Press, 1954.

Richman, John. *The United States and the Soviet Union: The Decision To Recognize*. Raleigh, NC: Camberleigh Hall, 1980.

Roosevelt, Franklin D. *On Our Way*. New York: John Day, 1934.

Schlesinger, Arthur M., Jr. *The Age of Roosevelt*. Vol. 1, *The Crisis of the Old Order, 1919–1933*. Boston: Houghton Mifflin, 1957.

Shepardson, Whitney H., and Scroggs, William O., eds. *The United States in World Affairs: An Account of American Foreign Relations, 1937*. New York: Harper, 1938.

————. *The United States in World Affairs: An Account of American Foreign Relations, 1939*. New York: Harper, 1940.

Sivachev, Nikolai V., and Yakovlev, Nikolai N. *Russia and the United States*. Translated by Olga Adler Titelbaum. Chicago: University of Chicago Press, 1979.

Tansill, Charles Calan. *Back Door to War*. Chicago: Henry Regnery, 1952.

Vanacke, Harold M. *A History of the Far East in Modern Times*. New York: F. S. Crofts, 1947.

Wehle, Louis B. *The Hidden Threads of History: Wilson Through Roosevelt*. New York: Macmillan, 1953.

Weil, Martin. *A Pretty Good Club: The Founding Fathers of the U.S. Foreign Service*. New York: W. W. Norton, 1978.

Williams, Robert C. *Russian Art and American Money, 1900–1940*. Cambridge, MA: Harvard University Press, 1980.

Williams, William Appleman. *American-Russian Relations, 1781–1947*. New York: Rinehart, 1952.

Yergin, Daniel. *Shattered Peace: The Origins of the Cold War and the National Security State*. Boston: Houghton Mifflin, 1977.

Articles in Journals and Magazines

Arootunian, U. V. "The Role of American Diplomacy in the Organization of the Munich Conference." *Voprosi Istorii*, no 2 (February 1958): 76–95.

"Background of War: The Bear that Shoots Like a Man." *Fortune* 16 (August 1937): 70.

Borg, Dorothy. "Notes on Roosevelt's 'Quarantine' Speech." *Political Science Quarterly* 72 (September 1957): 421–30.

Buell, Raymond Leslie. "An Epoch Making Address." *Foreign Policy Bulletin* 13 (January 5, 1934): 1–2.

Bullitt, William C. "How We Won the War and Lost the Peace." *Life* 25 (August 30, 1948): 83–97.

Current History 42 (June 1935): 279.

"Debt Offer Rejected." *Literary Digest* 119 (February 9, 1935): 7.

"Eagle Shows Bear Its Talons: Keep Out of My Nest!" *Newsweek* 6 (August 31, 1935): 16.

"The *Fortune* Quarterly Survey." *Fortune* 18 (July 1938): 37.

Furniss, Edgar S. "War Fear in the Soviet Union." *Current History* 43 (January 8, 1936): 435–38.

"In a Red Hole." *Time* 26 (September 9, 1935): 11.

"Litvinov Gives Up Office." *Christian Century* 16 (May 17, 1939): 628.

"Moscow Declines the American Protest Against Propaganda." *Newsweek* 6 (September 7, 1935): 13.

"A Newspaper Editorial Which May Be Historic." *Current History* 50 (May 1939): 47–48.

"Should the United States Government Recognize Soviet Russia?" *Congressional Digest* 12 (October 1933): 236–52.

Soloveytchik, George. "Litvinov and After." *Contemporary Review* 155 (June 1939): 666–73.

"Soviet Russia's 'Retort Contemptuous.' " *Literary Digest* 120 (September 7, 1935): 12.

Troianovskii, A. A. "The Foreign Policy of Soviet Russia." *Vital Speeches* 1 (August 12, 1935): 727–31.

"Twenty Years of Bolshevism: Soviet Policy Abroad." *International Conciliation* 335 (December 1937): 803–16.

"An Ultimatum." *Time* 26 (September 2, 1935): 19.

"Was the President's Chicago Speech a Move Toward Peace?" *Literary Digest* 124 (October 30, 1937): 12.

"What Will Russia Do?" *Christian Century* 56 (April 19, 1939): 503–05.

Unpublished Material

Balzarini, Stephen Edward. "Britain, France, and the 'German Problem' at the World Disarmament Conference, 1932–1934." Ph.D. dissertation, Washington State University, 1979.

Friedrich, Marlin K. "In Search of a Far Eastern Policy: Joseph C. Grew, Stanley Hornbeck, and American-Japanese Relations, 1937–1941." Ph.D. dissertation, Washington State University, 1974.

Newspapers

Christian Science Monitor
Izvestiia (Soviet Union)
New York Herald Tribune
New York Post
New York Times
Pravda (Soviet Union)
Washington Herald

Index

Dr. Edward M. Bennett is currently a professor of history at Washington State University. A specialist in twentieth-century US diplomatic history, Professor Bennett has written numerous books and articles in the field, including *Recognition of Russia: An American Foreign Policy Dilemma* and *As the Storm Clouds Gathered: European Perceptions of American Foreign Policy in the 1930s.*